GENEALOGY OF THE PAGE FAMILY IN VIRGINIA

ALSO A CONDENSED ACCOUNT OF THE

NELSON, WALKER, PENDLETON AND RANDOLPH FAMILIES,

WITH REFERENCES TO THE
BLAND, BURWELL, BYRD, CARTER, CARY, DUKE,
GILMER, HARRISON, RIVES, THORNTON,
WELLFORD, WASHINGTON,
AND
OTHER DISTINGUISHED FAMILIES IN VIRGINIA

Richard Channing Moore Page, M.D.

Life Member of the American Historical Association; of the New York Historical Society; and Member of the Virginia Historical Society. etc.

HERITAGE BOOKS
2026

HERITAGE BOOKS

AN IMPRINT OF HERITAGE BOOKS, INC.

Books, CDs, and more—Worldwide

For our listing of thousands of titles see our website
at
www.HeritageBooks.com

A Facsimile Reprint
Published 2026 by
HERITAGE BOOKS, INC.
Publishing Division
5810 Ruatan Street
Berwyn Heights, MD 20740

— Publisher's Notice —
In reprints such as this, it is often not possible to remove blemishes from the original. We feel the contents of this book warrant its reissue despite these blemishes and hope you will agree and read it with pleasure.

International Standard Book Number
978-0-7884-3062-6

To

THE MEMORY OF

COL. JOHN PAGE,

FIRST OF HIS FAMILY IN VIRGINIA,

WHOSE TEMPERATE AND INDUSTRIOUS HABITS, INDOMITABLE ENERGY,

AND STRICT INTEGRITY,

WON FOR HIM A HIGH PLACE IN THE CONFIDENCE OF THEIR MAJESTIES,

WILLIAM AND MARY,

AS A MEMBER OF THEIR COUNCIL IN THE

DOMINION OF VIRGINIA,

AND ARE WELL WORTHY OF IMITATION BY HIS DESCENDANTS,

THIS LITTLE BOOK

IS

Piously Dedicated.

THE WASHINGTON MONUMENT, RICHMOND, VA.

PREFACE TO THE SECOND EDITION.

TEN years have elapsed since the first edition of the "Genealogy of the Page Family in Virginia" was issued. During that time additional facts have been ascertained and minor errors corrected. There is also continued demand for the book. For these reasons the author has determined to issue a second edition. The following is a revised list of those who have furnished valuable information:

1. Prof. William Allen, decd., McDonough Institute, Maryland.
2. Miss Isabella Nelson Atkinson, Gonzales, Texas.
3. H. Farnham Burke, Somerset, College of Arms, London.
4. Mrs. George Byrd, New York City.
5. Capt. R. R. Carter, decd., Shirley, on James River, Virginia.
6. Mrs. Fanny Page Nelson Carter, Hollyoak, near Shirley, Virginia.
7. Wilson Miles Cary, Baltimore, Maryland.
8. John Esten Cooke, decd., Clarke County, Virginia.
9. Mrs. Nellie Deans Taylor, Norfolk, Virginia.
10. R. T. W. Duke, Jr., Charlottesville, Albemarle Co., Virginia.
11. Ernest A. Ebblewhite, College of Arms, London.
12. Mrs. John Bolling Garrett, Albemarle County, Virginia.
13. Mrs. Elizabeth H. Gordon, Baltimore, Maryland.
14. Miss Mary Jane Griffith, decd., Shelly, Gloucester Co., Virginia.
15. Hon. Hugh Blair Grigsby, Charlotte County, Virginia.
16. Mrs. Mary R. P. Harrison, The Rowe, on James River, Virginia.
17. Mrs. Ellen W. R. Harrison, Edge Hill, Albemarle Co., Virginia.

18. Genl. Roger Jones, Inspector-Gen., U. S. Army, Washington, D. C.

19. Mrs. Fannie B. P. Meade, decd., Washington, D. C.

20. Mrs. Fannie B. N. Mercer, Yorktown, Virginia.

21. Miss L. Page Nelson, New York City.

22. Dr. Robert W. Nelson, Charlottesville, Albemarle Co., Virginia.

23. Col. William Nelson, decd., Oakland, Hanover Co., Virginia.

24. Col. William N. Nelson, Clarke County, Virginia.

25. W. Steptoe Nelson, Bedford County, Virginia.

26. Mann Page, Esqr., Lower Brandon, on James River, Virginia.

27. Legh R. Page, Esqr., Richmond, Virginia.

28. John W. Page, Esqr., Petersville, Frederick Co., Maryland.

29. Peyton N. Page, decd., Gloucester County, Virginia.

30. Dr. John R. Page, Birmingham, Alabama.

31. William N. Page, Esqr., decd., Cumberland County, Virginia.

32. John Page, Esqr., Hanover County, Virginia.

33. Thomas Nelson Page, Richmond, Virginia.

34. Miss Lucy M. F. Page, Washington, D. C.

35. Thomas Walker Page, decd., Albemarle County, Virginia.

36. Carter H. Page, Esqr., Charlottesville, Virginia.

37. Frederick W. Page, Esqr., Librarian, University of Virginia.

38. Judge John E. Page, decd., Clarke County, Virginia.

39. Prof. Frederick M. Page, University of the South, Sewanee, Franklin Co., Tennessee.

40. Capt. John Page, decd., Argentine Navy.

41. Capt. Thomas Jefferson Page, U. S. N., Florence, Italy.

42. George C. Page, Rome, Italy.

43. Samuel H. Pendleton, Elizabeth, New Jersey.

44. Mrs. W. N. Pendleton, decd., Lexington, Rockbridge Co., Virginia.

45. Mrs. Judge Roger A. Pryor, New York City.

46. Mrs. D. Coupland Randolph, decd., Cumberland County, Virginia.

47. Dr. Robert C. Randolph, decd., Clarke County, Virginia.
48. Miss Polly Cary Randolph, Clarke County, Virginia.
49. Francis R. Rives, Esqr., decd., New York City.
50. William C. Rives, Esqr., decd., Newport, R. I.
51. Norborne Thomas Nelson Robinson, New Orleans, Louisiana.
52. Mrs. Lucy B. P. Saunders, decd., Washington, D. C.
53. Stephen Tucker, decd., Somerset, College of Arms, London.
54. Lyon Gardner Tyler, Esqr., Richmond, Virginia.

For the purpose of ascertaining the parentage of Col. John Page, progenitor of the Page family in Virginia, an exact copy of the coat-of-arms and inscription on his original tombstone at Williamsburg, James City Co., Virginia, was sent in 1879 to Mr. Stephen Tucker, of the College of Arms, London. At first Mr. Tucker concluded that he was the brother of Mary who, according to the record at Harrow, were the "sonne and daughter of Thomas Page, of Sudbury," and "baptized 26 Decr. 1628." But upon further examination it was found that both those children died soon after they were born. That theory, therefore, had to be abandoned.

In May, 1884, the author received a letter from Mr. Lyon Gardner Tyler, of Richmond, Virginia (son of Ex-President John Tyler, U. S. America), saying that while looking over the records in the Clerk's office at Yorktown, Virginia, for papers regarding his own family, he had accidentally discovered the recorded will of Col. John Page. It was through this will that the parentage of Col. Page was finally established. A legally authenticated copy was taken by the author to London in July, 1884, and placed in the custody of Mr. Tucker. Upon the death of the latter in January, 1887, his successor, Mr. H. Farnham Burke, son of the author of "Extinct and Dormant Baronetcies," took charge of the matter. From the names of persons and places mentioned in Col. John Page's will, search was made in St. Mary's Church, Bedfont Parish, Middlesex Co., England, with the result of establishing his parentage, as fully set forth elsewhere.

Regarding family portraits the same remarks hold good as in the preface to the first edition, except as follows:

Mrs. Belle Burwell Mayo, 110 West Franklin Street, Richmond, Virginia, has the portraits of MANN PAGE (father of Gov. John Page) and ANNE CORBIN TAYLOE, his second wife. They were formerly in possession of Mrs. Mary B. Whiting, decd., of Millwood P. O., Clarke Co., Virginia.

The portrait of MARY MANN is at present owned by Dr. R. C. M. Page, of New York, he having received it from Capt. Thomas Jefferson Page, of Florence, Italy, in August, 1892. This portrait had been in Captain Page's family for fifty-three years. It was first carried to the Argentine Republic, S. A., after the Civil War in the United States, and afterward to Florence. There are yet five other family portraits remaining in possession of Captain Page, as described elsewhere. The portrait of MANN PAGE, JR. (half-brother of Gov. John Page) and ELIZABETH, his sister, who afterward married Benjamin Harrison, of Brandon, is in the possession of Mrs. Lucy Gwyn Carter, of Winchester, Frederick Co., Virginia.

The portrait of ROBERT PAGE, of Broadneck, is thought to be in possession of Commodore William Hopkins, San Francisco, California.

R. C. M. PAGE, M.D.

31 West 33d Street,
NEW YORK, 1893.

PART I.

PAGE FAMILY IN VIRGINIA.

COAT-OF-ARMS OF COL. JOHN PAGE,

FIRST OF HIS FAMILY IN VIRGINIA,

AS EMBLAZONED BY J. S. AND A. B. WYON, CHIEF ENGRAVERS OF HER MAJESTY'S SEALS,
287 REGENT STREET, LONDON.

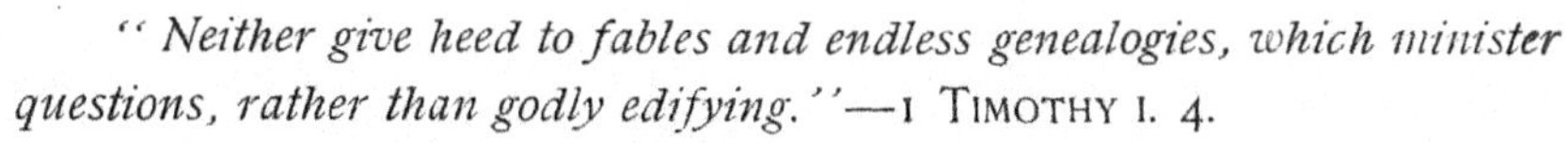

"*Neither give heed to fables and endless genealogies, which minister questions, rather than godly edifying.*"—I TIMOTHY I. 4.

"*But avoid foolish questions, and genealogies, and contentions, and strivings about the law; for they are unprofitable and vain.*"—TITUS III. 9.

(From the original portrait by Sir Peter Lely, London, 1660.)

COL. JOHN PAGE,

Williamsburg, James City County, Virginia,

FIRST OF THE PAGE FAMILY IN VIRGINIA.

DIED 23D JANUARY, 1692, AGED 65.

PAGE FAMILY.

I. JOHN PAGE, the first of the family in Virginia, is mentioned on his tombstone at Williamsburg, James City Co., Virginia, as "Colonel JOHN PAGE, of Bruton Parish, Esquire."

According to the record in the custody of the registrar of the College of Arms, London, he was the son of Francis Page, of the Parish of Bedfont, Middlesex Co., England.

Francis Page died 13th Oct., 1678, aged eighty-four and was buried in the chancel of St. Mary's Church, Bedfont. The inscription on the tombstone shows that it was placed there by "John Page, his son, of York County, Virginia, Merchant." The original tombstone was removed from the church in 1865 during repairs, and was placed in the churchyard against the eastern wall where it now stands. But in 1889 a brass plate was put in the chancel where the original tombstone formerly rested. On the brass plate is an exact copy of the coat-of-arms and inscription from the original, and a statement that it was placed there in 1889 by Dr. Richard Channing Moore Page, of New York.

The coat-of-arms found on the tombstone of Col. John Page, at Williamsburg, Va., is as follows, the arms being identical in outline with those of Francis Page, except the bordure:

ARMS.—A fesse dancette between three martlets, a middle chief crescent.
CREST.—A demi-horse forcene (rearing).

There are no marks on the tombstone to indicate the tinctures, and no motto. The latter, however, is unimportant. The crescent found on the arms signifies merely "second son." Col. John Page married, about 1656, Alice, whose surname, from the coat-of-arms on her tombstone at Williamsburg, Va., is supposed to be Luckin, of the County of Middlesex, England. It is thought that she was descended from the baronet of the same name whose coat-of-arms is as follows:

ARMS.—Sable, a fesse indented between two leopards' faces or.
CREST.—A demi-griffin or, issuing out of a tower paly of six of the last and sable.

This exactly corresponds in outline with that found on the tombstone of Alice, the wife of Col. John Page, except that in the latter case the arms have a bordure.

The omission of the bordure to the arms on the tombstone of Col. John Page appears to have been the error of a sculptor who placed it by mistake on the arms of the wife Alice, where it does not belong.

The arms of the Page family in Virginia are, therefore, the first above-named of Francis Page of Bedfont, County of Middlesex, England, as follows:

> ARMS.—Or, a fesse dancette between three martlets azure.
> CREST.—A demi-horse forcene (rearing) per pale dancette or and azure.
> MOTTO.—Spe Labor Levis.

The following is an accurate diagram of the fragments of the original tombstone of Col. John Page, placed, 1877, in the vestibule of the Episcopal Church at Williamsburg, James City Co., Va.

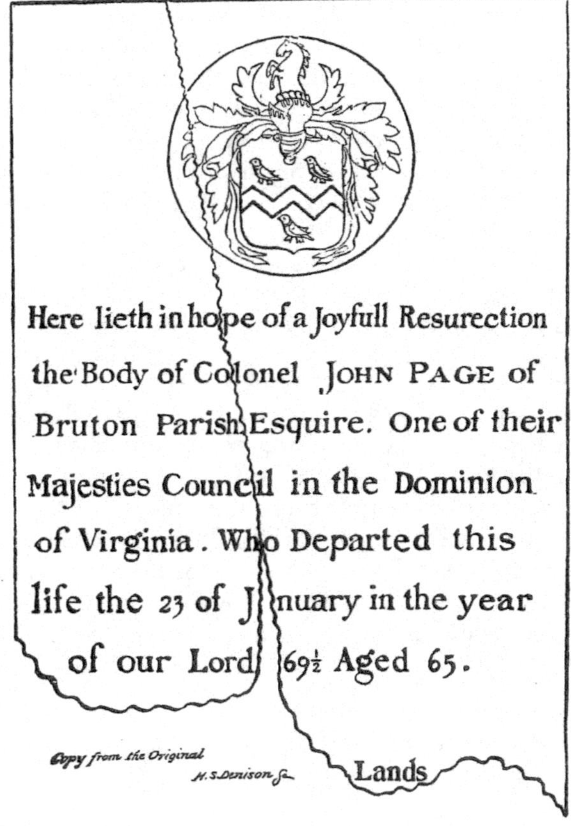

Col. John Page was born in England, 1627, and emigrated to Virginia about 1650 when he was about twenty-three years of age. According to his tombstone he died 23d January, 1692, aged sixty-five.

His wife Alice (Luckin?) died at Williamsburg, James City Co., Va., 22d June, 169– (last figure obliterated), aged seventy-three.

The following is an exact copy of the coat-of-arms and inscription on her tombstone:

Here lyeth the Body of ALICE PAGE
wife of JOHN PAGE of y[e] County of York
in Virginia. Aged 73 years. Who
departed this life the 22d day of June
Anno Domini 169–.

The last figure is obliterated, but it looks like 8: thus, 1698.

In regard to the above inscription on the tombstone of "ALICE PAGE, wife of John Page, of y[e] County of York in Virginia," it may be stated that the two counties of York and James City come together at Williamsburg, Va., so that Col. John Page might have lived in York County, although he is buried in James City County; or he may have lived in both counties at different times.

All records at Williamsburg, Va., up to recent times have been destroyed, as appears from the following certificate of Dr. Robert M. Garrett, lately deceased:

"WILLIAMSBURG, VA, 16th Dec., 1879.

"I do hereby certify that the records in the clerk's office of the city of Williamsburg and James City County, Virginia, contain no will of Col. John Page, and that the clerk thereof states that all records of both offices—up to a short period before the late war—were destroyed during the war.

"Given under my hand and seal as Justice of the Peace for the city of Williamsburg.

"RO. M. GARRETT, J P." [L. S]

In January, 1878, a new monument of Carrara marble was erected at the head of Col. John Page's grave, which was found by the side of that of his wife Alice. The following is copied from the Richmond, Va., *Weekly State*, of 15th Feb., 1878:

"A very chaste but substantial obelisk was erected last month over the grave of Col. John Page, in the old Episcopal churchyard, at Williamsburg, Va., by Dr. R. Channing M. Page, of New York. The fragments of about half the original tombstone were found and collected from various parts of the churchyard. By permission of the vestry, these were placed in the vestibule of the church for preservation The coat-of-arms and inscription are still visible, the latter reading as follows:

"'Here lieth in hope of a Joyfull Resurection the Body of Colonel JOHN PAGE, of Bruton Parish, Esquire. One of their Majesties Council in the Dominion of Virginia. Who Departed this life the 23 of January, in the year of our Lord -69½. Aged 65.'

"The date of the year has been obliterated in part, but it must have been, originally, 169½. The grave was marked by a mound of broken bricks, etc., by the side of his wife, Alice, whose tombstone is still in a fair state of preservation. The obelisk is about twelve feet high, and consists of a shaft, die, and base of the best Carrara marble, with a plinth of granite, the whole having been very neatly executed by Messrs. Draddy Bros., of Broadway, New York. It is erected on a solid foundation of brick and cement, extending six feet deep, at a total cost of five hundred dollars. The inscriptions, etc., are as follows, viz., Front face: coat-of-arms. Col. John Page died 23d January, 1692. Aged, 65. Name and date also on plinth beneath the ground. Reverse: 'He being dead yet speaketh.'—Heb. xi. 4. Right face: the original inscription copied from the old tombstone with a notice to that effect. Reverse: erected January, 1878, to replace the original tombstone."

(From a drawing by Draddy Bros., Broadway, New York, 1878.)

MONUMENT TO COL. JOHN PAGE,

WILLIAMSBURG, JAMES CITY COUNTY, VIRGINIA.

Erected January, 1878, to replace the original tombstone.

"Their Majesties," occurring in the inscription refers, of course, to William and Mary, who reigned 1690–1702. They were succeeded by Queen Anne, 1702–14.

It is evident that the fragment of date, –69½, found on the tombstone of Col. John Page, was, originally, 169½. This means 1691 or 1692, and was also written $16\frac{9}{9}\frac{1}{2}$, 1691–2, or 1691–'92, etc.

The error of the Julian calendar consisted in making the year 365¼ days, which was about eleven minutes too long. This in time amounted to days. In 1582, Pope Gregory XIII. ordered the 5th October to be called the 15th, and that the years 1700, 1800 and 1900 should not be accounted leap years. That is the Gregorian calendar.

The change from Julian to Gregorian reckoning was made in Great Britain by act of Parliament, Sept., 1752, the 3d of that month being called the 14th, and the following year to commence January 1st instead of March 25th. It appears that O. S. (old style) and N. S. (new style) refer only to the Julian and Gregorian calendars respectively, *e.g.*: George Washington, born 11th Feb., O. S.; 22d Feb., N. S.

From the fourteenth century up to 1752, in England, the legal and ecclesiastical year both began 25th March, which was the supposed date of the immaculate conception. After the change was adopted, in 1752, by which the legal year began 1st January, events which had occurred in January, February, and up to the 25th March of the old legal year, would, according to the new arrangement, be reckoned in the next subsequent year. In such cases, the dates of both years were given, and this custom prevailed for a long time after the change in 1752 was adopted.

Bishop Meade, in his "Old Churches, Ministers, and Families in Virginia," Vol. I., p. 146, states as follows:

"In 1678 it was proposed to erect, at Williamsburg, a good church to take the place of two indifferent ones in the parish. Rowland Jones was the first rector. John Page, first of the Family, headed the list of subscriptions with £20, and gave the ground for the church and graveyard. . . . Afterwards his eldest son, Francis, enlarged the church," etc. For a picture of this church see Bishop Meade, *opus citatum*, Vol. I., p. 146.

Bishop Meade, Vol. I., *op. cit.*, p. 195, also states that it was called Bruton Parish, in honor of Thomas Ludwell, who came from a parish of the same name in Somersetshire, England.

The church and wall around the churchyard are built of brick, and are both in a good state of preservation. It is usually said that the bricks used in the building of this and of other churches in those days, were imported. This, however, is probably a mistake. Rev. Philip Slaughter ("Hist. of Bristol Parish," p. 90) says: "There was no occasion for it, as brickmakers were among the earliest importations, and the bills for moulding and burning the brick for the capitol at Williamsburg, James City Co., Va., are still extant. (Palmer's Calendar of State Papers, 125; 1st Henning, 208.)"

The gates, both of wrought iron, are very ornamental. The ivy that now grows so luxuriantly at the east end of the church, originally came from Westminster Abbey, England.

The following is a copy of a letter from Col. John Page to his son Matthew:

"TO MY LOVING SON, CAPT. MATTHEW PAGE.

"SON MATTHEW: I herewith present you a New Year's gift, wherein you may observe the excellency of Scripture learning, which I desire that you may read, mark, and learn, that you may embrace and ever hold fast the blessed hope of everlasting life which God hath given you in the Gospel of our Saviour Jesus Christ. You will in this little book see what you are by nature—born in sin, having in you an original pravity, indisposition to do good, and proneness to evil. There is also taught you that Christ by His death vanquished death as Himself saith (John xi., 25), 'I am the resurrection and the life: he that believeth in Me, though he were dead, yet shall he live.' Therefore endeavor that Christ's death may become effectual to your soul, that you may rise from the death of sin to righteousness of life. Keep yourself from sin, and pray for God's Spirit to establish faith and sanctification in your heart, that you may live an heavenly conversation on earth; that, after death, eternal glory may be your portion. Set not lightly by my gift, but esteem those fatherly instructions above earthly riches. Consider the dignity of your soul, and let no time slip whereby you may, with God's assistance, work out your salvation with fear and trembling. I pray God bless you and give His blessing to what I have written for your everlasting happiness, which is the prayer of your truly loving father, JOHN PAGE.

"January 1st, 1688."

The little book referred to in this letter, and presented by Col. John Page to his son Matthew, on the first day of January, 1688, as a New Year's gift, was a MS. on parchment in Colonel Page's handwriting, and heavily bound. It contained practical instructions of a religious nature, together with quotations from the Bible. Though perhaps it was never intended for the press, yet it was so much esteemed by the late Bishop William Meade, of Virginia, that in the year 1856 he had it published. It was printed from the original MS. by Henry B. Ashmead, George St., above Eleventh, Philadelphia, Pa. There are a limited number of copies. These are distributed chiefly among Colonel Page's descendants, by whom the book is known as "The Deed of Gift."

Bishop Meade, in his preface to this book, states that Col. John Page died 23d January, 1691–2, aged sixty. This is an evident mistake, since, according to the inscription on his tombstone, he died at that time, aged sixty-five.

At the end of the book there is a notice—written by Bishop Meade presumably, though not signed—stating that the book was written by a titled personage. This mistake appears to be due to a statement made by Gov. John Page, in his brief autobiography, in which he says that Colonel Page was supposed to have been knighted (see Bishop Meade, *op. cit.*, Vol. I., p. 147, *note*). That he was not knighted, however, is a fact now well known and easily proved. It is not known what became of the original MS. of "The Deed of Gift." It is positively certain, however, that Mr. Henry B. Ashmead, of Philadelphia, after printing the book, returned the original MS. to Bishop William Meade. It is highly probable that the original MS. is now in possession of the family of Capt. Thomas Jefferson Page, U.S.N., now residing in Florence, Italy.

The following is a copy of the will of Col. John Page, taken from the records in the clerk's office at Yorktown, Va., in May, 1884:

In the name of God Amen. I, John Page, of Middle Plantation, in Yorke County, in Virginia, Esqr., being in good health, perfect memory & understanding (praised be God) doe make & ordain this my last Will & Testament in manner & form as following. Imprimis I surrender my soule into y[e] hands of God, my Creator, considering that my body being raised from nothing to what itt is now, is a mutation noe lesse than infinite; stedfastly believing after this mortall life ended, that by y[e] Divine power of God & merrit of my Saviour, Jesus Christ, y[e] ressurrection of my body and everlasting life, my body I remitt to y[e] Earth, to be decently buryed, with Christian buriall according to y[e] reights & ceremonies of y[e] Church of England, in y[e] Church yard of Bruton Pish, where I now live (if I happen to dye in or near that Pish) within ten foot of ye South side of ye Church wall from ye Chancill Door to ye East end of ye Church, And that over my grave erected with brick three foot six inches above ground, be laid a pollisht black marble stone of a good dimention. Itm. (in case itt shall happen that my dear and loving wife shall survive me) I give unto her so long as she shall live, and to my beloved son Francis Page & his heires forever, All of my seat, tract or divident of land situate lying and being att Middle Plantation, aforesaid, together with that other Plantation or tract of land situate neare James Citty, called ye Neck of land, formerly part of ye land & possession of my brother Mathew Page, deceased, which by and after his decease, was according to his will made over and given to his son Mathew Page, and which by ye Mathew Page ye son was mortgaged to me ye one and twentieth day of Decemb. one thousand six hundred and eighty three, and acknowledged in ye Gen^{ll} Court, ye nineteenth day of Aprill then next following, for security of ye payment of one hundred & four pounds Ster^{lg}, ye which sum (with twenty six pounds more I gave him) I paid and delivered for reedeeming him from Slavery out of Algiers & cloathing him att London) with all tenements houses out houses ediffices profitts emoluments & appurtenances what soever, to ye said several plantations or either of them belonging or appurtaining. And I doe also bequeath ye use possession and occupation of all & singular such servants slaves cattle horses sheep hogs, household stuffe lining woollen plate brass pewter, bedding furniture, utensills of household & husbandry both within dores & without, and all & singular other my goods chattells and personall estate whatsoever, which att ye time of my decease shall be remaining or being on my said plantations att Middle Plantation & Neck of land, or thereto or either of them belonging or therewith used and enjoyed, the rents proffits increase cropps neat proceeds, benefits & advantages, which shall arise, be made or had, of & from, my said plantations att Middle Plantation & Neck of land, or either of them, ye first and principall stock, being in the first place made good & undeminished both in quantity & quallity, And alsoe ye houses, fences orchards & plantations kept in as good order and repair as they shall be att ye time of my decease) to be equally devided, had and taken by and between my said wife & my said sonn Francis, his Executors, Adm^{rs} Assignes, And in case of ye death of my said wife either before or after me, then I doe give will & bequeath my said personall Estate, remaining or found at my said plantations att Middle Plantation and Neck of land or either of them unto my said sonn Francis, his Executors Adm^{rs} or Assignes forever, And I doe hereby declare that my said wife, by the true intent & meaning of this my Will is only to have a Joynt Estate for her life with my said sonn Francis and his heirs, in and to ye said two plantations att Middle Plantation and Neck of land, and to the personall estate on ye said plantations, shee is only to have ye joynt use thereof for her life, with my said sonn Francis, his Executors or Assignes, only ye neat proceeds of ye proffits arising thereby from & after my decease as aforesaid to be divided had and taken equally (that is to say) one moyety or halfe part by my said wife and the other half part by my said sonn Francis, his Executors and Assignes. And that in case of the death of my said wife before or after me, my son Francis is to have the aforesaid two plantations to him and his heires forever, and y[e] personall estate to the said plantations & either of them belonging as aforesaid to him his Execu[trs] Adm[rs] and Assignes for ever more, provided always and neverthelesse, that if my said nephew, Matthew Page, doe or shall at any time within tenn years, next after y[e] date of this my will pay or cause to be paid to me my Execut[rs] or Assignes y[e] aforesaid sum of one hundred and four pounds Ster[l] for which y[e] said plantation att y[e] Neck of land stands mortgaged to me as aforesaid, that then my devise or bequest of y[e] said plantation, called y[e] Neck of land, only to be voyd and of noe effect. And that my said cousin [NEPHEW?] Matthew Page, if then living shall be estated in and repossessed of so much of y[e] said plantation called y[e] Neck of land as the mortgage to me, but in case y[e] said Matthew dye before y[e] expiration of y[e] said terme of tenn years, then his heires executorrs or adm[rs] to have noe bennefitt or advantage of this provisoe. Itm forasmuch as I have been att great charge in y[e] purchase building & placeing on my plantation called Mehixton in New Kent County a competent number of Negroe slaves, cattle, horses sheep hoggs & other things convenient and necessary to mannage y[e] said plantation to advantage, & likewise a considerable expence in erecting repairing and keeping in order my Mehixton Water Mill on Tottapottamoys Creek, and as yett finde in my sonn Matthew Page noe inclination to take a wife, now to y[e] end my said plantation and Mill may not basely dessend or come to him or them, if I shall by this my last Will appoynt without y[e] stock that shall remaine upon my said plantation, and att y[e] said Mill att y[e] time of my death, therefore for y[e] better of such person or persons that shall succeed in y[e] inhabiting my sd plantation Mehixton, and enjoy my said Mill, my Will is, and I hereby give and bequeath unto my said dear and loving wife Alice, and my well beloved sonn Matthew Page for their respective lives all that my said seat tract or divident of land called Mahixton with all houses, outhouses ediffices profitts & appurtenences thereto belonging, situate on Tottapottamoys Creek, together with the use possession and occupation of all such of my servants, slaves, cattle horses sheep (y[e] one halfe of y[e] sheep being now my said sonn Matthew's) household stuff, linnen wollen, plate, brass, pewter, bedding, furniture utensills of household & husbandry, both within doores & without, & all & singular other my goods chattells and personall estate, whatsoever which att y[e] time of my decease shall be remaining or being on my said plantation called Mahixton, and the aforesaid Mill or thereto belonging, or therewith enjoyed, y[e] rents, profitts, encrease, advantage, bennefitt, cropps and cleare proceeds of y[e] same (y[e] principall stock not being diminished, but first made good both in quantity and quality) to be equally divided, had and taken by and between my said wife and my said son Matthew, share & share alike (that is one moyety to y[e] one, and the other moyety to y[e] other, for and towards their necessary support & maintainance. And further it is my Will and intent that my Mahixton plantation and Mill forever remain & continue insepable to whome y[e] right tytle or interest of y[e] said plantation shall come being dependant one on y[e] other, and in case of the death of my said wife before or after my decease, and before my said sonn Matthew, then I give and bequeath my said whole plantation called Mehixton with y[e] appurtences and ye aforesaid Mill & lands with ye appurtences to them or either of them belonging unto my said sonn Matthew, for ye terme of his natureal life & ye use possession and occupation of all & every, the servants, negroes, cattle goods chattells and other personal estate to ye said plantation called Mehixton and Mill belonging, only for his life, and after the decease of my wife and son Matthew, I give and bequeath my said plantation called Mahixton with ye appurtences and ye said Mill and lands thereto belonging unto ye heires male or female of ye body of my said sonn Matthew, lawfully begotten or to be begotten. And for want of such issue of my said son Matthew, then I give the said plantation called Mehixton with appurtences and Mill with ye land thereunto belonging, together with ye use bennefitt and occupation of all such of my servants, slaves, cattle, horses, household stuffe, and other my personall estate thereto belonging to my nephew, John Page, son of my brother Robert Page late of Hatton on Hownsley heath, for and during ye terme of ye natureall life of ye said John Page. And from and after his decease, I give and bequeath ye said plantation of Mehixton, and ye said Mill and appurtences with ye use of all the negroes, servts cattle household stuffe and other personall estate to the said plantation & Mill, belonging, to the heires male of the said John Page lawfully begotten or to be begotten, and for want of such heir maile on ye body of my said nephew John Page, then to the Rt heire of me ye testator, on this condition nevertheless, that if my said Cozen [NEPHEW?] John or his heir male, doe not personally come into Virga and actually live on my said plantation of Mehixton within eighteen monthes next after notice that ye same shall or may come to him, by ye true intent of this my will, then ye bequest hereby made to him or them shall be utterly voyd, and upon such refusall ye said plantation called Mehixton and Mill, with all my personall estate thereto belonging to goe and decend forever to such reight heir of me ye testator, as shall be actually living in Virginia. Itm. I give and bequeath to my said wife Alice and two sonnes Francis and Matthew, ye lease of those five tennements with ye appurtenances, situate on Longditch in ye Citty of Westminster (which I hould of ye Dean & Chapter of ye Collegiatt Church of St. Peeters in Westminster, for ye terme of twenty seven years from ye five and twenth day of March next to come and unexpired att ye yearly Rent of forty eight shillings and sixpence, for four acquitances) which houses I have lett to Francis Norris, Bricklayer, and Danl Finch, Carpenter, by lease dated ye four and Twentyeth day of March Anno Dom. one thousand six hundred eighty three for Twenty seven years to come the five and twentyeth day of December now last past under ye reserved yearly rent of forty pounds Sterl to have and to hold to my said wife and two sons and the longer liver of them his Executrs Admrs or Assignes with the improved rent thereby due and payable, for and dureing ye residue of ye terme which att my decease shall be to come of ye lease granted to me of ye same

Itm. I give ye remainder of my two hundred and ninety one acres of land situate in ye forks of Powhatan (not sold to Henry Malara) unto my said son Francis and the heirs male of his body lawfully begotten, and for want of such heirs maile, to my Grandson John Tyler sonn of my Grand daughter Eliz: Tyler, and his heires forever. Itm. I give to my said Grandson John Tyler the sum of fifty pounds Sterl to be paid att his age of eighteen years, and in case he dye before that age, then in lieu thereof I give the sum of thirty pounds Sterl to such other child of my said Grand daughter, Eliz: Tyler as shall attaine first to ye age of eighteen years. Itm. I give to the children of my brother Matthew Page one hundred pounds Sterl (that is to say) to my aforesaid Cozin [NEPHEW?] Matthew Page, thirty three pounds six shillings eight pence, to my Cozin [NEPHEW?] Luke Page thirty three pounds six shillings eight pence, and to my Cozin [NIECE?] Mary Page ye like sum of thirty three pounds six shillings eight pence Sterl, all which last mentioned sumes, in lett shall be sett apart and paid by my Executrs out of my Estate before any divission be made thereof among themselves, to ye person such legacy is before given & not to ye Executors or Admrs of such Legatee as shall happen to dye before me. And further it is my will, intent & meaning and soe I hereby declare that if it shall appeare by my booke written with my owne hand or if itt be with my owne hand indorsed on this my Will, that I have made payment in parte or in whole of any ye legacies before mentioned, that then such payment made by me in my life shall be accounted as so much paid of any of ye said legacies and what shall be behinde and unpaid, shall be only made good by my Executrs. Itm: I give and bequeath ye profitts of all and every part, parts, or share of such shipps, as at ye time of my decease, I shall have an interest or title to unto my said dear and loving wife, and two well beloved sonns Francis and Matthew, to be divided equally between them dureing ye natureall life of my said wife, and from and after her decease, I give my part and shares of ye ships called the Augustine, and ye East India Merchant (formerly called the Prince) unto my said son Francis his Executrs and Assignes forever. And my part of ye shipp Jeffreys to my said sonn Mathew his Executrs and Assignes forever. And as to all other my goods and chattells, debts, rights, and credits, due and owing to me by or from any person or persons whatsoever, in England, Virginia or elsewhere, my debts legacies and funerall charges being first paid and discharged, I give and bequeath to my said dear and loving wife and my two well beloved sonns Francis and Matthew or such of them as shall be living att ye time of my decease to be equally divided between them share and share alike. Itm, itt is my will and desire that such negroes or slaves as I shall dye possessed of at Midlde Plantations, ye Neck of land, and Mehixton, when they or any of them grow aged and past their labour, that such decrippitt slave or slaves be kept provided for and maintained by their respective owners and masters, with cloathes, dyatt & all other necessaries, in as good sufficient and like manner as when they were able to work. Itm. my Will is, that with as convenient speed as may be procured after my decease, eighteen funerall goold rings, one with another, of ye value of twenty shillings each, be given to those severall friends if living (Vizt) to my brother Francis and his wife,—to my brother Gibbs and his wife,—to my sister Ince, those to be given in England, —to my dear wife,—to my sonn Francis and his wife,—to my son Matthew,—to my Coz. Henry Tyler and his wife,—to my Grandson John Chiles,—to my honored sister Eliz: Diggs,—to my honored friend Willm Cole, Esquire,—to the Reverent Rowland Jones minister and his wife:—These to be given in Virginia, and to my brother Robert and his wife in England. And lastly, of this my last Will and Testament, I make my said dear wife, Alice, and my said two well beloved sonnes Francis Page & Matthew Page, Joynt Executors, having great confidence of my wifes love to our sons, shee being with this my last will right well pleased & contented, I charge & require my said sons to honor their mother with that filiall love duty & obedience as is pleasing to Almighty God, and due to parents, each to keep a just and true Acc^{t} of all things relating to their mother's interest, and faithfully & truly make paym^{t} of her just right & dues given her by this my last will, that noe dispute, strife, debate, or controversy may arise between my wife, sons or any other Relations claiming any bennefitt by this my Will, and if any question or doubt shall arise, my will is that ye exposition and determination thereof, shall be judged from time to time according to the litterall sense of this my last will in every behalfe, and by the discretion of my Execut^{rs} and two other discreet friends, and noe otherwise. And I doe hereby Revoke all former Wills, bequests, and legacies by me made, and establish this to be my last Will and Testament. In testimony that this (contained in two sheets of paper, is my last Will and Testament, I have in the presence of three witnesses sett my hand & affixed my seal the fifth day of March, in y^{e} third year of y^{e} Raigne of our Soveraign Lord King James y^{e} Second & Anno Dom. $168\frac{6}{7}$

JOHN PAGE

Signed by y^{e} Testator JOHN PAGE (& his wife Alice being also present) and also sealed and delivered as his last Will & Testament this fifth day of March Anno 1686 in presence of

[THE SEAL]

WM SHERWOOD
HENRY TYLER
ALEX. BONNYMAN

YORKE COUNTY Ss. Ffruary the 24th $169\frac{1}{2}$ presented in Court by Capt Ffrancis Page one of the joynt Executo^{rs} in y^{e} within Will mentioned, and was proved by y^{e} oathes of Henry Tyler and Alexander Bonnyman two of y^{e} witnesses hereunto. And is Recorded

WM SEDGWICK C^{d} Cur.

Memorand y^{e} Raseing of part of y^{e} first and second line, ye sixth, ninth, eleventh, nineteenth, twentyth, one two and three and twentyeth lines in ye second sheet of this my Will, was obliturated with mine own hand

JOHN PAGE.

Memorand That on ye thirtyeth day of September 1689 Mr. Geo: Richards by my order paid to my niece Mary Page, thirty three pounds six shillings eight pence, in full of all legacy within given, & signed a discharge for the same. That on ye 28th day of December 1689 ye like sume of thirty three pounds six shillings eight pence was paid to my nephew Luke Page in full of ye within Legacy as by both discharges inclosed herein, being fully paid by my order

JOHN PAGE.

Ffebruary y[e] 24th 169½ Recordant. die et Anno superadict

℘ WILL[M] SEDWICKE C[d] Cur. Ebor.

A copy

Teste

A. F. HUDGINS

Clk Court York County V[a].

VIRGINIA

YORK COUNTY TO WIT:

I, A. F. HUDGINS, Clerk of the County Court of York County, State of V[a], do hereby certify that the foregoing is a true copy of the last Will & Testament of John Page, deceased, as the same appears of record and on file in my office.

Witness my hand and the seal of said Court affixed this the 20th day of May A. D. 1884, in the 108th year of the Commonwealth of Virginia.

A. F. HUDGINS Clerk

York Co. Cts. V[a].

VIRGINIA

YORK COUNTY TO WIT:

I, H. B. WARREN, Judge of the County Court of York County, State of Virginia, do hereby certify that A. F. Hudgins who hath given the foregoing Certificate, is clerk of the County Court of York County, State of V[a] and was Clerk of said Court at the time of so giving it. And I further certify that his attestation is in due form of law. Given under my hand this 24th day of May 1884

H. B. WARREN Judge.

Résumé of the Will of Col. John Page.

Imprimis he surrenders his soul into the hands of God, and directs that his body shall be buried with Christian burial, according to the rites and ceremonies of the Church of England, in the churchyard of Bruton Parish, within ten feet of the south side of the church wall, and a black marble stone to be placed over his grave, on a brick foundation rising 3 ft. 6 in. from the ground.

I.—He gives equally to his wife Alice, during her life, and to his son Francis, and his heirs forever, his farm with houses, etc., at Middle Plantation, and the farm with houses, etc., near Jamestown, called Neck of Land; which latter belonged to his brother Matthew Page, deceased, whose son Matthew had mortgaged said farm, called Neck of Land, to the testator, John Page, 21st Dec., 1683, at £104 for redeeming said son Matthew from slavery out of Algiers. In addition he had given the said Matthew £26 for expenses, including clothing him, at London.

After the death of his wife Alice, the whole of both places to go to his son

Francis. If, however, the said Matthew redeem the Neck of Land farm of the mortgage of £104 in ten years, the said Matthew is to have the farm back. Otherwise it is to go to his son Francis.

II.—He gives his farm called Mehixton with water mill thereon, both situated on Tottapottamoy Creek, New Kent Co., Va., to his wife Alice and his son Matthew equally. After the death of his wife Alice, his son Matthew to have it all, and the farm and mill are not to be separated. After the death of his son Matthew, who as yet is not inclined to marry, the Mehixton farm, houses, etc., and mill to go to Matthew's lawful heirs if he have any. If not, the Mehixton farm, houses, etc., and mill, after Matthew's death without heirs, are to go to his nephew John Page, son of his brother Robert Page, late of Hatton, Hownsley Heath, during his life. After his death to his heirs if he have any. If not, or if he do not come to Virginia and actually live on the place eighteen months after notice, the property to go to his rightful heir then living in Virginia.

III.—He gives to his wife Alice and his two sons Francis and Matthew equally, or the longer liver of them, the profits arising from the lease of five tenements on Longditch, in Westminster, which he held from the Dean of St. Peter's, in Westminster, for twenty-seven years from 25th March, 1682, *at 48 shillings and 6 pence* (£2 8 6) per annum, but which he had rented out for twenty-seven years from 20th Dec., 1682, under lease dated 20th March, 1683, to Francis Norris, bricklayer, and Danl. Finch, carpenter, *at forty pounds* per annum!

IV.—He gives 291 acres of land, left over from some sold to Henry Malara, in the forks of Powhatan, to his son Francis and his heirs male. In want of which, it goes to his *grandson John Tyler*, son of his *granddaughter* Eliz. Tyler, and his heirs forever.

V.—He gives £50 to his *grandson*, John Tyler, to be paid when he becomes eighteen years old. If he die before then, £30 to such other child of his *granddaughter* Eliz. Tyler as shall first become eighteen.

VI.—He gives to each of his brother Matthew's children as follows: (1) to his nephew Matthew Page, £33 6 8; (2) to his nephew Luke Page, the same; and (3) to his niece Mary Page, the same. If any are paid off during his life, as was the case with Luke and Mary, they were not to get it after his death. [The record mentions them as *Cozins;* a term of consanguinity then used for relatives further than brother or sister—as O Tybault, my cozen, my own brother's son! (Shaks.) In a codicil, Luke and Mary are properly called *nephew* and *niece*, respectively.]

VII.—He gives his interest in ships equally to his wife Alice and his two sons Francis and Matthew during her life. After her death, his interest in the *Augustine* and *East India Merchant* (formerly called the *Prince*) is to go to his son Francis, etc., forever. His interest in the ship *Jeffreys* to go to his son Matthew, etc., forever.

All other dues, chattels, etc., not mentioned, to be equally divided between the three or such as shall be alive when he dies.

VIII.—All the negroes at either of the farms at Middle Plantation, Neck of Land, and Mehixton, when they become old, are to be taken care of, with clothes, diet, and all other necessaries as when they were able to work.

IX.—Eighteen gold rings, each costing twenty shillings, to be given to the following friends if living when he dies: (1 & 2) his brother Francis and his wife; (3 & 4) his brother Robert and his wife; (5 & 6) his brother Gibbs and his wife; (7) his sister Ince (Jure—*Tyler*); those to be given in England. And in Virginia the following: (8) to his wife Alice; (9 & 10) to his son Francis and his wife; (11) to his son Matthew; (12 & 13) to his cousin Henry Tyler and his wife; (14) to his grandson John Chiles; (15) to his honored sister Eliz. Diggs; (16) to his honored friend Wm. Cole, Esq.; (17 & 18) to Rev. Rowland Jones and his wife.

X.—Lastly he makes his dear wife Alice and his two well-beloved sons Francis and Matthew joint executors. Should any doubt or dispute arise, it is to be settled by the executors and two other discreet friends. He revokes all other wills, etc., and signs this on the 5th March, $168\frac{6}{7}$, and 3d year of the reign of James II., in the presence of Wm. Sherwood, Henry Tyler, and Alex. Bonnyman.

Col. John Page died 23d January, 1692. On the 24th Feby., 1692, the will was presented in court by Capt. Francis Page, one of the joint executors, and was proved by the oaths of Henry Tyler and Alexander Bonnyman, two of the witnesses. And was recorded.

Signed by WM SEDGWICK C^{d} Cur. (also written C^{d} Cur. Ebor.)

Mr. Lyon G. Tyler, son of the late John Tyler, ex-President U. S., writes under date of April 29th, 1884, Richmond, Va., as follows:

I inclose you the testimony I collected and hastily jotted down, from which you will perceive that Col. Page speaks of a *grandson* named *John Chiles*. It appeared to me at the time that Elizabeth, wife of Henry Tyler, was sister of John Childs. You will observe also that there was a Mr. John Page, of Gloucester Co., Adm^{r} of Matthew Page of Rosewell. (This John Page was undoubtedly the husband of Eliz. Page, only child of Capt. Francis Page, brother of Matthew.) Ann Tyler, mother of Henry Tyler, husband of Elizabeth in question, makes a Mr. John Page trustee in her deed of gift, June 24, 1672. She speaks of him as her "trusty and well-beloved friend." Deed Book 1671-76, p. 17.

It appears that John Tyler lived to become eighteen years old, and received the fifty pounds according to Colonel Page's will. Mr. Lyon G. Tyler, under same date, incloses the following copy of the record:

Received by me, John Tyler, son of Mr. Henry Tyler, of Yorke County in Virginia, and grand son of $Coll^{ll}$ John Page, formerly of y^{e} said County in

Virginia, dece[d], of John Page of y[e] County of Gloucester, fifty pounds of lawful mony of England, by bills of Exchange on Mr. Micajah Perry and Comp[a] Merch[ts] in London at ten days sight. The said Sum being due to me, the said John Tyler, for a legacy left me by y[e] last Will & Testament of y[e] said Coll[ll] John Page Dec[d], which I do hereby acknowledge to have received and discharge and acquit the said John Page of y[e] said County of Gloucester & Mary his wife, Admin[rs] of Matt. Page Esq[r] late of y[e] said County of Gloucester dece[d], one of y[e] Exec[rs] of y[e] last Will & Testament of y[e] said Coll[ll] John Page deced., and hold myself fully satisfied, contented and paid. In witness whereof I have hereunto set my hand and seal this nineteenth day of August 1706.

JOHN TYLER

Signed, sealed, and delivered in y[e] presence of

MARY WHALEY
HEN. CARY

At a Court held for Yorke County June the 24th, 1707, John Tyler the above mentioned came into Court & acknowledged y[e] above writing as his act and deed, & according to order is Recorded.

WILLIAM TUNLEP JR., Dep. Clerk.

This "John Page and Mary his wife, Admin[r] of Matt. Page, Esqr late of y[e] said County of Gloucester dece[d]," was the same John Page who married, first, Elizabeth, the only child of Capt. Francis Page, and, secondly, Mary Mann, the widow of Hon. Matthew Page, deceased.

Col. John Page, first of his family in Virginia, mentions brothers and sisters as follows: (1) Matthew Page, of Virginia, wife unknown. Had three children, viz.: Matthew, Luke, and Mary. (2) Francis Page, of England, wife and children unknown. (3) Robert Page, of Hatton, Hownsley Heath, England, wife unknown. One son mentioned, viz., John Page, who was offered some inducements by Colonel Page, his uncle, to come to Virginia. He probably married, first, Elizabeth Page, his first cousin, only child of Capt. Francis Page, eldest son of Col. John Page. She died very young, aged 19, without known issue. John Page then married, second, Mary Mann, widow of Hon. Matthew Page, and removed to Gloucester County, where he was administrator of Hon. Matthew Page, of Rosewell. (4) Gibbs Page and wife unknown, of England. (5) Ince (Jure—*Tyler*), sister, England.

Other Relations.

(1) Grandson John Tyler, son of his granddaughter, Eliz. Tyler (wife of his cousin Henry Tyler and probably sister of John Chiles).

(2) His cousin Henry Tyler—wife Elizabeth (Chiles?).

(3) Grandson John Chiles.

(4) Sister Eliz. Diggs.

Colonel Page had only two sons, Francis and Matthew. Of these Matthew alone had surviving male issue—one, Mann Page, who was the *only real grandson.* How could he have *grandsons John Tyler* and *John Chiles?* Eliz. Diggs was his sister by courtesy and mother of his daughter-in-law. John Tyler was great-grandfather of John Tyler, ex-President of the United States.

Col. John Page may have had a daughter married Chiles, who had John; and Eliz. married Henry Tyler. If so, their son, John Tyler, would have been great-grandson of Col. John Page and not grandson. Mr. F. R. Rives stated that in those days grandchildren and grandchildren's children were probably all called grandchildren only. On the other hand, nephew meant grandson; niece meant any relation in general, especially aunt; and cousin meant any relation more distant than sister or brother. It was frequently used for nephew.

Eliz. Diggs (mother of Mary Diggs, wife of Francis?) was either sister by courtesy or else sister who married Diggs.

Memoranda of Papers Carried to England per Cunard Steamship Aurania, Captain Hains, 9th July, 1884.

I. Probate Order. Ordo[d] for A probate of y[e] last Will & Testament of John Page Esq[r] deceased was this day granted unto Alice his wife Executrix and his two sonnes Capt ffrancis and Capt Mathew Pages joynt Executors appointed by y[e] said Will, which was this day proved in Court by y[e] Oathes of Henry Tyler & Alexander Bonnyman, two of y[e] Witnesses to y[e] said Will

A Copy

Teste

A. F. HUDGINS

Clk Court, York County, V[a].

II. Will of JOHN PAGE foregoing.

III. Certificate of British Vice-Consul as follows:

BRITISH VICE CONSULATE,
RICHMOND, VIRGINIA, U. S. A.

I, William Marshall, British Vice-Consul at Richmond, State of Virginia, Do hereby Certify That A. F. Hudgins, whose genuine Signature, and Seal of his Court, are respectively subscribed, and affixed to the foregoing Certificate, was on the day of the date thereof, the Clerk of the County Court of York County, State of Virginia, duly qualified, to whose official acts, faith and credit are due—and that the signature of H. B. Warren to his certificate is that of the Judge of the aforesaid County Court of York County, State of Virginia.

In Testimony whereof I do hereunto set my hand and Seal of office, at the City of Richmond, Va. on this Sixth day of June, A. D. 1884.

WILLIAM MARSHALL,
British Vice-Consul.

IV. Coat-of-arms drawing and Draddy's and Smith's Certificates, same as in first edition of this book, but Consul's and County Clerk's certificates somewhat different, as follows:

STATE OF NEW YORK,
CITY AND COUNTY OF NEW YORK, } *ss.*

I, PATRICK KEENAN, Clerk of the City and County of New York, and also Clerk of the Supreme Court for the said City and County, the same being a Court of Record, DO HEREBY CERTIFY, That A. P. Smith whose name is subscribed to the Certificate of the proof or acknowledgment of the annexed Instrument, and thereon written, was, at the time of taking such proof and acknowledgment, a Notary Public in and for the City and County of New York, dwelling in the said City, commissioned and sworn, and duly authorized to take the same. And further, that I am well acquainted with the handwriting of such Notary and verily believe that the signature to the said certificate of proof or acknowledgment is genuine. *I further certify that said Instrument is executed and acknowledged according to the law of the State of New York.*

IN TESTIMONY WHEREOF, I have hereunto set my hand and affixed the Seal of the said Court and County, the 26th day of June, 1884.

PATRICK KEENAN, Clerk.

HER BRITANNIC MAJESTY'S CONSULATE-GENERAL, NEW YORK.

(Arms of Great Britain follow.)

I, J. PIERREPONT EDWARDS, Esqr., HER BRITANNIC MAJESTY'S ACTING CONSUL GENERAL, DO HEREBY CERTIFY (old Eng.), That I have reason to believe that the Signature subscribed and Seal affixed to the Certificate hereunto annexed, are the true Signature and Seal of A. P. Smith who was on the day of the date of said Certificate, a Notary Public in and for the State of New

York, duly commissioned and sworn, to whose Official acts faith and credit are due.

IN WITNESS WHEREOF (old Eng.), I do hereunto set my hand and seal of Office at the CITY OF NEW YORK, this Twenty-sixth day of June, in the year of our Lord, one thousand eight hundred and eighty-four.

J. PIERREPONT EDWARDS.

V. Two Land Office Certificates endorsed by British Vice-Consul etc., as follows:

John Page 200 Land Reg. Vol. 3, p. 66.

(1). To all et, whereas et. Now Know y[ee], That I the said Richard Bennett Esq[r] et give and grant unto John Page, Merchant two hundred acres of Land Situated on the North side of Yorke river beginning at a little run joyning to the Land of Colt[o] William Clayborne running West by South by the river ten perches West North West behind Sunken Ground one hundred forty two perches and Soe North by West fourteen perches to a creeke runing East North East three hundred and Seventy perches by the said Creeke thence South by East to the back of Colto: Clayborne and Soe West by South halfe a point Southerly and thence South halfe a point Westerly one mile to the place where it began. The said Land being due unto the said John Page Merchant by and for the transportation of four persons into this Colony to have and to hold et. Yielding and paying et which payment is to be made Seven years after the first grant or Sealing thereof and not before, provided et. Dated the 23[d] of August *1653 Ut in Alys*

JOHN PAGE Merchant
NOICE — -- —
WILLIAM ORD
JOHN COX

LAND OFFICE, RICHMOND, VIRGINIA.

I hereby certify the foregoing to be a true copy from the Records of this Office as Witness my hand and Seal of Office this 27th day of June, 1884.

I. A. WINGFIFLD,
Reg. Land Office.

BRITISH VICE-CONSULATE,
RICHMOND, VIRGINIA, U. S. A.

I hereby certify, That I. A. Wingfield, whose true signature and seal of his Office are respectively subscribed and affixed to the foregoing Certificate, was on the day of the date thereof the Registrar of the Land Office of the State of Virginia, to whose official acts faith and credit are due.

In Testimony whereof I do hereunto set my hand and seal of office at the City of Richmond on this 27th day of June, A. D. 1884.

WILLIAM MARSHALL,
British Vice-Consul.

John Page 850, Land Reg. Vol 3, p. 212.

(2). To all et. Whereas et. Now know y^{ee} that I the said Richard Bennett Esqr et give and grant unto M^{r}. John Page, Merchant Eight hundred and fifty acres of Land Situated on the south side of the freshes of Yorke river. Beginning by a little run at a marked Beech tree running East South East down the river to another marked beech tree by a runn adjoyning to the now Land of M^{r}. Anthony Langstone runing one mile South South West into the Maine woods and Soe West halfe a point Northerly on the back side four hundred and eight perches from thence North, North East one mile to the place where it begann. The said Land being due unto the said John Page by and for the transportation of Seventeen persons into this Colony et. and also by order of the Governo^{r} and Councill bearing Date the blank to have and to hold et. Yielding and paying et. which payment is to be made Seven years after the first grant or Sealing thereof and not before provided et. Dated the blank.

Sam Smith	Mary Page	Andrew Coster
Jno. Binias	Thomas Pevinn	George Beashill
Alice Page	Thomas Wadlowe	Mary Middleton
Eliz^{a} Page	Morris Garrett	Jane Vallm

Anne Hill
Anne Cooper
Eliz^{a} Parsons

Then follows certificate of registrar; also British Vice-Consul, same as the one before this.

This one bears no date, but occurred during Richard Bennet's governorship of Virginia, 30th April, 1652, to 30th March, 1655.

It may be stated here that other branches of the Page family owned land in the colony of Virginia at various times, as evidenced by the following extracts taken from the old land register in Richmond, Va.:

1. Robert Page, patent for 500 acres of land, on Elizabeth City River, April 13th, 1636, Land R. Vol. I. p. 416.

2. John Page, Gent.—2700 acres, Lancaster Co., within the freshes of the Rappahannock River, eighteen miles above Nansemum town, on North side of said river—the 2700 acres of land being by the said John Page called "Pages Pilgrimage"— Dated last of Oct. 1656, 1400 acres purchased from Nicholas Meriwether, and 1300 acres due for 26 persons. L. R. N° 4, p. 132.

3. Thomas Page 281½ acres on south side of Rappahannock River for transporting six persons—Apr. 21, 1657. L. R. N° 4, p. 132.

Also same patentee—600 acres—south side Rappahannock river—Date 1662. L. R. N° 5, p. 246.

4. Richard Page, County of York—100 acres—land formerly granted to Daniel Wyld and assigned to said Page. Date Sept. 13, 1664. L. R. N° 5, p. 424.

5. Thomas Page and others—3075 acres in Rappahannock Co. 3[d] Apr. 1667 —N° 6, p. 182.

Same, 783 acres in Rap. Co. 16 immigrants 3 Aug. 1667. L. R. N° 6, p. 183.

6. John Page, 1900 acres in New Kent Co., V[a], on southe side of York River—38 immigrants—March 14th, 1672—L. R. N° 6, p. 107.

Ditto 34 immigrants, same date. L. R. N° 6, p. 108.

7. John Page Esqr. 330 acres Mid. Plantation in York Co., on the north side of the road leading through Mid. Plantation to J. Cittie Apr. 16, 1683.

8. Francis Page, 1600 acres in New Kent Co. on north side of the Pamunky river—Dated 20 Apr. 1685—L. R. N° 7, p. 457.

The following is a copy of the will of Alice Page, wife of Col. John Page, taken from the records in the clerk's office at Yorktown, Va., in April, 1890:

In the name of God Amen, I Alice Page of Middle plantation in Yorke County Virg. being sick and weak in body but of pfect memory & understanding praised be God Doe make and Ordain this my last Will and Testament in manner & forme following, ffirst I comend my Soule into y[e] hand of Almighty God my Creator hoping y[t] through the Death and merritts of his blessed Sonne, my Lord and Savior Jesus Christ I shall be raised again & receive eternall life My body I committ to y[e] Earth to be decently burried according to y[e] Reights and Ceromonies of y[e] Church of England in y[e] Church yard att Middle plantation between my late dear husband John Page Esqr his grave and my well beloved Sonn Capt ffrancis Page his grave, And itt is my desire y[t] over my Grave Erected with brick with equal highth with my Dear husband & Sonn's graves there be laid a polisht black Marble Stone, And for such Worldly goods as itt hath pleased God to bestow on me I give and dispose of y[e] same as followeth (that is to Say)

Im primis, ffirst I doe give and bequeath unto Bruton pish for y[e] use of y[e] Church one good pulpit Cloth and Cushion of y[e] best Velvitt Att y[e] discretion of my Executor hereafter named.

Item. I doe give & bequeath unto my Sonne Matthew Page his sonne Mann Page And to his daughter Alice Page each of them one hundred pounds sterl to be paid when they shall arrive at y[e] age of one & twenty years, And in case eyther or both of them depart this life before that age, Then to his daughter Mary Page, And all y[e] remaining part of my Estate both Reall and ꝑersonall wheresoever eyther in England or Virginia I doe give and bequeath unto my loveing Sonne Matthew Page hee paying all my just debts, And lastly I doe hereby make ordaine and appoint my said loveing sonne Matthew Page whole & sole Executor of this my last Will & Testament, not doubting his care to see y[e] same fulfilled in every respect, And I doe hereby Revoake & make voyd all former and other Guifts Wills, or legaces, by me heretofore made or spoken And establish this to be my last Will and Testament. In Witness whereof I the said Alice Page have to this my last Will and Testament Sett my hand & Seal the twelveth day of November In the year of our Lord one thousand six hundred ninety six.

ALICE PAGE (The Seal)

Signed, Sealed, & delivered by ye within named Alice Page for and as her last Will & Testament. In presence of us,

BRIDGETT TAYLOR
ALLEXANDER BONNYMAN

Att A Cort held for Yorke County August ye 24th 1698 The within written Will was then proved in Co^rt^ by the oath of Bridgett Taylor one of ye Witnesses thereto & according to order is received.

Test. WILLM SEDGWICK C^d^ Com. Ebor.

Att a Co^rt^ held for Yorke County September ye 26th 1698 P. adjournm^t^ from August Co^rt^ ye 24th last past, the within will was then proved in Co^rt^ by ye oath of Alexander Bonnyman ye other witness thereunto.

Teste. WILLM SEDGWICK C^e^ Com. Ebor.

STATE OF VIRGINIA, COUNTY OF YORK, to wit:

I, Chidley Wade, Clerk of the County Court of the County of York, in the State of Virginia, do hereby certify that the foregoing is a true copy of the will of the said Alice Page as recorded in my said office

Seal of the County Court of York, Virginia.

In testimony whereof, I hereunto set my hand and annex the seal of the said Court, this 2d day of April A.D. 1890.

CHIDLEY WADE, Clerk.

STATE OF VIRGINIA, JAMES CITY COUNTY, to wit:

I, W. G. W. Farthing, Judge of the County Court of York County, do hereby certify that Chidley Wade, whose name is signed to the foregoing certificate bearing date April 2d, 1890, is the Clerk of the said County Court of York in the State of Virginia, and as such is entitled to the custody of the records in the Clerk's Office of said County Court, and duly authorized to copy and certify the same.

Seal of the County Court of York, Virginia.

Given under my hand this 3d day of April, 1890.

W. G. W. FARTHING.

BRITISH VICE-CONSULATE,
RICHMOND, VIRGINIA, U. S.

I, WILLIAM MARSHALL, BRITISH VICE-CONSUL AT RICHMOND, VIRGINIA, DO HEREBY CERTIFY, That W. G. W. FARTHING, whose true SIGNATURE and OFFICIAL SEAL, are respectively SUBSCRIBED AND AFFIXED to the foregoing and above written CERTIFICATE, was on the day of the date thereof the JUDGE OF THE

COUNTY COURT of YORK COUNTY, STATE OF VIRGINIA, duly COMMISSIONED and QUALIFIED, and to whose OFFICIAL ACTS, FAITH AND CREDIT ARE DUE.

Seal of the British Vice-Consulate, Richmond, Va.

In TESTIMONY WHEREOF I do hereunto set my HAND AND SEAL OF OFFICE on this SEVENTH day of APRIL, A. D. 1890, at the CITY OF RICHMOND, Va., State of Virginia.

5 Shilling, Stamp Consular Service.

WILLIAM MARSHALL,
British Vice-Consul.

As already stated in the preface, it was by reason of the names of persons and places mentioned in Col. John Page's will that Mr. Burke, successor to Mr. Tucker in the College of Arms, London, was led to make searches in the parish of Bedfont. The following is a copy of his first report:

PAGE FAMILY IN ENGLAND.

FIRST REPORT AS TO THE PARENTAGE OF COL. JOHN PAGE, OF VIRGINIA.

On the 25th July, 1884, after the publication of his "Genealogy of the Page Family in Virginia," Dr. R. C. M. Page wrote to the late Stephen Tucker, Esqr., Somerset Herald, asking him to proceed with the investigation into the parentage of his ancestor, John Page, Esqr., of Middle Plantation, in York County, Virginia, by making the searches suggested by Mr. Tucker in March, 1880. A complete list of all wills and administrations of the name of Page was then made in the Prerogative Court of Canterbury from 1500 to 1700 and careful abstracts taken of those referring to the County of Middlesex from 1633 to 1681. On the supposition that the entry of baptism of 1628 in the parish registers of Harrow, Co. Middlesex, referred to Dr. Page's ancestor, and that consequently he was a member of the branch of the family of Page, of Harrow, which was then seated at Sudbury in that parish, the records of the Heralds College, and of the old Grammar School at Harrow, as well as other likely sources were carefully exhausted with a view of corroborating and elaborating this conjectural pedigree. In 1886, Mr. Tucker's assistant, E. A. Ebblewhite, who had been conducting these searches under that gentleman's direct instructions, carefully examined and made extracts from the parish registers of Harrow on the Hill, from their commencement in 1558 to 1700. It was then discovered that the John Page who was baptized 26th December, 1628, was buried on the following day and his twin sister, Mary, nine days later. The theory, therefore, that he was identical with the John Page who emigrated to America, about 1650, was entirely upset, and the whole matter had to be gone over again.

Mr. Tucker died on the 6th January, 1887, and Mr. Ebblewhite became my assistant on my succeeding to the office of Somerset Herald.

In April, 1887, I was instructed by Dr. Page to proceed with the investigation and having obtained all the papers from the administratrix of Mr. Tucker's estate, and after a careful examination of the whole case, I decided to act upon a clue in the will of John Page, of Virginia, dated 1686-87, in which he men-

Brass from the Chancel of St. Mary's Church, Bedfont, Co. Middlesex, England.

tions his brother Robert as "late of Hatton on Hounslow Heath." I found Hatton to have been in the parish of Bedfont, Co. Middlesex, and therefore instructed Mr. Ebblewhite to go there and examine the parish registers and monuments. We were informed by the Vicar that the parish chest did not contain any books prior to 1678, and after a careful search this was found to be the case. Extracts were taken down to 1723, at which period the family appeared to have died out there, but without much hope of their proving to be of assistance. In the chancel of Bedfont church is a brass to the memory of Matthew Page gent. 1631, and his mother Isabell 1629, of which a painting was made.

After thoroughly examining the church and surroundings, Mr. Ebblewhite discovered a large marble stone, with the Page arms, fixed against the churchyard wall. The inscription seemed only to record the death of Francis Page in 1678, aged 84, but having carefully removed the grass and mould from the foot of the stone, my assistant discovered a further statement to the effect that it had been placed there at the instance and cost of John Page, of York County, in Virginia, Merchant, the son of the deceased Francis.

We now know, therefore, that Dr. Page's ancestor was second son (as shown by the crescent in the arms in America) of Francis Page, senior, of Bedfont, Co. Middlesex, gent., who died on the 13th and was buried there on the 16th October, 1678, aged 84. It is very probable that this Francis was brother to Matthew Page whose brass is in the chancel, and that consequently his mother was the Isabell Page who died on the 9th day of January, 1629-30.

The Pages were seated at Bedfont at a very early period—Rowland Page having held the manor of Pates there in the time of Edward VI. In the following reign Alice, daughter of John Page, of Bedfont, married Paul Garway, of Tingereffe, in Bedfordshire, who died in 1619.

The arms on the monument to Francis Page give the birds with legs, thus indicating swallows or house martins, but they are usually depicted as martlets or swallows without feet.

The descendants of John Page, of York County, Virginia, are therefore representatives of the family of Page, of Bedfont—a branch of the old family of Pages of Harrow on the Hill, and are entitled to the arms borne by them, namely—Or, a fesse dancette between 3 martlets azure, a bordure of the last. Crest: a demi-horse forcene per pale dancette, or and azure.

With this report I send:

1. A collection of evidences bound in morocco and lettered "Page Family in England."

2. A painting, framed, of the monument to the memory of Francis Page, 1678.

3. A painting, framed, of the Brass, 1631, and

4. A mezzo-tint engraving of Bedfont Church.

H. Farnham Burke,
Somerset.

Heralds College, London.
11th October, 1887.

[seal]

Original Tombstone of Francis Page, Removed, 1865, from the Chancel of St. Mary's Church, Bedfont, Co. Middlesex, England, and now Standing Against the East Wall of the Churchyard.

From the foregoing report it might be supposed that the tombstone of Francis Page, father of Col. John Page, had been placed by the latter against the churchyard wall. This, however, is a mistake, for, as already mentioned, this tombstone was originally placed by Col. John Page over the grave of Francis Page in the chancel of the church, but was removed in 1865 during repairs, and was never replaced. The new brass plate in the chancel is an exact copy of the original tombstone, but cannot be seen without removing the matting placed over it. Any one visiting the church would never suppose that such a memorial existed unless they rolled up the matting. The latter was placed there at the suggestion of Vicar Pilkington to preserve the brass plate and prevent its being scratched by nails in the boots of country folk.

The following is Mr. Burke's second and final report on the parentage of Col. John Page, of Williamsburg, James City Co., Va.:

THE PAGE FAMILY IN ENGLAND.

Second Report.

Since my report of the 11th October, 1887, on my researches into the history of the Page Family in England, I have compiled a full pedigree showing the genealogical history of the descendants of Francis Page, of Bedfont, Co. Middlesex, who died in 1678.

The particulars contained in the papers I sent to Dr. R. C. M. Page, of New York, on the 12th October, 1887, were supplemented by information collected by him and other members of the family in the United States, and the draft pedigree was authenticated by the signature of Dr. Page, dated 7th September, 1888, and by that of Mary Maria (Page), wife of the Rev. George W. Dame, of the Episcopal Church, Danville, Pittsylvania Co., Virginia, dated 4th August previous. The pedigree was then handed in by me at the Heralds College, Chapter of the 6th December, 1888, and it was referred for proof to Windsor Herald and Rouge Croix as official examiners.

It then became necessary for me to make some further investigations with a view of showing that Francis Page, of Bedfont, was descended from some family of the same name who had previously registered their family genealogy in the records of the Heralds College. This I have not actually succeeded in doing, though from the notes I have made I have every reason to believe in the following conjectural descent:

At the visitation of Bedford, taken in the year 1566, John Page, of Arlesey, in that county, Esquire, son and heir of Richard Page, of the same place, Esquire (by Cicelie, his wife, daughter and one of the heirs of John Greene of Stoutfold, Co. Bedford, by Edith, daughter and one of the heirs of Sir Nicholas

Latymer of Dountoysh, Co. Dorset, Knight), who was son and heir of John Page, of London, Esquire, entered his family pedigree and arms.

Mr. John Page, who attested the pedigree, had been twice married—first to Mary, daughter of William Broke, of Broughing, Co. Herts, and secondly to Margaret, daughter of Lawrence Snowe, of Neither Gravenhurst, Co. Bedford—by whom she had issue, Richard Page, son and heir, Thomas, second son, and four daughters, Mary, Elizabeth, Anne and Dorothy—all of which children were living in 1566. Mr. John Page also had a sister Elizabeth, who was married first to Michael Cooper of Arlesey, and secondly to Jasper Smith of the same place, yeoman.

The arms admitted to this family were Or, a fesse dancette between three martlets Azure (quartering Greene, viz.: Azure, three stags trippant Or, and Latymer, viz.: Gules, a cross patonce Or) and the Crest of Page, a demi-horse forcene per pale indented Or and Azure named of the first. [Philipot, No. 49, p. 16, Her. Coll.]

It seems probable that John Page, of London (the grandfather of Mr. John Page, of Arlesey), had a younger son, John Page, of Bedfont, Co. Middlesex—whose family may have added the bordure to their arms—as the distinction of a cadet line, which was at that early period a very usual practice. This John Page (sometimes called Rowland Page), of Bedfont [1c., 2b., 11b.—Her. Coll.] was father of Alice who was born about 1555, and who was subsequently twice married: first to George Brettridge of Iver, Co. Bucks, and afterward of London (son of William Brightridge, of Iver, aforesaid) and secondly, to Paul Garaway (or Garway), of Acton, Co. Middlesex, and afterward of Tingereffe, Co. Bedford, who died in Feb., 1619, and was buried in St. Martins-in-the-Fields, Co. Middlesex (G. 3., 98b: C24., 153c: 122.20c; C2., 330c. and C24.298c.—Heralds College).

I believe that "John Page, of East Bedfont, Co. Middlesex," who was living in the years 1603, 1610, 1616, 1621, 1625, and 1628 (see Public Record Office Extracts at p. 139—*sequitur*) was the son of John Page, of Bedfont, above mentioned—the father of Alice, Mrs. Garaway.

John Page, of East Bedfont, seems to have died in 1628, leaving a widow, Isabel, who died 9th January, 1629 (see my first report of Oct. 11th, 1887). They seem to have had three children: (1) Mary, who was married by license 29th June, 1610 (Bishop of London's office) at East Bedfont, to John Walker, of the City of London; (2) Matthew Page, of Bedfont, who died unmarried, 1st February, 1631 (see my report of October 11th, 1887) and (3) Francis Page, senior, of East Bedfont (the ancestor of the Pages of Virginia), who was born in 1595 and died in 1678.

I do not depart from the suggestion in my previous report that the Pages of Bedfont were akin to those of Harrow on the Hill—for the identity of the arms proves this.

Although there is a good deal to be urged in favor of this descent, I have been unable definitely to prove it—and when it is remembered that the parish registers of Bedfont and the wills for that district (Archdeaconry of Middlesex) were destroyed by fire—it will be seen that the task is no easy one.

My investigations have comprised the wills and administrations of Page from 1600 to 1740 (pp. 9 to 45 *seq.*) and extracts from the Public Record Office (p. 139 *et seq.*) as well as various incidental searches.

On the 6th June, 1889, having satisfactorily proved the Page pedigree (together with the additions afforded by the will of John Page, of Gloucester County—see pp. 47, 65) I handed it in at the Chapter for Record, when it was referred to the official examiners, and another officer, "for a precedent as to what pedigree has been entered of an alien from an English ancestor not on record in the Heralds College."

On this resolution of chapter I went diligently through all our records for the desired precedent; but, although I discovered some very similar entries and offered them for the consideration of the committee, the officers were not unanimously in favor of the registration.

It was then suggested that, as I had failed in proving the earlier paternal descent, owing to the destruction of evidence, it would be taken as sufficent if I were to show a descent through Alice, wife of Col. John Page, from a Luckin family recorded in the College books. I accordingly examined the records here, the wills and administrations in the various Courts of Probate, and the registers of various parishes in Essex to discover the parentage of Alice Luckin —but all to no purpose (see pp. 69 to 134 *seq.*).

As will be seen from the accompanying papers (pp. 67, 135, and 137) similar searches were made as to Digges—with a more gratifying result, and the facts were added to the pedigree. This connection with the College Records, however, was not considered as sufficient, and the pedigree could not be actually recorded. The Draft Pedigree—every statement in which I have thoroughly vouched for—remains in the custody of the registrars of the Heralds College and will always be accessible for future reference; and I quite believe that the technical difficulty which prevents its further registration will hereafter be removed or overcome.

In the meantime I have prepared a vellum copy of the whole pedigree to which I have certified (in the following form) under date the 3d September instant: "I hereby certify that the above pedigree of the descendants of Francis Page, of Bedfont, has been faithfully compiled from authentic sources, that it has been fully proved before the official examiners of the College, and handed in by me at the Chapter for record."

I also certify that the whole of the documents attached to this report are faithful copies from the originals.

H. Farnham Burke,
Somerset Herald. [seal]

Heralds College, London,
6th day of September, 1889.

From the foregoing reports of Mr. Burke it appears that Col. John Page, progenitor of the Page Family in Virginia, was the son of Francis Page, of Bedfont, Middlesex County, England, as stated on the tombstone at St. Mary's Church, but beyond this all is, for the present, conjecture, owing to destruction of the records in that parish. It is highly probable that he was a relative of Sir Gregory Page, Bart., of Greenwich, County of Kent, England, as their arms closely resemble each other and their crests are identical. Mrs. Gregory Page died and was buried in Bun Hill Fields Cemetery, London, where rest also Daniel De Foe, John Bunyan, Isaac Watts, Mrs. Susannah Wesley, and others. The inscription on the tombstone of Lady Page attracted the attention of Rev. S. Halsted Watkins while visiting this cemetery among other places in London in August, 1892, and he copied it for the author. It runs thus:

Here lyes Dame Mary
Page, Relict of Sir Gregory
Page, Bar^t^. She departed
this life Mar. 11, 1728. In
the 56th year of her age.

And on the opposite side as follows:

In 67 months she was tap'd
66 times. Had taken away
240 gallons of water without
ever repining at her
case or ever fearing the
operation.

This beautiful little Church of St. Mary's, Bedfont Parish, Middlesex County, England, was built about the twelfth century and is of Norman architecture, as indicated by the zigzag (dogs' teeth it is called) ornamental work about the arches and doorways. The little village of Bedfont is near Feltham, on the London and South Western Railway, about thirteen miles from London. In order to get to Feltham it is necessary to take the train at Waterloo station, London, on what is called the Loop Line. There are always vehicles at Feltham station in readiness for conveying passengers to their destination, wherever they may wish to go. Near this church is a beautiful little vicarage, the residence of the vicar, Rev. Mr. Pilkington. In front of the church stand two ancient yew trees, curiously trimmed to represent peacocks, and in their foliage are still preserved the initials of parish officers dated 1704 (see also *Gentlemen's Magazine*, Vol. XCV., July to Dec., 1825, p. 201). In the churchyard are tombstones to the memory of several who had lived at Williamsburg, Va. Beneath the large yew tree on the south side of the churchyard is a tombstone containing the following inscription:

Here Lieth the Body
of MARY WHALEY,
Granddaughter to
FRANCES PAGE
of Hatton, and Widdow
of IAMES WHALEY
Gentleman in ye County
of York in ye Coloney of
Virginia.
She Died ye 31 of Ian^ry^
1742.

In August, 1889, this church was visited by Dr. R. C. M. Page, of New York, and his two cousins, Thomas Nelson Page, the author, and his brother, Rosewell Page, of Virginia, who had gone to Europe during the Paris Exposition. They were very handsomely entertained by Vicar Pilkington, who with the assistance of the young ladies, all of whom were very beautiful, prepared some ivy slips which were taken to America and planted in the rear of Dr. Page's house in New York, where they now flourish.

This church was also visited by Dr. Page and his friend, Rev. S. Halsted Watkins, while travelling in Europe during the summer of 1892. It has also been visited at various times by Dr. and Mrs. Page.

To return to Williamsburg, Va. According to the original tombstones at Williamsburg and Rosewell, Col. John Page and Alice, his wife, had two children, viz.:

1. Francis Page, eldest, born at Williamsburg, Va., A.D. 1657.
2. Matthew Page, born at Williamsburg, Va., A.D. 1659.

II. FRANCIS PAGE, of Williamsburg, James City Co., Va., eldest son of Col. John Page, of England and above-named place, and Alice Luckin, his wife, was born at the first-named place, in 1657, and died there 10th May, 1692, aged thirty-five years.

The inscription on his tombstone, at Williamsburg, Va., is as follows:

St. Mary's Church, Bedfont.

Here lieth in hope of a Joyfull Resurection
the Body of Captain FRANCIS PAGE of
Bruton Parish in the Dominion of Virginia.
Eldest Son of Colonel JOHN PAGE of the
same Parish, Esquire. Who Departed
this life the tenth Day of May
in the year of our Lord
1692. Aged 35.

Bishop Meade, *op. cit.*, Vol. I., p. 196, says that "he died at this early age, not without, however, being much distinguished as a lawyer. To him, according to Henning, were committed several trusts: among them the revision of the laws of the colony. He was a vestryman of the parish of Bruton, and contracted for the building of that part of the present church that was built before the time of Governor Spottswood."

He was also Clerk of the House of Burgesses, as appears from the following copy from Calendar of Virginia State Papers, Vol. I.

VIRGINIA, *S. S.*

BY HIS EXCELLENCY.

For as much as I, Francis Lord Howard, Baron of Effingham, and his Maj[ties] Lieut. Gov[r] Gen[ll] of Virg[a], am by his most sacrd Maj[ties] Especiall Commands, Given, at his Maj[ties] Court at Windsor, the first day of Aug[st], An[o] Dom, 1686, and in the second y[ar] of his Maj[ties] Reigne, Required upon the Convening Assembies, to appoynt a fitt person to Execute the office of the Clerke of the House of Burgesses. In Obedience to which commands of his most Excellent Maj[ties], I, the s[d] Francis Lord Howard, Baron of Effingham, being well assured of the Loyalty, Integrity and ability of you, Capt. Francis Page, of the execution and performance of the said place and office, and trust thereto belonging, I have thought fitt, and hereby doe, by and with the advice and approbation of the Councell of State, ordaine, nominate and appoynt you, the said Capt. Francis Page, Clerke of the House of Burgesses, with power to take, receive and Injoy to y[or] owne use and behoofe, all fees, dues and perquisites to the said place usually belonging or appertaining, and that you continue Clerke to the House of Burgesses till I shall signifye my Will and pleasure to the contrary.

Given under my hand and the Seale of the Colony, this twenty-fourth day of April, An[o] Dom. 1688.

EFFINGHAM.

Capt. Francis Page married, about 1682, Mary Diggs, the inscription on whose tombstone is as follows:

Here lieth in hope of a Joyfull Resurrection
the body of Mary the wife of Captain
FRANCIS PAGE of Bruton Parish in
the Dominion of Virginia. Daughter of
EDWARD DIGGS of Hampton Parish in
the same Dominion, Esquire. Who Departed
this life the Eighteenth Day of March in
the year of our Lord 169$\frac{0}{1}$. Aged 3-.

The last figure is partially obliterated, but it looks like 2. Thus: aged 32.

Capt. Francis Page and Mary Diggs, his wife, had an only child, Elizabeth Page, the inscription on whose tombstone is as follows:

Here lyeth the Body of ELIZABETH PAGE dec'd
late wife to JOHN PAGE of York County, Gent.
and Daughter of Cap. FRANCIS PAGE late of the
same county deceased. Who Departed this
life the 12th November Anno Domini 1702
and in the 20th year of her age.

The following is the will of Capt. Francis Page, copied from the records in the Clerk's office at Yorktown, Va.:

IN THE NAME OF GOD, AMEN, I, Ffrancis Page of Middle Plantation in Yorke County, Gentl^m^, being sick of body but of sound and perfect minde and memory, all laud and praise be given to God for ye same, considering with myself the certainty of Death and uncertainty of time when to make this my last Will & Testament in manner following, Ffirst I commend my soule unto the hands of Almighty God, my Creator, hopeing that through the death and meritts of his blessed sonn my Lord and only Saviour Jesus Christ, I shall be raised againe, and receive eternall life, my body I comitt to the Earth to be decently buryed according to the rites & ceremonies of the Church of England, in the Churchyard at Middle Plantation as near and att as a convenient distance from my late dear wifes grave as may be for laying of a gravestone over each of our graves, the ordering whereof, and of my funerall, I leave to the order and discretion of my Honored Mother M^rs^. Alice Page, and my dear and loving brother Capt Matthew Page. And itt is my desire that over my grave erected with brick of equall highth with my dear fathers and wifes graves, there be laid a pollisht black marble stone. And for such worldly goods and Estate as itt hath pleased God to bestow on me, I give and dispose of ye same as follows: (That is to say) I well knowing ye intent of my late deceased father John Page Esqr was to give to my coz: John Page, son of my unkle, M^r^. Robert Page, y^e^

plantation called Muskimino, doe hereby not only to perform the desier of my said father but alsoe for the love and affection I have to my said loving cosen John Page; Give and bequeath to him, all that y[e] aforesaid plantation called Muskimino containing seven hundred and ninety acres (more or lesse) situate lying and being att or near Chickahominy. Three hundred acres part there of lying in James Citty County, being purchased by my said deceased father of Christopher Chant, and y[e] other four hundred and ninety acres lying in New Kent County purchased by my said father parte from Robert Booth, and the other parte of John Boswell son & heir of David Boswell deceased; To have and to hold y[e] said whole divident of land with y[e] appurtenances, to him my said Cusen John Page, and the issue of his body lawfully begotten forever, And for want of such issue to revert to y[e] reight heire of me y[e] testator, And whereas I have (as one of y[e] Executors of my said deceased father) a right to the third parte of the negroes, stock, and other personall estate on and belonging to the said plantation; I doe hereby give to my said Cusen John Page and the issue of his body lawfully begotten, the use, possession and occupation of my part of all and every y[e] servants, negroes, cattle, stock, goods & chattells to y[e] said plantation called Muskimino belonging, and if my said Cusen John Page dye without having issue of his body lawfully begotten, then y[e] same to come and revert to my Reight heire. Item, I give and bequeath to my dear and only child Elizabeth Page (after my debts and legacies paid) all and singular my Estate both reall and personall whatsoever and wheresoever to me belonging, eyther discending to me as heir of my said desceased father, or given by his Will or by me purchased or otherwise belonging. And I hereby comitt her next to the blessing of God to the care, tuition, and government of my honored mother and after the decease of my said mother, to the care, tuition, and government of my well beloved brother in law Dudley Diggs, who I desire to bestow on my said child, the best education this country can afford. And itt is my Will, and soe I doe hereby order and appoynt that my Execut[rs] imploy my negroes labour and Cropps, with my other part of my personall estate to the best bennefitt and advantage of my said daughter, by settling another quarter on my land called Pamputike in King and Queen County, and purchasing more negroes to be settled thereon, and on my other plantations and quarters, and by secureing or imploying y[e] mony that shall arise by y[e] neat proceeds of the cropps and other part of my Estate as they my Execut[rs] shall think fitt, for the best advantage of my said daughter. And itt is my Will and desire that my Execut[rs] pay to my said daughter on the day of her marriage (in which I charge her to take the advice of her Grandmother, and two unkles, my Execut[rs] & their conssents) the sum of two hundred pounds ster[l], besides that part of her Grandmother M[rs] Eliz: Diggs' Estate which is due to her, and that y[e] other part of my said daughters estate be paid to her at her age of one and twenty years. And I desire my Execut[rs] to take care, that my brick mault house, and brick barne, with all other my houses att Middle Plantation be forthwith finished, and from time to time kept in good and sufficient repairs, and that y[e] same be leased out by my Excut[rs] till my said Daughter come to y[e] age of one and twenty years, for such reasonable rent as they my Executrs shall think fitt, and that care be taken, and ye tenants bound to keep and leave ye same in good and sufficient repair. All my Reall Estate, houses, land, and plantations whatsoever, I give to be held by my said Daughter, and the issue of her body forever, and for want of such issue then I give and bequeath the same to my said Brother Matthew Page his heires and Assignes forever. Item itt is my earnest request and desire to my said Brother Dudley Diggs, that he take ye trouble on him and care (and if occassion be, to take ye assistance of my other Executrs forthwith to settle and secure for my said child that part of the Estate to her belonging out of the Estate of her Grandmother Mrs. Eliz: Diggs deceased, to ye end the same may be imployed or securely putt oute for the best advantage of my said child. Item, I give to a poor man that lives on the Queen's Mill in Pomunkey Neck (whose name I cannot well remember, but is well known to my brother Matthew Page) the sum of five pounds Sterl, to be laid out to the best advantage, by my said Brother, of the said poor man. Itm, I give to Evan Roberts of Mill Swamp in Bruton Pish five pounds Sterling to be laid out by Mr. Samuell Timpson for the best advantage of the said Evan, Itm I give to each of my Executrs hereafter named twenty pounds Sterl apeece to buy them and their wife's mourning. Item I give mourning rings to the several persons hereafter named, Vizt William Cole Esqr and his wife, William Diggs Esqr and his wife, my loving Brother Matthew Page and his wife, and Mr. Dudley Diggs and his wife, Edward Jenings Esqr and his wife, William Sherwood and his wife, Mr. Dannll Parke and his wife, Mr. Saml. Timson and his wife, my Cussen Tyler and his wife, and John Page, Mrs. Mary Jones, Mr. Samuell Eborne and his wife, Mr. Martin Gardner, Mr. Thomas Thorpe and his wife and Capt James Archer, and desire that ye same be produced & disposed of by Executrs with the first conveniency Item I give to my loving friend William Sherwood five pounds Serling for writing this my Will. And lastly I hereby make, ordaine and appoint my said dear and loving Brother Capt Matthew Page and Mr. Dudley Diggs Executrs of this my last Will & Testament, not doubting but they will take care to see the same fulfilled in every respect. And I hereby revoke and make voyd all former and other guifts wills or legacies by me heretofore made, or spoken, and establish this to be my last Will and Testament. In witnesse whereof, I the said Ffrancis Page have to this my last Will and Testament sett my hand & seale the Three and twentyeth day of Aprill, in the year of our Lord One thousand six hundred ninety two.

FFRANCIS PAGE [THE SEALE]

Signed, sealed, published, & declared by the within named Ffrancis Page for and as his last will an Testament and by him soe delivered (the words, if fulfilled, Mr. Thomas Thorpe and his wife) being interlined before signing.

In presence of

WILLM SHERWOOD
JAMES DORAN
JOHN NEWSAM

YORKE COUNTY May the 24th 1692

Proved in Cot by the Oathes of all the witnesses. And is Ordered to be comitted to Record, which is accordingly performed.

WILLM SEDGWICKE Cd Cur. Ebor.

A copy

Teste

A. F. HUDGINS

Clk Court York County Va.

VIRGINIA.

YORK COUNTY, to wit:

I, A. F. HUDGINS, Clerk of the County Court of York County, State of Virginia, do hereby certify that the foregoing is a true copy of the Last Will and Testament of Francis Page, decd and also a true Copy of the Probate Order for said Will as the same appears of record and on file in my Office. Witness my hand and the seal of said Court affixed this the 21st day of May A. D. 1884, in the 108th year of the Commonwealth of Virginia.

A. F. HUDGINS,

[L. S.] Clerk of York County Court, Virginia.

VIRGINIA

YORK COUNTY, to wit:

I, H. B. WARREN, Judge of the County Court of York County, State of Virginia, do hereby Certify that A. F. Hudgins, who hath given the foregoing Certificate, is Clerk of the County Court of York County, State of Virginia, and was Clerk of said Court at the time of so giving it. And I further Certify that his attestation is in due form of law. Given under my hand this 24th day of May A D. 1884.

H. B. WARREN, Judge.

PROBATE ORDER.

Capt Mathew Page and Mr. Dudley Diggs upon their petition to this Cort have Ordered granted for a probate of ye last Will and Testament of Mr. Ffrancis Page deceased they being appointed Executrs by the said Will which was this day proved in Cort by ye Oathes of all ye Witnesses thereunto subscribed. And it is ordered to be comitted to Record.

A copy

Teste

A. F. HUDGINS

Clk Court York County Va.

There are at present (1893) five graves of the Page family at Williamsburg, Va., and the foregoing inscriptions are exact copies, in every respect, of those found on the tombstones. These copies were made 18th October, 1881, by Dr. R. Channing M. Page, of New

York City, in the presence of Francis R. Rives, Esq., of the same place, the two being at that time on a visit together to the centennial anniversary of the Yorktown surrender.

Elizabeth Page, only child of Capt. Francis Page and Mary Diggs, his wife, was born at Williamsburg, Va., in 1683. She married, about 1701, John Page, an eminent lawyer, by whom she had no issue, and died 12th November, 1702, aged nineteen.

Bishop Meade, *op. cit.*, Vol. I., p. 197, says:

> There is also in the Williamsburg churchyard the tomb of a Mrs. Page, wife of John Page, and the daughter of Francis. This John Page was, doubtless, Col. John Page, the lawyer, to whom the Vestry intrusted their rights, when Nicholson and others sought to invade them. . . . The Vestry directed Mr. John Page (who was grandson of the old vestryman of that name, who was now dead), an eminent lawyer and member of the Council, to present the case to the House of Burgesses, requesting them to take action on the subject, etc.

This John Page was not grandson, as Bishop Meade supposed, but was grandson-in-law "of the old vestryman of that name who was now dead" and afterward his son-in-law; for he married, first, Elizabeth, the granddaughter, and, secondly, the daughter-in-law, Mary Mann, the latter being the widow of Hon. Matthew Page. The following is the will of this John Page, the lawyer, furnished by Mr. Burke, of the College of Arms, London:

(*P. C. C., Browning 14.*)

IN THE NAME OF GOD AMEN. I John Page of Gloucester County in Virginia, being in good health and perfect memory and understanding (praised be God) and designing by the grace of God shortly á voyage for England do make and ordain this my last will and Testament in manner and form following:—

Imprimis, I give and bequeath to my dear and loving daughter Elizabeth Page all her Mother's Cloathes, Rings and Jewells, and five Guineas to lay out on such Jewell or Ornament as she shall think proper, at the age of twelve years—which will be on the fourth day of November in the year of our Lord one thousand seven hundred and fourteen, and such a certain sum of money besides as, with what is due to her from the Estate of Cap[t] ffrancis Page and M[rs] Elizabeth Page (her Mother) deceased, (which will appear by my account of the said Estates given into the Generall Court), will make the full sum of three thousand pounds of lawfull English Money—to be paid her at the age of twenty one years.

Item I give and bequeath to my dear and loving daughter Mary Page the full sum of three thousand pounds of lawfull English money :—That is to say two thousand pounds of the said summ to be paid her three months after the day of her marriage or at the [age] of twenty one years which shall first happen and the other one thousand pounds to be paid her at the age of twenty one years, which will be on the twenty-sixth day of January in the year of our Lord One thousand seven hundred and twenty seven. And I give my said daughter Mary a pair of gold earings sett with rubies and Rose Diamonds in a Shaggreen case, and one large gold wedding ring one gold ring enameld with blew and another with Black, which were her Mothers, and the one half of all my China ware in my now dwelling house in the said Gloucester County. Item I give and bequeath to my loving daughter in Law Martha Page all her Mothers rings and Jewells, except the Earings and the other three Rings already bequeathed to my daughter Mary, And the other half of my China ware in my now dwelling house in the said Gloucester County and one large Comon Prayer book with a Shagreen Cover plated with silver and clasps, which was her mothers. Item I give and bequeath unto my loving son in Law Mann Page upon his arrivall in Virginia a saddle horse such as he shall choose upon any of my plantations, also a large folio Bible with a Turkey leather cover plated with silver and clasps, a silver Watch, a Silver hilted sword a Torter shell and Silver hilted hanger and Belt, one Torter shell and Silver handed Horse whip, Crimson Velvett Howsen and Holster caps trimm'd with Silver Lace and a Silver Tobacco box which were his ffathers. I also give and bequeath to my said Son in law five Pictures in double lacker'd frames now hanging in the parlor of my said dwelling house in Gloucester County (viz[t]) of his father Cole [sic, a contraction for "Colonel"] Mathew Page, of his Mother M[rs]. Mary Page, of himself and of his two Sisters Alice and Martha; And whereas by an Instrument of writing, bearing date the twentieth day of September in the year of our Lord one thousand seven hundred and five made by me before marriage with my late wife mother of the said Mann Page—wherein I did oblige myself to pay to the said Mann Page to the value of two thousand pounds sterling in Negroes, Cattle horses, mares and sheep, and hoggs household necessaries, and working Tooles, as the same should be appraised by four honest men upon their oathes whereof the said Mann Page to choose two of them if the said Mann Page and myself my Executors &c. should not otherwise agree and forty hogsheads of prized Tobb[a] at the rate of thirteen shillings and sixpence for every hundred pounds weight upon the Plantations of the said Mann Page in New Kent County which is to be in full payment of so much as part of what is due to the said Mann Page out of his said ffathers Estate. Now my will is if I should depart this life before the said Mann Page attain to the age of twenty one years that, Imediately after the finishing the Crop upon hand at my death, my Trustees of this my last will and Testament hereafter menconed do have so much of the said Estate in the said New Kent County appraised as with the said forty hogsheads of Tobacco (which is to be leaf tobacco) shall amount to the said Sum of Two thousand pounds sterling and deliver the same to the said Mann Page or his Guardian in part of payment of what is due to him from his said ffathers Estate; Nevertheless if the said Mann Page or his Guardian in Trust for him be willing to take the said Stock of Negroes, Cattle, horses, mares, hogs, household necessaries and working Tooles upon the said Plantations [after the rates (in proportion to their quality) they were formerly appraised as will appear by Inventory in the Secretaries office] then my will and desire is (if he like of it) that he may have the whole stock of Negroes, Cattle, horses, mares, hogs, household necessaries and working Tooles, and all the Indian Corn and other grain upon the said Plantations in New Kent County, at the said rates, discharging my Estate from so much as the same shall amount to as part of his due out of his said ffathers Estate; And Whereas it would be a very great hindrance and loss to my said Son in law Mann Page to have his plantations in Gloucester County unstockt when they shall come into his hands therefore my will is that he may have the whole Stock of Negroes, (Except George and Jemmy two of my Carpenters and Doll and Poll two house wenches and their Children), Cattle, horses and mares, sheep, hogs, household furniture and working Tooles, as near as can be computed by four honest men upon their Oathes at the rates they were formerly appraised which will appear by Inventory in the Secretaries Office, having due regard to the quality of the said Negroes, and my will also is that my said Son in Law Mann Page may have one half of my Store goods upon the said Plantations which are properly for the use of the Plantations at the rate of Tenn p' Cent upon what they cost in England which is for charges of Importation but if the said Mann Page shall refuse to take the whole stock, goods and chattells aforesaid in Gloucester County then my will and intention is that he have no part thereof And whereas the aforementioned goods and chattles will amount to considerably more than what will be due to him of his said ffathers Estate my will is if it should so happen that the said Mann Page hath not nor cannot have the Guardianship of his sister Martha whereby to have his porcon in his hands that he the said Mann Page giving Bond with sufficient security, if under twenty one years of age, but if at that age, his own Bond shall be sufficient for the payment within three years from the date of the said Bond for the use of my Executor hereafter named the overplush with the said stock of Negroes Goods and Chattells shall amount to more then what shall be due to him from his said ffathers Estate. Item I give and bequeath to my Godson Bouth Napier son of Robt. Napier formerly of New Kent County the Sum of Twenty pounds St^g^. to be paid Six months after my decease to buy him a young Negro. Item I give and bequeath to my Godson Edward Diggs son of Co^ll^. Dudley Diggs twenty pounds St^g^., to be paid him at the age of twenty one years to buy him a peice or peices of plate. Item I give and bequeath to my godson Matthew Walker Son of M^r^. Joseph Walker of York County thirty pounds S^tg^. to be paid within Six months after my decease to be laid out the first opportunity in pur chasing two negro children which said two negroes and their Increase to go to him dispose of as he shall think fitt as soon as he shall attain to the age of Eighteen years. Item I give and bequeath to my dear and loving Son John Page all the remainder of my Estate both reall and personall in England and Virgini or elsewhere (Except forty pounds sterling hereafter bequeathed) and do make my said son John Page sole Executor of this my last Will and Testa-

4

ment and my will is that he have full and absolute possession of the said Estate and full power in the Execucon of this my last Will and Testament as soon as he shall attain to the age of Eighteen years, which will be on the twenty second day of December in the year of our Lord one thousand seven hundred and seventeen, and untill my said son John Page shall attain to the age of Eighteen years, I appoint my loving ffriends M^{r}. Edmond Barkley of Gloster County, M^{r}. Robert Anderson jun^{r}. of New Kent County and M^{r}. Richard Wiltsheir of Gloster County Trustees to see this my last Will and Testament duely executed, and for the better managem^{t} of my said sons Virginia Estate my will and desire is that my said Trustees appoint one or two of themselves or some other capable person at a reasonable Sallary to look after and manage the same as a Gen^{ll} overseir or Baylif and to ship the Crops of Tob^{co}, but that the bills of loading be taken in all my Trustees names.

Item I give and bequeath to each of my said Trustees ten pounds st^{g} to buy mourning, and my will is, as soon as my Son in law Mann Page shall attain to the age of Twenty one years and have received full payment of my said Trustees out of my Estate for what is due to him from his said ffathers estate, that my said son in Law Mann Page by joined to my said Trustess, in Trust for my said son John Page's Estate. In Witness whereof I have hereunto sett my hand and seal the twentieth day of Aprill in the year of our Lord Christ One thousand seven hundred and nine. J. Page. Signed sealed and delivered by the within named John Page for and as his last Will and Testament In the presence of Guy Smith Cler :, John Pratt, Hugh Hughes.

2^{d} January 1718 Which day appeared personally Micajah Perry and Richard Perry of the Parish of S^{t}. Catherine Cree-church London merchants, and John Page of York County in Virginia, Gentleman, and by vertue of their corporall Oaths deposed as followeth to wit the said Micajah and Richard Perry deposed that they were well acquainted with John Page the elder, late of Gloucester County in Virginia, but at Bethnal Green in the parish of Stepney in the County of Middx Merchant deceased, and with his hand-writing for severall years next before and till the time of his death which happned sometime in the year 1710—having severall times seen him write and received severall Letters and Bills of Exchange from him whereby they became well acquainted with his hand-writing and the Dep^{ts} several times visited the said deceased at his lodging at Bethnal Green afores^{d} during the time of his sickness whereof he dyed and he then told the Depon^{ts} that he had made his will and left the same at Virginia and the Deponents shortly after his Death found amongst his the deceaseds papers of importance in his Escrutore or desk at his said lodgings the Schedule Testamentary hereunto annexed purporting his the deceaseds last Will and Testament beginning thus vizt :—In the Name of God Amen I John Page of Gloucester County in Virginia &c., and ending thus, vizt :—In witness whereof, I have hereunto sett my hand and seal. And the Dep^{ts} verily believe the same to be all wrote by and with the proper hand of him the said deceased and the said Micajah Perry further deposed that he hath had in his custody the aforesaid Schedule ever since the same was so found as aforesaid. And the said John Page the younger deposed that he was well acquainted with his said ffathers hand writing and verily believes the aforesaid Schedule to be all wrote by and with the proper hand of his said ffather and that the same agrees with his said ffathers originall will remaining in the Secretaries office in Virginia and the Dep[t] about nine months since received from M[r]. Joseph Walker of York County aforesaid Merchant one of the Trustees therein named the other Schedule Testamentary hereunto annexed bearing date the twentieth day of April in the year of our Lord one thousand seven hundred and nine who then told him the Dep[t] that the same was a Copy of his fathers last will and Testament which the Dep[t] believes to be true—

Micajah Perry, Richard Perry, J. Page—eōd die p[r]fati Micajah et Rich'us Perry et Jolies Page Jurat. fuer. super veritati p[r]missorum coram me E. Kinaston, Surr.

Probatum fuit hujusmodi Testamentum apud London coram venerabili viro Edvardo Kinaston Legum Doctore Surrogato venerabilis et egregij viri Johannis Bettesworth Legum etiam Doctoris Curiæ Prerogativæ Cantuariensis Magistri Custodis sive commissarij legitime constituti secundo die mensis Januarij anno Domini millesimo septigentesimo decimo octavo, Juramento Johannis Page filij dicti defuncti et Executoris unici in dicto Testamento nominat. Cui commissa fuit administratio omnium et singulorum bonorum jurium et creditorum dicti defuncti de bene et fideliter administrando eadem ad Sancta Dei Evangelia jurat, etc:

From the foregoing will it appears that the John Page who first married Elizabeth, daughter of Capt. Francis Page, married secondly Mary Mann, widow of Hon. Matthew Page, of Rosewell, and had issue, all of whom lived in England. John Page himself died in 1710 at Stepney, England. His widow, Mary Mann, returned to Rosewell, where she died and was buried, as will appear when speaking of her as the wife of Hon. Matthew Page.

It was the case above mentioned of the Vestry of Bruton Parish *versus* Parson Whately and his supporter, Governor Nicholson, about 1702, that led Bishop Meade, *op. cit.*, Vol. I., pp. 150, 151, to write as follows:

In the history of the Vestries we may fairly trace the origin not only of that religious liberty which afterward developed itself in Virginia, but also of the early and determined stand taken by the Episcopalians of Virginia in behalf of civil liberty. The Vestries, who were the intelligence and moral strength of the land, had been trained up in the defence of their rights against governors and bishops, kings, queens, and cabinets. They had been slowly fighting the battles of the Revolution for one hundred and fifty years. Taxation and representation were only other words for support and election of ministers. The principle was the same. It is not wonderful, therefore, that we find the same men, who took the lead in the councils and armies of the Revolution most active in the recorded proceedings of the Vestries. Examine the vestry books and you will find prominent there the names of Washington, Peyton Randolph, Gen'l Nelson, Gov. Page, Richard Henry Lee, George Mason, and hundreds of others who might be named as patriots of the Revolution.

The Williamsburg branch of the Page family in Virginia became extinct upon the death of Capt. Francis Page without surviving issue. The second son, Matthew Page, had an only son, as we shall see, from whom all the others are descended.

II. MATTHEW PAGE, OF ROSEWELL, Gloucester Co., Va., second son of Col. John Page, of England and Williamsburg, James City Co., Va., progenitor of the Page family in Virginia, and Alice Luckin, his wife, was born at the last-named place in 1659, and removed to the first-named place. He died 9th January, 1703, aged forty-four years, and on his tombstone at Rosewell he is mentioned as "Honourable Collonell MATTHEW PAGE, Esqr."

The following is a copy of the inscription:

Here lieth Interred ye Body of ye Honourable
Collonell MATTHEW PAGE Esqr. One of Her Majesties
most Honourable Councell of the Parish of
Abington in the County of Gloucester in the
Collony of Virginia.
Son of the Honourable Collonell JOHN & ALICE
PAGE of the Parish of Bruton in the County
of Yorke in ye aforesaid Collony. Who Departed
this life in the 9th day of January Ann.
Dom. 1703 in ye 45th year of his age.

In the above inscription "Her Majesties most Honourable Councell" refers to Queen Anne, who reigned 1702–14. Hon. Matthew Page was one of the members of the original Board of Trustees for the College of William and Mary, and his name appears in the charter of that Institution as "Matthew Page, Gent." This charter is dated "at Westminster, the eighth day of February, in the fourth year of our reign" (1692). A MS. of this charter may be seen at the College of Arms, London. For a picture of the College of William and Mary see Bishop Meade, *op. cit.*, Vol. I., p. 157.

He married, about 1689, MARY MANN, only child of John and Mary Mann, of Timberneck, Gloucester Co., Va., where he probably lived several years before removing to Rosewell. The house in which he lived at the latter place does not now exist. It was simply a temporary wooden structure, like many others erected in the early colonial days, and has since been replaced by the present brick mansion, a description of which appears further on.

Mary Mann was an heiress, and alone survived her parents; hence the reason for naming her only surviving child, MANN.

She was born at Timberneck, in 1672, and died at Rosewell, 27th March, 1707, aged thirty-five. She was buried at Rosewell, and the following is a copy of the inscription on her tombstone there:

Here lyeth Interred the Body
of MARY PAGE wife of the
Honble MATTHEW PAGE Esquire
one of Her Majestys Councel
of the Collony of Virginia and
Daughter of JOHN and MARY
MANN of this Collony. Who
Departed this life ye 24th Day
of March in ye year of our
Lord 1707 in ye thirty Sixth
year of her Age.

She married first, as already stated, Hon. Matthew Page, about 1689; after his death in 1703 she married her cousin John Page, the lawyer, whose will has already been given.

In regard to John and Mary Mann, the parents of the wife of Hon. Matthew Page, the following are copies of the inscriptions on their tombstones at Timberneck:

Here Lyeth ye Body of JOHN MANN of
Gloucester County in Virginia. Gent.
Aged 63 years. Who Departed this life
y^{e} 7th Day of January Anno Domini 1694.

That of Mary, his wife, reads as follows:

Here Lyeth Interred the Body of Mrs
MARY MANN of the County of Gloucester in
the Collony of Virginia. Gentle Wo^{m}. Who
Departed this life the 18th day of March $170\frac{3}{4}$.
Aged 56 years.

Of the four children of Hon. Matthew Page and Mary Mann, his wife, three died infants. One of these, Elizabeth, the eldest,

(From the original oil portrait.)

MARY MANN,

TIMBERNECK, GLOUCESTER CO., VA.

was buried at Timberneck, and the inscription on her tombstone there is as follows:

> Here Lyeth y^{e} Body of Elizabeth Page
> Daughter of Matthew Page of ye Colony of
> Virginia. Gentleman. Aged three years.
> Who departed this life ye 15th day of March
> Anno Domini 1693.

The other two children were buried at Rosewell, and the inscription on their joint tombstone reads as follows:

> Neare this Place lye Interred the Body of
> Matthew Page Son of ye Honourable Colon^{ell}
> Matthew Page Esqr. and Mary his wife.
> Who departed this life the 31 day of December
> An^{n}. Do^{m}. 1702 in y^{e} 5th month of his Age.
> Allso the Body of Mary Page Daughter
> to Colon^{ell} Matthew Page Esqr. & Mary
> his wife. Who Departed this life y^{e} 14th day of
> Jan: An^{n}. Do^{m}. 170$\frac{2}{3}$ in the 7th yeare of her Age.

The children of Hon. Matthew Page, of Rosewell, Gloucester Co., Va., and Mary Mann, his wife, were therefore as follows:

1. Elizabeth Page, eldest, born 1690; died at Timberneck, 15th March, 1693, aged 3 years.
2. Mann Page, born 1691; only survivor.
3. Mary Page, born 1697; died at Rosewell, 14th January, 1703, aged 6 years.
4. Matthew Page, born 1702; died at Rosewell, 31st December, 1702, aged 4 months.

The location known as Rosewell, Gloucester Co., Va., was originally settled by Hon. Matthew Page about the year 1700, although the house that was built there by him does not now exist. Why he should have selected that particular site is not certainly known. It is no more conveniently situated than the location now called Shelly, and the latter is of a considerably higher elevation than the former, which is quite a consideration in that rather flat portion of the country. It is claimed by some that Powhatan had his headquarters at Rosewell, and it is supposed that Hon. Matthew Page settled there in commemoration of the event of the saving of the life of Capt. John Smith by Pocahontas. Many Indian relics have been found at Rosewell and in its immediate vicinity, and from various accounts it would appear that Rosewell was about the location of Powhatan's headquarters. On the other hand, Howison, in his "History of Virginia," is quite positive that Shelly, which was formerly called *Werowocomico*, is the correct location that marks the spot where that celebrated Indian chief, or "Emperor of Virgina," once resided. Bishop Meade (*op. cit.*, Vol. I., p. 335) inclines to Howison's statement of the case. The two localities are not very far distant from each other, and are separated by Carter's Creek, which flows into York River. They are both situated on the left bank of York River, Rosewell being on the right bank of Carter's Creek, while Shelly is on the left bank of that stream.

III. MANN PAGE, I., OF ROSEWELL, Gloucester Co., Va., the first of that name, second and only surviving child of Hon. Matthew Page, of the same place, and Mary Mann, his wife, second child (and only one having surviving male issue) of Col. John Page, of England and Williamsburg, James City Co., Va., progenitor of the Page Family in Virginia, and Alice Luckin, his wife, was born at the first-named place in 1691, and died there 24th January, 1730, aged 39 years. He was the half-brother of John Page of England, who was the son of Mary Mann, by her second husband, John Page.

The following is an exact copy of the inscription on the tombstone at Rosewell:

Here lie the remains of the Honourable MANN PAGE Esq.
One of His Majesties Council of this Collony
of Virginia.
Who departed this life the 24th Day of January 1730
In the 40th year of his Age.
He was the Only Son of the Honourable MATTHEW PAGE Esq.
Who was likewise a member of His Majesties Council.
His first wife was JUDITH Daughter of RALPH WORMELEY Esq.
Secretary of Virginia;
By whom he had two Sons and a Daughter
He afterwards married JUDITH Daughter of the Honble ROBERT CARTER Esq.
President of Virginia
With whom he lived in the most tender reciprocal affection
For twelve years:

Leaving by her five Sons and a Daughter.
His publick Trust he faithfully Discharged
with
Candour and Discretion
Truth and Justice.
Nor was he less eminent in His private Behaviour
For he was
A tender Husband and Indulgent Father
A gentle Master and a faithfull Friend
Being to All
Courteous and Benevolent Kind and Affable.
This Monument was piously erected to his Memory
By His mournfully Surviving Lady.

According to Governor Page's autobiography, quoted in Bishop Meade, *op. cit.*, Vol. I., p. 147, *note*, Hon. Mann Page was educated at Eton in England.

He was a member of His Majesty's Council in Virginia at the time of his death which occurred in the early part of the reign of George II. (1727–60). He was also a member of the Council during the latter part of the reign of George I. (1714–27). He inherited a vast landed estate, and was the founder of the present Rosewell Mansion.

According to Bishop Meade, he made a financial mistake in building such a large and costly house. Others say that the account of Bishop Meade, *op. cit.*, Vol. I., pp. 331, 332, is based on inaccurate information, and is greatly exaggerated. However this may be, he was only sixteen years old when his parents and grandparents on both sides were dead, and it is hardly surprising that a youth thus left alone in the world should be tempted into extravagance under the idea that he was rich because he had inherited vast forests.

The present Rosewell House was commenced about 1725. It was barely completed in 1730, when Hon. Mann Page died, and his body was laid out in the great hall, where it remained a short time before it was buried. The house is situated on the right bank of Carter's Creek, near the junction of the latter with York River, and just opposite Shelly. It is built of brick, with imported marble casements, and is three stories high, exclusive of the basement. It was then, and for many years afterward, the largest house in Virginia. The rooms are cubes in their proportions. The large hall was wainscoted with polished mahogany, and the balustrade of the grand stairway was made of the same material. The latter is carved by hand to represent baskets of fruit, flowers, etc. From the roof can be seen the Nelson House, at Yorktown, about fifteen miles away. It is the tradition of the place that Jefferson drafted the Declaration of Independence in this house before going to Philadelphia. This

(From the original oil painting by unknown artist, 1696.)

MANN PAGE, I.,

FOUNDER OF THE PRESENT ROSEWELL MANSION, 1725.

Died 24th January, 1730, aged 39.

tradition is not only not impossible, but is highly probable, as Jefferson was an intimate friend of Gov. John Page, and frequently visited Rosewell. For a picture of this house, see Bishop Meade, *op. cit.*, Vol. I., p. 332. It remained in the possession of the Page Family until about 1838, when it was sold, together with the land belonging to it, to Thomas B. Booth, of Gloucester Co., Va., for the paltry sum of twelve thousand dollars.

Mr. Booth changed the original flat roof to its present shape, covering it with galvanized iron instead of the lead, which he sold. After selling $35,000 worth of lumber and wood from the estate, he sold the latter to John Tab Catlett, of Gloucester Co., Va., for $22,500. The present owner, Mrs. Deans, says that her husband, lately deceased, bought it from Catlett, in 1855, for the last-named sum. The above-mentioned Mr. Booth evidently had an eye to profit when he bought the place. The lead was stripped from the roof, as already stated, and sold—galvanized iron being used instead. A letter is still in existence wherein Edmund Pendleton urges Gov. John Page to accept pay for the lead weights taken from the window casements for the purpose of being cast into American Revolutionary bullets. The grand old cedars bordering the avenue, some of which are said to have been of enormous size, were cut down and the wood sold for tub timber. The mahogany wainscoting was detached from the walls of the hall and sold, but being unable to dispose of the carved wood of the stairway, it was whitewashed. Even the bricks of which the wall of the graveyard was made were removed. The very foundations of the tombstones themselves appear to have been taken away, and the large marble slabs are scattered about on the surface of the ground. For a very interesting account of Rosewell, the reader is referred to *Scribner's Monthly Magazine* for Oct., 1881, published in New York by The Century Company.

Hon. Mann Page was quite prominent in politics, and according to Governor Page (Bishop Meade, *op. cit.*, Vol. I., p. 147, *note*), he was influential in "checking the British merchants from claiming even freight on their goods from England," etc.

The following copy of an old document, in possession of the author, is published, as it refers to Mann Page and is a Colonial relic:

MR. PRATT'S CASE WITH MR. STE. COMYNS'S OPINION, IN AUG., 1744.

12th Decr 1722, Mr. Wm Pratt of Virginia by his will of this date Gives to his only Daughter Elizabeth Pratt £1000 payable as therein is mentioned and in case his wife shod be ensient with a Son then he disposes of all the residue of his Estate in manner following "I Give all my real Estate unto such after born Son & his Heirs for Ever, and as to my personal Estate I give the Same to such after born Son when he shall marry or attain the age of 21 years for Ever. But if such after born Son happen to die before such time or in case my Wife shod not be ensient with a Son as afd I give all the residue of my sd Estate to my Father William Pratt of Peterhead in the kingdom of Great Britain

Gent, and his Heirs for ever. But if my Father sho^{d} die in my life time and so my Will become void as to him then I Give the residue to my Uncle John Pratt of London Merchant and his Heirs for Ever. And if he sho^{d} die before me then I Give the same to be equally divided among all my Brothers and their Heirs." He further willed that his Ex^{tors} sho^{d} allow out of the profits of his s^{d} Estate such Sum or Sums of Money as sho^{d} be sufficient to maint^{n} and Educate his s^{d} Child or Children in such manner as sho^{d} be fitting for them and appointed Mann Page Esqr, Mr. John Pratt his Uncle and John Randolph Guardians to his s^{d} Child or Children & Ex^{tors} of his Will.

The Test^{r} died the 22^{d} Feby 1723 leaving the s^{d} Elizabeth his Daughter and Keith William Pratt his only Son and who was born after making the said Will and Mr. John Pratt alone proved the Will.

It does not appear the Test^{r} had any real Estate but died poss^{ed} of a personal Estate of about £7000, one 3^{d} whereof his Widow was intitled to and the residue (after payment of the s^{d} Legacy of £1000) amounting to about £3600 was to be paid to the said Keith William Pratt or to such Person as sho^{d} be intitled upon the Contingencies mentioned in the said Will.

Wm Pratt ye Test^{rs} Father died in the Life time of the Testator 12th Feby 1731. The s^{d} John Pratt by his will of this date Gave to the s^{d} Elizabeth Pratt £500 to be paid her at her age of 21 or Marriage, and gave to the s^{d} Keith William Pratt his Gold Watch and his great Bible Two Silver Salvers and several other pieces of Plate therein particularly mentioned to be delivered to him at his Age of 24 years and Gave all the rest and residue of his Estate to the s^{d} Keith William Pratt to be paid him at his age of 24 years, but if he sho^{d} die before such age then he gave a further Legacy of £1500 to the said Elizabeth Pratt if she sho^{d} be then living and the residue of his Estate to his Nephew James Pratt willing that his Ex^{tors} do first thereout pay to his Bro. Wm Pratt and his wife Greeswell Thirty Pounds and directed his Ex^{tors} to maintain and Educate the s^{d} Keith Wm Pratt in the manner mentioned in his Will & appointed Joseph Windham, Philip Terry & Roger Tublay Ex^{tors}.

The s^{d} John Pratt died the 7th June 1731, and his Ex^{tor} duly proved his Will & maintained & educated the s^{d} Keith Wm Pratt and placed him in a Merchants House at Lisbon where he died lately under the age of 21 years & unmarried, but whether he made any will is not yet known.

The s^{d} Eliz^{a} Pratt is the only Sister of the s^{d} Keith Wm Pratt and was married to Mr. Walter King.

Mr. King has rec^{d} of the Ex^{tors} of Mr. John Pratt the Legacy of £1000 left to his Wife by her Fathers Will & the £500 left her by the Will of the s^{d} John Pratt.

Q. What is Mr. King in right of his Wife, the Representatives of Keith W^{m}. Pratt, & ye s^{d} James Pratt respectively intitled unto under ye Wills of Wm Pratt & Jno Pratt upon ye death of ye s^{d} Keith Wm Pratt unmarried & before attaining ye age of 21.

If Mr. Wm Pratt left any real Estate, the same was well devised to Keith Wm Pratt, & upon his death Mrs. King his Sister became intitled thereto as his Heir at Law ; as to ye residue of Mr. Wm Pratts personal Estate given to

Mr. Jno Pratt upon ye contingencies of Keith Wm Pratt dying unmarried and before 21, I apprehend is now to be considered as part of ye personal Estate of ye sd Jno Pratt, both ye contingencies of K. W. Pratt dying unmarried & before 21 having happened, but ye Interest and annual Increase of such residue from ye death of ye sd Wm Pratt is I conceive to be looked upon as part of the personal Estate of ye sd K. W. Pratt & go according to his Will (if he has made any) if no Will made, then to go to his Sister & her Mother if living to be distribuuted equally between them & not to go over with ye residue to Jno Pratt, there being no express words for that purpose, nor will a Court of Equity construe it to be ye intention of ye Testr that it shd go over to ye prejudice of an only child. As to ye Plate &c given by John Pratts Will to K. W. Pratt to be delivered to him at his age of 24 years was a vested Legacy on K. W. Pratt, & ye time of delivery only postponed, & will consequently go to his Representatives & not to James Pratt as ye same is not devised over to him upon ye death of K. W. Pratt. Mr. King in right of his Wife is intitled to ye Legacy of £1500, & Mr. James Pratt to ye residue of ye personal Estate of John Pratt after payment of Debts & legacies

STS : COMYNS
Inner Temple Augst 4th, 1744.

He married, first, at the age of 21, in 1712, Judith Wormeley, aged 17, daughter of Hon. Ralph Wormeley, Secretary of the Colony of Virginia. The following is an exact copy of the inscription on her tombstone at Rosewell:

Sacræ et Piæ Memoriæ
Hoc Monumentum positum doloris
ab Honorato MANN PAGE Armigero
charissimæ suæ conjugis
JUDITHÆ
In ipso ætatis flore decussæ
Ornatissimi RALPHI WORMELEY
de Agro Middlesessiæ
Armigeri
Nec non Virginiani Secretaij quondam Meritissimi
Filliæ dignissimæ
Lectissimæ dilectissimæque fœminæ
Quæ vixit in Sanctissimo Matrimonio
quatuor annos totidemque menses.
Utriusque Sexes unum Superstitem
reliquit
RALPHAM et MARIAM
vera Patris simul et Matris ectypa.
Habuitque tertium MANN nominatum
vix quinque dies videntem

Sub hoc Silenti Marmore Matre suâ inclusum
Post cujus partum tertio die
Mortalitatem pro Immortalitate
commutavit.
Proh dolor!
Inter uxores amantissima
Inter matres fuit optima
Candida Domina
Cui summa Comitas
Cum venustissima suavitate morum et sermonum
conjuncta
Obiit duodecimo die Decembris
Anno Milessimo Septingessimo decimo Sexto
Ætatis Suæ vicessimo Secundo.

The following is a translation of the inscription on the tombstone of Judith Wormeley:

"To the Sacred and Pious Memory of his most beloved wife, Judith, cut down in the very flower of her age, this Monument of grief was erected by the Honourable Mann Page, Esquire. She was a most worthy daughter of the very illustrious Ralph Wormeley of County Middlesex, Esquire, formerly also a most deserving Secretary of Virginia. She was a most excellent and choice lady who lived in the state of most holy matrimony for four years and as many months. She left one survivor of each sex, Ralph and Maria, true likenesses together of Father and Mother. She also had a third named Mann, who, scarcely five days surviving, under this silent marble was inclosed with his mother. On the third day after his birth she exchanged mortality for immortality. Alas, grief! She was a most affectionate wife, the best of mothers, and an upright mistress of her family, in whom the utmost gentleness was united with the most graceful suavity of manners and conversation. She died on the twelfth day of December in the One Thousand Seven Hundred and Sixteenth year and the twenty second of her age."

The following is copied from the old Family Bible now in possession of Frederick M. Page, son of Capt. Thomas Jefferson Page, U. S. Navy:

"Mann Page son of Judith & M. Page born the 8th of December, about three of the clock in the morning, 1716. On the twelfth day of December (the most unfortunate that ever befel me) about seven of the clock in the morning, the better half of me, my dearest dear wife, was taken from me, after she had endured the bitterest pangs of death about thirty hours, with the greatest patience imaginable, and most absolute resignation to the blessed will of God."

The said Family Bible was printed in London, 1696, and contains, besides the Bible, the Episcopal Prayer Book, Hymns, and the Apocrypha.

The records contained in it are very meagre and written by different people at different times. The above-quoted memorandum was probably written by Hon. Mann Page himself, unless it is a copy. That and a memorandum regarding the births of Ralph and Maria Page (which see) are the only satisfactory entries, the rest being in different handwritings and without dates.

Armiger literally means armor-bearer, but in heraldry it signifies Esquire.

In a letter from William C. Rives, Esqr., of Newport, R. I., to Dr. R. C. M. Page, of New York City, dated 18th February, 1879, he says:

"One of our nearest neighbors at Newport is Miss Catharine P. Wormeley, daughter of Admiral Ralph Wormeley, of the British Navy. He was a Virginian by birth, and beyond doubt of the same blood with the lady whose beautiful epitaph you have transcribed."

Hon. Mann Page married, secondly, in 1718, Judith, third child and second daughter of Hon. Robert (King) Carter, of Corotoman, Lancaster Co., Va., President of the Colony of Virginia, and Judith Armistead, his first wife. In regard to Hon. Robert Carter, Capt. R. R. Carter, of Shirley, on James River, Charles City Co., Va., writes as follows, 18th May, 1879:

Robert Carter (King) was the son of John Carter by his third wife, Sarah Ludlowe. The said John Carter was born in England, moved to Corotoman, Lancaster County, Virginia, in 1649, built the house and a church there, and died there in 1669, Robert "The King" being then six years old.

King Carter married, first, in 1688, Judith Armistead, and secondly, in 1701, Betty Landon. By each of these wives he had five children. Judith Carter, the second wife of Mann Page, of Rosewell, was his third child, and second daughter by the first wife, and was born about the year 1694.

My great-grandfather, Charles Carter, of Shirley, married, secondly, in 1770, Anne Butler Moore, of Chelsea, King William County, Virginia. Their daughter, Anne Hill Carter, was born in 1773, and married Gen. Lee (Light Horse Harry) 18th June, 1794. Miss Moore was granddaughter of Gov. Spottswood.

It may be stated here that Sir Alexander Spottswood, governor of Virginia, was aid-de-camp to Marlborough at the battle of Blenheim. He built the house now known as the Moore House, at Yorktown, Va., in which the terms of surrender were signed by Lord Cornwallis, in October, 1781.

Judith Carter was about 23 years of age when she became the second wife of Hon. Mann Page, of Rosewell, in the year 1717–18. When she died, or at what age, is not known. Bishop Meade, *op. cit.*, Vol. I., p. 351, says: "There were tombstones over each of the wives of this the first Mann Page—one in Latin and the other in English. The latter was first broken, and then crumbled away." The children of Hon. Mann Page and Judith Wormeley, his first wife, were as follows:

1. Ralph Wormeley Page, eldest, born at Rosewell, 2d December, 1713. He lived to become a student at William and Mary College, but died single and probably young.
2. Maria Page, born at Rosewell, 24th February, 1714. She was called Judith after the death of her mother, and married, about 1735, William Randolph, of Tuckahoe, Goochland Co., Va. She was the grandmother of Gov. Thomas Mann Randolph, of Edge Hill, Albemarle Co., Va. (See Randolph.)
3. Mann Page, born at Rosewell, 8th December, 1716; died infant.

The following is a copy of the record in the old family Bible in regard to these three children of Hon. Mann Page and Judith Wormeley, his first wife:

Ralph Page, the son of Judith & Mann Page, was born at Rosewell the second of December about half an hour after twelve at night, 1713.

Mary P., the daughter of Judith & M. Page, was born the 24 day of February, about 8 o'clock in the morning, 1714.

Mann Page, son of Judith & M. Page, born the 8th of December about three of the clock in the morning, 1716.

The children of Hon. Mann Page, of Rosewell, Gloucester Co., Va., and Judith Carter, his second wife, were as follows:

1. Mann Page, eldest, born at Rosewell, Gloucester Co., Va., about 1718, resided there. He married, first, 1743, Alice Grymes. Their eldest child was Governor John Page. Mann Page married, secondly, about 1748, Anne Corbin Tayloe.
2. John Page, second son and child, born at Rosewell, Gloucester Co., Va., about 1720; removed to North End, Gloucester (now Matthews) Co., Va. He married, in 1746, Jane Byrd, of Westover, on James River, Charles City Co., Va.
3. Robert Page, third son and child, born at Rosewell, Gloucester Co., Va.,

about 1722; removed to Broadneck, Hanover Co., Va. He married, 20th January, 1750, Sarah Walker.

4. Carter Page, born at Rosewell about 1724. He was a student at William and Mary College, but died single and young.
5. Matthew Page, born at Rosewell about 1726. He also became a student at William and Mary College, but died young and without issue.
6. Daughter Page, born at Rosewell about 1728, and died infant.

The three surviving brothers, MANN, JOHN, and ROBERT, became the heads, respectively,, of the three branches of the Page family in Virginia, viz.: (1) ROSEWELL, also called the White Pages. (2) NORTH END, or Black Pages. (3) BROADNECK Pages. The latter removed to Clarke County, Va.

After completing the history of the Rosewell Pages, we will consider the North End and Broadneck branches.

IV. MANN PAGE, the second of that name, OF ROSEWELL, Gloucester Co., Va., eldest son of Hon. Mann Page, of the same place, and Judith Carter, his second wife (by whom alone he had surviving male issue), only survivor of Hon. Matthew Page, of the same place, and Mary Mann, his wife, second (and only son having male issue) of Col. John Page, of England, and Williamsburg, James City Co., Va., progenitor of the Page family in Virginia, and Alice Luckin, his wife, was born at the first-named place about the year 1718.

He was probably buried at Rosewell, but at what age he died is not known. Bishop Meade, *op. cit.*, Vol. I., p. 352, correctly states that "there is no tombstone over the second Mann Page."

According to the Catalogue of William and Mary College, he was a member of the Board of Visitors of that institution in 1758, and is designated as "Mann Page, Gent." His son, Governor John Page, in his autobiography, as quoted in Bishop Meade, *op. cit.*, Vol. I., p. 147, *note*, says: "He declined the office of Councillor in favor of his younger brother, John Page (of North End), who, my father said, having been brought up in the study of the law regularly, was a much more proper person for that office than he was."

He married, first, in 1743, Alice Grymes, daughter of Hon. John Grymes, of Middlesex County, Va., who was a member of the Colonial Council during the reign of George I. The following is a copy of the inscription on her tombstone at Rosewell:

HON. MANN PAGE, II.,

Rosewell, Gloucester Co., Va.

Here lies the Body of Mrs. ALICE PAGE
Wife of MANN PAGE Esq.
She departed this life the 11th Day of January 1746
In child-bed of her second Son
In the 23rd year of her Age
Leaving
Two Sons and one Daughter.
She was the third Daughter
of the Honourable JOHN GRIMES Esquire
of
Middlesex County
one of His Majesty's Council in this Colony
of Virginia.
Her personal Beauty
and the uncommon Sweetness of her Temper
Her affable Deportment and Exemplary Behaviour
Made her respected by all who knew
The spotless Innocency of her Life
and her singular Piety
Her Constancy & Resignation at the Hour of Death
Sufficiently testified
Her firm & certain Hopes of a joyfull Resurrection.
To her sacred Memory
This Monument is piously erected.

The children of Mann Page, of Rosewell, and Alice Grymes, his first wife, were as follows:

1. John Page, eldest, born at Rosewell, 17th April, 1744, and afterward Governor of Virginia.
2. Judith Page, born at Rosewell about 1745, married Lewis Burwell, of Carter's Creek, Gloucester Co., Va.
3. Son Page—died infant.

Mann Page married, secondly, about 1748, Anne Corbin Tayloe of Mt. Airy, Spottsylvania Co., Va., and they had the following children:

1. Mann Page, Jr., born at Rosewell about 1749; removed to Mansfield, Spottsylvania Co., Va.
2. Robert Page, born at Rosewell about 1751; removed to Hanovertown, Hanover Co., Va.
3. Tayloe Page, born at Rosewell, 1756; died there, 1760, aged 4 years. The following is a copy of the inscription on his tombstone at Rosewell:

Here lyeth interr'd the Body of
TAYLOE PAGE
Third Son of MANN and
ANN CORBIN PAGE.
Who Departed this life
the 29th Day of November 1760
in the 5th year of his Age.

4. Gwynn Page, born at Rosewell about 1758; removed to Kentucky.
5. Matthew Page, born at Rosewell about 1760; died single.
6. Elizabeth Page (called Betsey), born at Rosewell about 1762. Married, about 1782, Benjamin Harrison, of Brandon, on James River, Prince George Co., Va. Their daughter, Lucy Harrison, married Richard Byrd, and their children were:
   (1) Addison Byrd; married Miss Custis.
   (2) Otway Byrd, and
   (3) Mary Anne Byrd, who married Beverly Kennon, and had two sons.
7. Lucy Burwell Page, born at Rosewell about 1764; married, first, about 1784, Col. George W. Baylor, and had the following children:
   (1) John Baylor; married Nancy Fitzhugh.
   (2) Lucy Baylor; married William Brent.
   (3) Molly Baylor; married Horner.
   (4) Nathaniel Baylor; died unmarried.
   (5) Eliza Baylor; married Horner.
   (6) Francis Baylor; died unmarried.

Lucy Burwell Page, the widow Baylor, married, secondly, about 1798, Col. Nathaniel Burwell, of Carter Hall, Clarke Co., Va., and had:
   (1) Tayloe Burwell; died unmarried.
   (2) William Burwell; married Mary Brooke.
   (3) Eliza Burwell; married Dr. James Hay and had issue. One of the daughters married Robert Dunbar, of Baltimore, Md.
   (4) Mary Burwell; married Francis Whiting, of Clay Hill, Millwood P. O., Clarke Co., Va. She died in 1881, leaving the portraits of Mann Page, of Rosewell, her grandfather, and Anne Corbin Tayloe, his second wife, to Mrs. Belle Burwell Mayo, 110 West Franklin Street, Richmond, Va.
   (5) George Burwell; married, first, Isabella Dixon; and, secondly, Agnes Atkinson.
   (6) Thomas H. Burwell; died unmarried.

In regard to the Burwell Family in Virginia, the first was Lewis Burwell, who emigrated from the north of England, 1640, and settled on Carter's Creek, Gloucester Co., Va. He married Lucy Higginson and had issue.

Of the children, Nathaniel Burwell, the fourth son, was born about 1680, and died in 1721, aged about forty-one years. He married, about 1709, Elizabeth, eldest daughter of Robert (King) Carter, and sister of Judith, the second wife of the Hon. Mann Page, of Rosewell.

Of the known children of Nathaniel Burwell and Elizabeth Carter his wife, may be mentioned: Elizabeth Burwell, their only daughter and called Betty, married in February, 1737, Prest. William Nelson (see Nelson); Col. Robin Burwell, of Isle of Wight Co., Va., married Sally, only daughter of Scotch Tom Nelson and the widow Tucker, his second wife, and was the father of Gov. John Page's first wife; and Lewis Burwell, the eldest son, born in 1710. After the death of Nathaniel Burwell in 1721, his widow, Elizabeth Carter Burwell, married Dr. George Nicholas and was the mother of Robert Carter Nicholas, Speaker of the Virginia House of Burgesses and Treasurer of Virginia.

Lewis Burwell, the eldest son, and born 1710, as already stated, removed to The Grove, James City Co., Va., which was built for him by President William Nelson, about 1740.

The house is situated on James River and is not far from Williamsburg. It is still standing and is said to contain the finest marble mantelpiece ever brought to Virginia in olden times. Lewis Burwell married, 1736, Mary Willis; and Col. Nathaniel Burwell, who married the widow Baylor, as already stated, was probably his son.

Col. Nathaniel Burwell first lived at The Grove, near Williamsburg, James City Co., Va., but subsequently removed to Clarke Co., Va., where he founded Carter Hall. After the death of his first wife, Susan Grymes, Col. Burwell was so afflicted that he went to Rosewell and requested Gov. John Page to send for his young and beautiful widowed half-sister, Mrs. George W. Baylor, for him to marry. The widow came, but refused to listen to Col. Burwell's addresses. The latter put it all to rights by saying: "Lucy, you don't know what is good for you. Your brother John and I arranged it all before you came!" Their marriage took place soon after. The ceremony having been performed, he said: "Now, Lucy, you can weep for your dear George, and I will weep for my beloved Suky!"

Colonel Burwell built Carter Hall soon after the Revolution, and before 1790. He left The Grove to his eldest son, Carter Burwell.

The foregoing copies of inscriptions on the tombstones at Rosewell were furnished by Miss Nellie Deans, of that place, in 1879, and they are accurate in every respect. The Timberneck inscriptions were furnished, about the same time, by Peyton N. Page, Esqr., of Gloucester Court House, Virginia.

V. JOHN PAGE, OF ROSEWELL, Gloucester Co., Va., GOVERNOR OF VIRGINIA, eldest son and child of Mann Page, of the same place and Alice Grymes, his first wife, eldest son and child of Hon. Mann Page, of the same place, and Judith Carter, his second wife (by whom alone he had surviving male issue), second and only surviving child of Hon. Matthew Page, of the same place, and Mary Mann, his wife, second child (and the only one having male issue) of Col. John Page, of England and Williamsburg, James City Co., Va., progenitor of the Page Family in Virginia, and Alice Luckin, his wife, was born at the first-named place, 17th April, 1744, and died at Richmond, Va., 11th Oct., 1808, aged 64 years. He was buried in St. John's Episcopal Churchyard, near the present east side entrance.

A tombstone of Carrara marble was placed to his memory, November 26th, 1881. It was made by Messrs. Rogers & Miller, of Richmond, Va., and has upon it the following inscription:

GOV. JOHN PAGE
(coat-of-arms)
Died
Oct. 11th 1808
AGED 64 YEARS.
Blessed are the dead
Which die in the Lord.

In the diagram on the following page furnished by William G. Strange, Esqr., of Richmond, Va., may be seen the relative positions of St. John's Church, Richmond, Va., and Governor Page's grave —the latter marked *g:*

The portion marked A was built first, and at H, near the present door *f*, stood Patrick Henry when he uttered the memorable words, "GIVE ME LIBERTY OR GIVE ME DEATH!" It was in this portion, also, that the Virginia Convention met for the ratification of the Federal Constitution in 1788.

The shaded portion marked B is said to have been added in 1836.

c is the new main entrance to the church.

d is a door—it originally led to a gallery.

e on the south side was the old main entrance, but has been converted into a window.

f was originally the position of the old pulpit, which was subsequently moved, and the present east side entrance was placed here.

p is the location of the new pulpit facing the new main entrance *c*.

g is the grave of Gov. John Page.

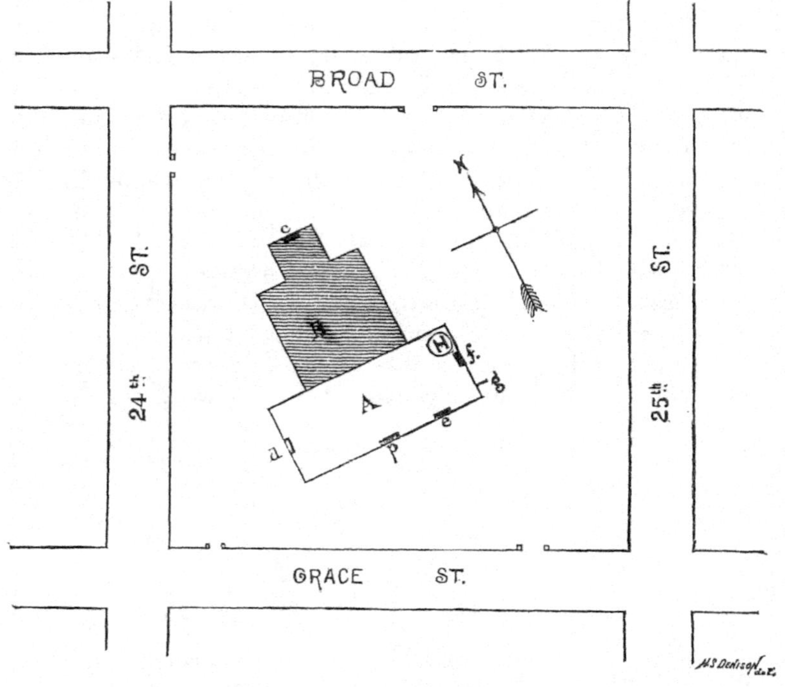

For a picture of this church, see Bishop Meade, *op. cit.*, Vol. I., p. 141.

According to the same authority, he was educated at William and Mary College, where he was the associate and intimate friend of Thomas Jefferson, and his follower in politics afterward, though entirely differing with him on religious subjects.

The following letters written by him in his earlier years will be read with interest:

(From the original portrait by Benjamin West, 1758.)

GOV. JOHN PAGE AT THE AGE OF 16,

ROSEWELL, GLOUCESTER CO., VA.

Died 11th October, 1808, aged 64.

ROSEWELL, Sept. 18th, 1772.

DEAR SIR: The bearer of this, Mr. Robert Andrews, a native of Pennsylvania, was educated and took his degrees with credit at the College of Philadelphia. He has lived as tutor in my father's family several years, has applied himself to the study of divinity, and now offers himself a candidate for holy orders. His morals, abilities and orthodoxy are such that it gave me pleasure, when I found he was determined to enter into that sacred office in our church. As his character is truly amiable, I heartily recommend him to your notice; every civility shown to him will be deemed as shown to myself; and if you will please introduce him to the most ingenuous gentlemen of your acquaintance, as he is very ingenuous himself, you will lay an additional obligation on your much obliged and most obedient servant, JOHN PAGE, JUN.

John Norton, Esq., London.

ROSEWELL, July ye 21st, 1773.

DEAR SIR: I must beg leave to introduce to you Mr. Thos. Davis, a candidate for holy orders, and a late usher of our college. I need say but little of him, as I suppose you are acquainted with his father, and make no doubt he will carry many recommendations to you. . . . I had observed for several years past a great inequality of the quantity of rain which fell, and judged that in the gust of 1769 and some other heavy showers, there fell as much as fell in the same time in any part of Europe; and I had fancied that our dews were greater than in most parts of the world. I had also supposed that not only our crops, but our health must be greatly affected by this inequality of moisture, and that both must depend upon a certain due proportion of heat and moisture. To be satisfied on this point, I contrived a simple instrument by which I could easily measure the $\frac{1}{300}$th part of an inch of rain. Mr. David Jameson, by Mr. Hunt's means, procured such an instrument from London, Mr. Hunt causing it to be made after his direction. Mr. Jameson imported two, and gave me one. We have now for thirteen months kept an exact journal of the weather, and most accurately measured the rain and dews which fell. I measured at Rosewell, $40\frac{346}{1000}$, and Mr. Jameson, at York, $41\frac{321}{1000}$ (inches?), which fell from June 14th, 1722, to June 14th, 1773. We several times found nearly four divisions of dew in our glasses, which were equal to $\frac{1}{100}$th of an inch on the earth. I have troubled you with this long account of our observations, partly because I thought it might be acceptable to you and your curious friends, as being the first that ever were made of this kind in America, and I may say, with such an instrument, in the world. With best wishes, etc., your much obliged humble servant, JOHN PAGE, JUN.

John Norton, Esq., London.

ROSEWELL Jany ye 2^{d} 1794

SIR: I am still confined by Lameness in my Foot but hope to be able to set out to Philad^{a} early next Week. I wish before I go, to receive a Copy of the Account of Sales of the Tob^{o} which Mr Charlton shipped in the Year 1792 to Mrs Donald's House; & shall also be obliged to you for an Account of the Tob^{o}

which you put into M[rs] Shedden's Hands at New-York. A few Lines by Monday's Stage will reach me.

I am y[r] obliged
h[ble] Serv[t]
JOHN PAGE

Ja[s] Brown Esq[r]
Merchant in Richmond.

The following account is taken from Bishop Meade, *op. cit.:*

He was with Washington in one of his western expeditions against the French and Indians. Afterward he was a Representative in the House of Burgesses. In 1776, he was a visitor of the College of William and Mary; at which time he is mentioned in the Virginia Almanac as John Page, Junior, Esqr., to distinguish him from his uncle, Hon. John Page, of North End, Gloucester (now Matthews) Co., Va.

It was about this period of his life that Governor Page opposed Lord Dunmore in the attempt of the latter to place John Randolph (who went to England when the war commenced) among the visitors of the College, and succeeded in having Mr. Nathaniel Burwell (afterwards of Frederick County, Va.), chosen, Lord Dunmore's vote alone being cast for Mr. Randolph. During the Revolutionary struggle Governor Page rendered important services as a member of the Committee of Public Safety, and as Lieutenant-Governor of the Commonwealth. He also contributed freely from his private fortune to the public cause, and was an officer for the County of Gloucester, Va., during the war. He was elected one of the earliest Representatives in Congress from Virginia, upon the adoption of the Federal Constitution, and continued to act in that capacity from 1789 to 1797.

In the *Congressional Record* of 1789, we find, among others, that John Page and James Madison, Representatives from Virginia, resided at No. 19 Maiden Lane, New York City—the seat of government being at that time in New York, and its removal from that city was opposed by Mr. Page. (See "Repub. Court," p. 166, *note.*) In reference to changing it, Dr. Benjamin Rush, of Philadelphia, wrote to a friend, saying, that he was glad that there was a prospect of moving it from "*such a sinkhole of vice.*" Mr. Page, of Virginia, on the other hand, who was sagacious, moral, and without local interest, except in his own State, declared that New York was superior to any place he knew, for the orderly and decent behavior of its inhabitants. ("Repub. Court," p. 322.)

In 1796 and 1799 he published addresses to the people, and in 1800 he was chosen one of the electors for President. In December, 1802, he was chosen Governor of Virginia, in the place of James Munroe. After serving three terms he was succeeded by Mr. Cabell in

1805. (The State Constitution at that time required the Governor to be elected annually by the General Assembly, and permitted the same person to serve only three years in succession. At least four years must then elapse before the same person could be elected again to that office.)

The following is a copy of a paper formerly in possession of the late Thomas W. Page, Esqr., of Keswick (Turkey Hill), Albemarle Co., Va., signed in Governor Page's handwriting:

The *Commonwealth* of *Virginia*,
To JACOB C. CLARKE, GREETING:

Know You, that from the special trust and confidence reposed in your fidelity, courage, activity and good conduct, and upon the recommendation of the Court of the County of Albemarle, our Governor, in pursuance of the act, intituled (*sic*), "An act to amend and reduce into one the several acts of the General Assembly for regulating the Militia of this Commonwealth," doth appoint you the said Jacob C. Clarke, LIEUTENANT in the Eighty Eighth Regiment third Brigade, and second Division of the said Militia, to rank as such agreeably to the number and date hereof.

In testimony whereof, these our letters are sealed with the Seal of the Commonwealth and made patent.

Witness John Page our
said Governor, at Richmond, this
13th day of July, 1805.

JOHN PAGE.

Registered.
SAM: COLEMAN.

At the time of his death, in 1808, he was Commissioner of Loans, a Federal office, which had been conferred upon him by President Thomas Jefferson.

"Hon. John Page was, from his youth, a man of pure and unblemished life. He was a patriot, a statesman, a philosopher, and a Christian. From the commencement of the American Revolution to the last hour of his life, he exhibited a firm, inflexible, unremitting, and ardent attachment to his country, and rendered her very important services. His conduct was marked by uprightness in all the vicissitudes of life—in the prosperous and calamitous times through which he passed—in seasons of gladness and of affliction.

"He was not only the patriot, soldier, and politician, the well-read theologian and zealous churchman—so that some wished him to take orders, with a view to being the first Bishop of Virginia—but he was a most affectionate domestic character."

He was born about the same year with Thomas Jefferson and Col. John Walker—the latter of Castle Hill and Belvoir, Albemarle Co., Va.

The following is a copy of a very interesting letter from Gov. John Page to Arthur Lee, in March, 1778:

Wmsburg March the 12th 1778

DEAR SIR

My former Acquaintance with you & my Knowledge of your great Abilities constantly exerted in Support of your Country's Cause & the Liberties of Mankind have long excited in me a Desire of being admitted into the Number of your Correspondents; but the Fear of interrupting your Attention to the important Affairs you are engaged in, has hitherto prevented me from attempting to enjoy that Happiness.

However, I am so selfish that I can no longer refrain from asking you to permit me to engross Part of your Attention. For this Interruption I will endeavour to make some amends by writing to you the best Accounts I can collect of the State of Affairs in America in general & Virginia in particular, as often at least as the Multiplicity of my public Business will admit of.

You will have heard long before this reaches you that Howe is in quiet Possession of Philada, & that Burgoyne with his Army are detained at Cambridge till the Convention of Sarahtoga shall be ratified by the King his Master. By the unhappy Error Congress & the different States fell into of raising their Troops upon short Inlistments, & from the wretched Accommodations the Clothiers & Commissaries afforded them when raised, we have not been able to keep our Troops long enough together to introduce amongst them proper Discipline, nor indeed have we been able to collect ⅓ of the Men voted by Congress. Whereas had it been determined at first that they should be inlisted for the War, & had the Clothiers & Commissaries done their Duty, & been properly assisted by the Legislature & Executive of each State, I have no Doubt we should have had our Quotas of Men compleat, & by this Time they would have been as well disciplined as the british Troops. Indeed by this Time we should have no Occasion for Troops, for had we been able to produce ½ of our Quota in Field when General Howe landed at the Head of Elk, it is certain his whole Army must have been cut off if we may judge from what was done at Brandywine with an ½ Part of that Number—for I have been well assured by good authority that we had not an eighth Part of the Troops voted by Congress that Day in the Field. We are now reduced to the Necessity of drafting the Militia to fill up the Vacancies occasioned by the Expiration of Inlistments &c &c—but although this seems to be an expeditious and certain Method of raising Troops, it is by no Means so good as that by voluntary Inlistments—Numbers are dissatisfied and others desert. However I hope we shall have Men enough in the Field to bring Howe to a Capitulation or Convention, at least, if he does not receive considerable Reinforcements in the Spring—and from the considerable Importations made this Winter on public Account & by private Adventurers, added to some late Regulations of Congress, & the different States, we may expect to see our Troops well clothed & armed & in a more respectable & comfortable Situation than they have ever been. The Enemy have left Virgi[a] almost in a State of Peace ever since Dunmore was driven away, till this Winter, when they began to be troublesome on the Bay & at the Mouths of some of our Rivers—their Frigates seem to be very shy of our Gallies and Batteries, but I hope before this Summer is out they will be more so.

I take this Opportunity, Sir, of informing you that you were elected a corresponding Member of our Society for promoting useful Knowledge at one of our last Meetings—which have been for some Time past discontinued, the critical Situation of our Country engrossing the Attention of all the Members—However we have made some Progress in our Business having received some valuable Astronomical Observations, Meteorological Journals and other Papers, Models of Machines &c, & are collecting Materials for compleating the natural History of Virginia. Not only the Arts & Sciences, but Manufactures & Agriculture are objects of our Attention. By the next Opportunity I will send you some Extracts from some of our Papers. The Society will think themselves happy to receive any thing you may think proper to communicate. I have engrossed so much of your Time, & intruded so much on you, that I must beg your Pardon, & conclude after desiring you to present my Comp[ts] & best Wishes to your Brother, his Lady & Family—I am dear Sir your

affectionate h[ble] Servant
JOHN PAGE
of
Rosewell.

Gov. John Page married twice. He married, first, about 1765, Frances (called Fannie), daughter of Col. Robin Burwell, of Isle-of-Wight County, Va., and Sallie Nelson, his wife. The latter was the only child of Thomas Nelson (Scotch Tom), of Yorktown, York Co., Va., and the widow Fannie Tucker (whose maiden name was Houston), of Bermuda Islands, his second wife. Col. Robin Burwell was the brother of Betty Burwell, who was the wife of President Nelson.

Frances Burwell, first wife of Gov. John Page, died in 1784, aged 37, and was buried at Rosewell, although no tombstone appears to have been erected to her memory. Three of their children died infants. Their names are unknown. The remaining nine were as follows:

1. Mann Page, eldest, born at Rosewell, 1766; removed to Shelly, Gloucester Co., Va., and married, 5th June, 1788, Elizabeth, eldest daughter and sixth child of Gov. Thomas Nelson, of Yorktown, York Co., Va.

2. John Page (No. 1), born about 1768; died infant.
3. Robert Page, born about 1770; died unmarried, at Yorktown, Va., aged about 25 years.
4. Sally Burwell Page, born about 1771; married, about 1790, William, eldest son and child of Gov. Thomas Nelson, of Yorktown, Va.
5. John Page (No. 2), born about 1773; drowned in Carter's Creek, in 1784, aged about 11 years.
6. Alice Grymes Page, born at Rosewell about 1775; married, first, 1793, Dr. Augustine Smith, of Yorktown, Va., by whom she had as follows:
   (1) Robert Nelson Smith, first of Louisville, Ky., and then of Lexington, Mo.; died 1877, aged about 82 years. He married, 1815, Mary Fry, of Albemarle Co., Va., and had issue. F. Coleman Smith, of Butler, Bates Co., Mo., is one of the sons.
   (2) John Page Smith; died in 1859 in Louisville, Ky. He married twice, and had several daughters and two sons, one of whom was killed in the late war.
   (3) Augustine Smith; removed to Alabama, and died in Mobile, leaving three sons and two daughters. One of the sons, Rev. Dudley D. Smith, now resides in Philadelphia; married twice.
   (4) Lucy Calthrope Smith; married, 1835, Ralph Diggs, of Louisa Co., Va. He removed to Alabama, and died in 1836. The widow now lives in Shepherdstown, Jefferson Co., W. Va., with the widow of her late nephew, Dudley Diggs Pendleton.
   (5) William Smith; removed to Alabama.
   (6) Frances Burwell Smith.

   Alice Page (the widow Smith) married, secondly, in 1812, Col. Dudley Diggs, of Louisa Co., Va., and had Elizabeth Diggs, who married, in 1840, Hugh N. Pendleton, and was his second wife. (See Pendleton.)
7. Frances Page, born at Rosewell about 1777; married, first, in 1795, Thomas Nelson, Jr., second son of Gov. Thomas Nelson, of Yorktown, Va. Their daughter, Thomasia, married, 1821, Bishop William Meade, of Virginia, and was his second wife.

   Frances Page (the widow Nelson) married, secondly, about 1811, Dr. Carter Berkeley, of Edgewood, Hanover Co., Va.
8. Francis Page, born at Rosewell about 1781, removed to Rug Swamp, Hanover Co., Va., and married, in 1806, Susan, fourth daughter and tenth child of Gov. Thomas Nelson, of Yorktown, Va.
9. Judith Carter Page, born at Rosewell about 1783; married, about 1803, Robert, ninth child and youngest son of Gov. Thomas Nelson, of Yorktown, Va. Being Chancellor of William and Mary College, he was called Chancellor Nelson.

Thus there were twelve children of Gov. John Page and Frances Burwell, his first wife, three of whom died infants, names unknown

Of the remaining nine, five married sons and daughters of Gov. Thomas Nelson, of Yorktown, Va.

Gov. John Page married, secondly, 1789, in New York City, Margaret, daughter of William Lowther, of Scotland. She was visited by General Lafayette, 20th October, 1824, at Williamsburg, Va., while he was on his way from Yorktown to Richmond, during his last visit to America. Although Governor Page was now dead, his name appeared among those of other patriots of the Revolution, on the obelisk that was temporarily erected at the main entrance to the Capitol Square at Richmond, Va., during the celebration of General Lafayette's visit.

There were eight children by the second marriage, as follows:

1. Margaret Lowther Page, born at Rosewell about 1790; married, first, about 1810, John H. Blair, of Elmington, Hanover Co., Va., and had:
   (1) Archie Blair; died in Kentucky, leaving a widow and daughter.
   (2) Margaret McLean Blair; unmarried.
   (3) Mary Anne Beverly Blair; married a son of Richard Anderson, of Richmond, Va., by his first wife.
   (4) Fanny Adams Blair; married another son of Richard Anderson, of Richmond, Va., by his first wife.

   Margaret Lowther Page (the widow Blair) married, secondly, the above-mentioned Richard Anderson, of Richmond, Va., and was his second wife. He was the father of her two sons-in-law. By the second marriage, she had:
   (1) Richard Lowther Anderson; died infant.
   (2) Margaret Anderson; brought up by her aunt, Mrs. John Minor Botts.
2. William Lowther Page; died infant.
3. Mary Mann Page; ditto.
4. Gregory Page; a very talented youth; was drowned while a student at William and Mary College.
5. John Page; died unmarried in 1838. He was a very cultivated and polished gentleman, who had travelled a great deal.
6. John William Page; died infant.
7. Barbara Page, born at Rosewell about 1795; died, unmarried, at Williamsburg, Va., about 1864, aged 69 years.
8. Lucy Burwell Page, youngest of the twenty children of Gov. John Page, was born at Rosewell, in 1807. She married, 1828, Hon. Robert Saunders, of Williamsburg, James City Co., Va. He died about 1870. After the death of her husband, Mrs. Saunders removed to the Louise Home, established in Washington, D. C., by the liberality of Hon. W. W. Corcoran, of that city. The children of Hon. Robert Saunders and

Lucy, his wife, were Barbara, Lelia, Robert (died infant), Robert, Lucy (died infant), John (ditto), Page, and Mary Anna, who married Rev. George T. Williams of Virginia, and had issue.

We now return to the children of Mann Page, the second, of Rosewell, Gloucester Co., Va., and Anne Corbin Tayloe, his second wife.

V. Mann Page, of Mansfield, Spottsylvania Co., Va., better known as Mann Page, Jr., eldest son and child of Mann Page, of Rosewell, Gloucester Co., Va., and Anne Corbin Tayloe, his second wife, was born at the last-named place about 1749, and removed to the first-named place. He was a member of the Continental Congress from Virginia, in 1777, along with Thomas Jefferson, Thomas Nelson, Jr., and George Wythe.

He married, 18th April, 1776, Mary Tayloe, fifth child and daughter of John Tayloe, of Spottsylvania County, Va., and Rebecca Plater, his wife.

John Tayloe died 18th April, 1779. He married, 11th July, 1747, Rebecca, daughter of Hon. George Plater, of Maryland. The children of Mann Page and Mary Tayloe, his wife, were as follows:

1. Maria Page, born about 1777; married Lewis Burwell.
2. Lucy Gwynn Page, born about 1779; married Josiah Tidball.
3. Mann Page, born about 1781; married, but name of wife is unknown. Their son, Mann Page, married, 1827, at Willis' Grove, Orange Co., Va., Miss Mary Champe Willis, daughter of William C. Willis, and resided at Orange Court House. She subsequently died, leaving only one surviving child. Mann Page subsequently studied medicine and removed to Mississippi. Nothing more is known.

V. Robert Page, second son and child of Mann Page, of Rosewell, Gloucester Co., Va., and Anne Corbin Tayloe, his second wife, was born at Rosewell, about 1751, and removed to Hanovertown, Hanover Co., Va.

He married, about 1776, Elizabeth Carter, daughter of Charles Carter, of Fredericksburg, Va. Their children were:

1. Elizabeth Page (called Betsey), born about 1777; married, about 1797, Philip Burwell, of Chapel Hill, Frederick Co., Va., son of Col. Nathaniel Burwell, of Carter Hall, Clarke Co., Va., and Susan Grymes, his first wife. No issue known.
2. Charles Page, born about 1778; married, in September, 1799, Sally Cary,

fourth daughter and sixth child of Col. William Nelson, of The Dorrill, Hanover Co., Va., who was the eldest son and child of Secretary Thomas Nelson, of Yorktown, Va. (See Nelson.)

3. Mann Page, born about 1780; married, about 1803, Mary Chiswell Nelson, sister of his brother Charles' wife.

V. Gwynn Page, fourth son and child of Mann Page, of Rosewell, Gloucester Co., Va., and Anne Corbin Tayloe, his second wife, was born at Rosewell, about 1758, and removed to Kentucky.

He married, first, Miss Herreford, by whom he had one child, viz.:

Dr. Matthew Page, born about 1789; removed to Clarke County, Va., and married, about 1814, Mary Randolph (called Polly), daughter of Archie Cary Randolph, of that county, who was the eldest son of Thomas Isham Randolph, of Dungeness, Goochland Co., Va. (See Randolph.) Their children were (1) Archie Cary Page, (2) Gwynn Page, (3) Dr. William Meade Page, of San Francisco, Cal., and (4) Matthewella Page (called Mattie), who married, 1858, Benjamin Harrison, Jr., of Berkeley (Harrison's Landing), on James River, Charles City Co., Va., by whom she had Dr. Benjamin Harrison and others. (See Broadneck.) Benjamin Harrison, Jr., and Mattie Page, his wife, were the last of the Harrison family to reside at Berkeley (Harrison's Landing). They removed to Longwood, Clarke Co., Va.

He married, secondly, Miss Hoe, of Caroline County, Va., by whom he had:

1. Gwynn Page, of Louisville, Ky., an eminent lawyer. He removed to San Francisco, Cal., and amassed a large fortune. He died unmarried, at the Greenbrier White Sulphur Springs, W. Va., and left his money to his sister Lucy.
2. Lucy Page, of San Francisco, Cal., unmarried.

VI. Mann Page, of Shelly, Gloucester Co., Va., eldest son and child of Gov. John Page, of Rosewell, same county, Va., and Frances (called Fannie) Burwell, his first wife; eldest son and child of Mann Page, of the same place, and Alice Grymes, his first wife; eldest son and child of the Hon. Mann Page, of the same place, and Judith Carter, his second wife (by whom alone he had surviving male issue); second and only surviving child of Hon. Matthew Page, of same place, and Mary Mann, his wife, second son (and only one having male issue) of Col. John Page, of England and Williamsburg, James

(From the original oil painting in possession of Mrs. Lucy Gwyn Carter, Winchester, Va.)

MANN PAGE, JR., AND HIS SISTER ELIZABETH.

City Co., Va., progenitor of the Page Family in Virginia, and Alice Luckin, his wife, was born at Rosewell, the second above-named place, in 1766, and died 24th August, 1813, at Mt. Air, Hanover Co., Va., aged 47 years. He was buried at Airwell, the seat of the Berkeleys, in Hanover County, Va.

He founded Shelly, on York River, Gloucester Co., Va., in 1794. It is situated on the hill opposite Rosewell, across Carter's Creek. The original house was destroyed by a fire in 1883, but was subsequently rebuilt.

The Indian name for this place was Werowocomico, and is said to have been the location of Powhatan's Headquarters, where Pocahontas is said to have saved the life of Captain John Smith. The name being difficult of pronunciation, it was changed by Governor Page to Shelly, on account of the great quantity of shells found there. (See Bishop Meade, *op. cit.*, Vol. I., p. 335.)

The following is copied from the record in the clerk's office at Yorktown, Va.:

This Indenture made the twenty third day of November in the year of our Lord, One Thousand Seven Hundred & forty nine, between Mann Page of the County of Gloucester in the Colony of Virginia, Esqr: Heir at Law of Mary Whaley late of the Parish of Saint Margaret Westminster in the County of Middlesex in Great Britain, widow deceased, of the one part, & Thomas Dawson, Clerk John Custis and John Blair Esq^{rs}, Thomas Jones, Peyton Randolph, Thomas Cobbs, Henry Tyler, Mathew Pierce, Lewis Burwell, Benjamin Waller and William Parks Gent., all of the Parish of Bruton in the said Colony, of the other part. Whereas, the said Mary Whaley being in her lifetime and at the time of her death seised in Fee Simple of certain lands lying and being in the said Parish of Bruton in the County of York and Colony aforesaid, made her Last Will and Testament in writing bearing date the Sixteenth day of February One Thousand Seven Hundred and forty one, and therein did give, devise and bequath as follows: "I give, devise and bequath to the Minister and Church Wardens for the time being of the said Parish of Bruton in the County of York in the said Colony of Virginia, and their successors, a certain piece or parcel of land in the said Parish of Bruton, Containing by estimation, ten acres, little more or less, together with Mattey's School House and Dwelling House lately erected and built thereon for the use of a School Master to teach the neediest Children in the said Parish, who shall be offered, in the art of Reading, Writing and Arithmetick, and bounded by the Main Road leading to Queen's Creek and beginning at a Gully of running water surrounding the said ten acres of land & adjoining upon Mr Pope's land, which said piece or parcel of land School House and Dwelling House together also with all outhouses, gardens and appurtenances thereunto belonging I give and devise to the said Minister and Church Wardens for the time being and their successors for ever, upon Trust, to continue the same for the use, benefit and behoof of the said Mattey's School for the purposes aforesaid to eternalize Mattey's School by the name of Mattey's School for ever to and for no other use, intent or purpose whatsoever as in the said Will more fully is contained: And whereas, in a suit in Chancery lately depending in the General Court of the said Colony between Peyton Randolph Esqr: Attorney General of our Lord, the King in the Colony aforesaid at the relation of the Minister and Church Wardens of the said Parish of Bruton, Plaintiff, and the said Mann Page and James Frances Executor of the last Will & Testament of the said Mary Whaley Defendants, it is, among other things, decreed and ordered that the said Mann Page do convey the Fee Simple Estate of the lands with the houses and appurtenances herein before mentioned and described, unto the said Thomas Dawson, John Custis, John Blair, Thomas Jones, Peyton Randolph, Thomas Cobbs, Henry Tyler, Mathew Pierce, Lewis Burwell, Benjamin Waller and William Parks and James Wray deceased, their heirs and assigns for ever. In Trust, and to and for the uses and purposes mentioned in the Last Will and Testament of the said Mary Whaley as in the said decree, dated and signed the fourteenth day of October last past, more fully is Contained. Now this Indenture Witnesseth, that in compliance of the recited decree, and for and in consideration of the sum of Five Shillings to the said Mann Page in hand paid by the said Trustees, the receipt whereof is hereby acknowledged, he, the said Mann Page, hath given, granted, bargained, Sold, aliened and confirmed, and by these presents, doth give, grant, bargain, Sell, alien and confirm unto the said Thomas Dawson, John Curtis, John Blair, Thomas Jones, Peyton Randolph, Thomas Cobbs, Henry Tyler, Mathew Pierce, Lewis Burwell, Benjamin Waller and William Parks, their heirs and assigns for ever, all that piece or parcel of land in the said Parish of Bruton, Containing by estimation, ten acres, little more or less, and bounded as herein before is mentioned and expressed, being the Lands devised by the Will of the said Mary Whaley as aforesaid, together with all houses out houses, edif..ces, buildings, yards, gardens, orchards, woods, underwoods, trees, ways, waters, watercourses, profits, commodities, hereditaments and appurtenances whatsoever to the same in anywise belonging, and the reversion and reversions remainder and remainders, rents and issues thereof, and all the estate, right, title and interest, Claim and demand whatsoever of him, the said Mann Page, of in and to the same, or any part thereof. To have and to hold all & singular the premises with the appurtenances unto the said Thomas Dawson, John Custis, John Blair, Thomas Jones, Peyton Randolph, Thomas Cobbs, Henry Tyler, Mathew Pierce, Lewis Burwell, Benjamin Waller and William Parks, their heirs and assigns for ever. In Trust, and to and for the uses and purposes mentioned in the Last Will and Testament of the said Mary Whaley according to the said decree and to no other use, intent or purpose whatsoever. In witness whereof, the parties to these presents have hereunto interchangebly set their hands and affixed their seals the day and year first within written

Sealed and delivered in presence of MANN PAGE [L. S.]

THOS. EVERARD
J. PALMER
GEORGE WYTHE

At a Court held for York County The 18th day of December 1749. This Indenture was proved by the oaths of Thomas Everard John Palmer and George Wythe, the witnesses thereto, and ordered to be recorded

Examd Teste,

THOs EVERARD Ct Curn

A copy,

Teste,

A. F. HUDGINS, Clerk

VIRGINIA,

YORK COUNTY, to wit:

I, A. F. HUDGINS, Clerk of the County Court of York County, State of Virginia, do hereby Certify that the foregoing is a true copy of the Deed of Mann Page to the said Trustees therein named as the same appears in the Record on file in my Office.

Witness my hand and the seal of said Court affixed this the 20th day of May A.D. 1884, in the 108th year of the Comth of Va.

[L. S.] A. F. HUDGINS, Clerk.

VIRGINIA,

I, H. B. WARREN, Judge of the County Court of York County, State of Virginia, do Certify that A. F. Hudgins, who hath given the foregoing Certificate, is Clerk of said Court, and that his said attestation is in due form.

Given under my hand this the 24th day of May A.D. 1884, in the 108th year of the Comth of Virginia.

H. B. WARREN, Judge.

Mann Page, of Shelly, married, 5th June, 1788, Elizabeth Nelson, eldest daughter and sixth child of Gov. Thomas Nelson, of Yorktown, York Co., Va., and Lucy Grymes, his wife, and their children were as follows:

1. John Page, eldest, born at Shelly, 7th March, 1789; died there 31st January, 1817, aged 28 years—from disease contracted during service in the war of 1812, and from excessive blood-letting by his physicians. He married, in 1812, Elizabeth (called Betsy) Perin, of Gloucester County, Va. No surviving issue. She married, secondly, the eminent lawyer, Thomas J. Michie, of Staunton, Augusta Co., Va. No issue.
2. Lucy Mann Page, born 9th February, 1790; married, about 1811, Dr. Nathaniel Nelson, of The Lodge, Hanover Co., Va. He was the youngest son and fourth child of Col. Hugh Nelson, of Yorktown, Va., and Judith Page, his wife. (See Nelson.)
3. Frances Burwell Page (called Fannie), born 15th July, 1791; married, about 1813, Major William Perin, of Goshen, Gloucester Co., Va. She died 20th May, 1819, aged 28 years. Their daughter, Anna Louise Perin, married, about 1838, Wyndham Kemp, of Gloucester County, Va., and

died, leaving three children, viz. : (*a*) Perin Kemp, lawyer; Gloucester Court House, Va. (*b*) Emily Kemp, married Peyton N. Page, of same place. (*c*) Wyndham Kemp, Jr., of Texas. Ellen Perin, sister of Anna Louise Perin, died single.

4. Thomas Nelson Page, born 5th October, 1792; married 1st February, 1827, Juliana, daughter of Isham Randolph, of Richmond, Va. She was the sister of Fanny P. Randolph, the wife of William N. Page, of the North End branch. (See Randolph.)
5. Mann Page, born 9th June, 1794; married, first, 1819, Judith Nelson, of Hanover County, Va. He married, secondly, Anne Page Jones, of Gloucester County, Va.
6. Eliza Nelson Page, born 15th October, 1795; married, 1830, Benjamin Pollard, of Norfolk City, Va. Their only child, Ellen Pollard, married, about 1853, Mr. Marsden, of the same place.
7. William Nelson Page, bron 20th July, 1797, died unmarried at Mt. Air, Hanover Co., Va., in 1829, aged 32 years.
8. Mary Jane Page, born 30th October, 1798; married, about 1832, Archie McGill, of Winchester, Frederick Co., Va., and afterward of Barley Wood, same county, Va. No issue.
9. Dr. Warner Lewis Page, born 10th March, 1800; died unmarried, at Rugswamp, Hanover Co., Va., 26th March, 1822, aged 22 years.
10. Sally Burwell Page, born 8th May, 1802; died single, at Shelly, in 1869, aged 67 years.
11. Ann (called Nancy) Page, born 10th February, 1803; married 24th April, 1823, Francis K. Nelson, of Cloverfields, Albemarle Co., Va., and was his first wife. He was the eldest son and child of Hon. Hugh Nelson, of Belvoir, same county. (See Nelson.)
12. Philip L. G. Page, born 28th September, 1804; died single, at Shelly, 1st April, 1821, aged 16 years.
13. Robert Nelson Page, born 13th December, 1805; died single, 15th August, 1824, aged 18 years.
14. Thomas Jefferson Page, born 4th January, 1807; married, in 1838, Benjamina Price, of Loudon County, Va.
15. Cornelia Mann Page, fifteenth and last child of Mann Page, of Shelly, and Elizabeth Nelson his wife, was born 29th April, 1809, and died at Shelly, 15th December, 1890, aged 81. She married 23d December, 1835, at Shelly, Lieutenant Alberto Griffith, U. S. N. During a storm on the Pacific Ocean he burst a blood-vessel on board ship and died. He was buried at Kingston, Jamaica. Their only child, Mary Jane Griffith, recently died unmarried at Shelly.

VI. Francis Page, of Rugswamp, Hanover Co., Va., eighth child and fifth son of Gov. John Page, of Rosewell, Gloucester Co., Va., and Frances (called Fannie) Burwell, his first wife, was born at Rosewell, about 1781, and married, in 1806, Susan (called

Suky), fourth daughter and tenth child of Gov. Thomas Nelson, of Yorktown, Va., and Lucy Grymes, his wife. Their children were as follows:

1. Anzolette Page, born 1807; married, in 1831, Rev. William N. Pendleton, of Lexington, Va.; died 15th January, 1884, aged 77. (See Pendleton.)
2. Thomas Lucius Page, eldest son, resided at Rugswamp, Hanover Co., Va., and died there, single, in 1861, aged 52 years.
3. Francis Mann Page, born about 1813; married, 1854, Victorine Valette, of Baltimore, Md., and had five children, viz.: (1) John Randolph Grymes, (2) Victorine, (3) Rosalie Rosewell, (4) Marie, and (5) Edmund Shelly.
4. Anne Rose Page, born 1815; unmarried, removed to Oakland, Hanover Co., Va., the residence of Capt. Thomas Nelson.
5. Frances Burwell Page (called Fannie), born about 1818; married, 1838, Philip N. Meade. Their children were: (1) William; married in Louisa County, Va. No issue. (2) Everard, minister in the Episcopal Church. (3) Philip N., Jr., (4) Harry Vernon, (5) Susan Page, (6) Mary Nelson, (7) Fannie. Four others died infants. Philip N. Meade resided at Mountain View, Clarke Co., Va. He was the eldest son of Bishop William Meade, of Virginia, and Mary Nelson, his first wife, daughter of Philip Nelson, of Clarke County, Va. After the death of her husband, Mrs. Fannie B. P. Meade removed to the Louise Home, Washington, D. C., where she died about 1885.
6. John Page, born about 1822; removed to Oakland, Hanover Co., Va., where he married, 1847, Elizabeth Burwell (called Betsey), fourth daughter and eighth child of Capt. Thomas Nelson, of the same place. Three children, as follows: (1) Rev. Francis Page, of the Episcopal Church; (2) Thomas Nelson Page, lawyer and author, Richmond, Va.; (3) Rosewell Page, lawyer, Danville, Va.
7. Hughella Page, born about 1824, died, single, 1844, aged about 20 years.

VI. Charles Page, of Hanovertown, Hanover Co., Va., eldest son and second child of Robert Page, of the same place, and Elizabeth Carter, his wife, second son and child of Mann Page, of Rosewell, Gloucester Co., Va., and Anne Corbin Tayloe, his second wife, was born at the first-named place about 1778.

He married, in September, 1799, Sally Cary, fourth daughter and sixth child of Col. William Nelson, of The Dorrill, Hanover Co., Va., eldest son and child of Secretary Thomas Nelson, of Yorktown, Va., and was her first husband. (See Nelson.) Their children were as follows:

1. Elizabeth Burwell Page (called Betsey), born about 1800; married, about 1820, Dr. B. R. Wellford, of Fredericksburg, Va., and was his first wife. She died leaving one child, who married Joseph Atkinson, of North Carolina.
2. Caroline Page, born about 1802; married, about 1822, John C. Pollard, of Hanover County, Va.
3. Norborne Page, born about 1804; married, about 1829, Mary Jones. No known issue.
4. William A. Page, born about 1806; married, about 1831, Caroline Jones, and died leaving four children, names unknown.
5. Robert C. Page, born about 1808; married, about 1833, Martha Temple, and died without issue, in California. His widow resided in Richmond, Va.

VI. Mann Page, of Hanovertown, Hanover Co., Va., about the third child and second son of Robert Page, of the same place, and Elizabeth Carter, his wife, second son and child of Mann Page, of Rosewell, Gloucester Co., Va., and Anne Corbin Tayloe his second wife, was born at the first-named place about 1780.

He married, about 1803, Mary Chiswell, eighth child and fifth daughter of Col. William Nelson, of The Dorrill, Hanover Co., Va., eldest son of Secretary Thomas Nelson. Their children were as follows:

1. Robert Page, born about 1804; died unmarried.
2. Charles Page, born about 1806; married, about 1831, Lucy, daughter of Wilson Cary Nelson, of Hanovertown, who was the son of Capt. Thomas Nelson, the third son and child of Secretary Thomas Nelson. No issue known.
3. John F. Page, born about 1808; married, about 1833, Catherine, also a daughter of Wilson Cary Nelson. They had one child, viz.: Mary Mann Page, born about 1834, and married, about 1854, William B., son of Hon. Willoughby Newton, of Westmoreland County, Va., and brother of Rev. John B. Newton, of Richmond, Va., who married Roberta P. Williamson, of Orange County, Va. William B. Newton died leaving a widow and three children, viz.: (*a*) Lucy P., (*b*) Willoughby, and (*c*) Kate. They resided at Summer Hill, Old Church P. O., Hanover Co., Va. After the death of John F. Page his widow Catherine married Dr. Brockenborough, who died, leaving her a second time a widow.

VII. Thomas Nelson Page, of Shelly, Gloucester Co., Va., second and eldest surviving son and fourth child of Mann Page, of same place, and Elizabeth Nelson, his wife, eldest son of Gov. John

Page, of Rosewell, Gloucester Co., Va., and Frances (called Fannie) Burwell, his first wife, eldest son and child of Mann Page, of the last-named place, and Alice Grymes, his first wife, eldest son and child of Hon. Mann Page, of same place, and Judith Carter, his second wife (by whom alone he had surviving male issue), second and only surviving child of Hon. Matthew Page, of same place, and Mary Mann, his wife, second son (and only one having male issue) of Col. John Page, of England and Williamsburg, James City Co., Va., progenitor of the Page Family in Virginia, and Alice Luckin, his wife, was born at Rosewell, 5th October, 1792, and died at Shelly, in October, 1835, aged 43 years. At his own request he was buried at Rosewell.

He married, 1st February, 1827, Julianna, second child and daughter of Isham Randolph, of Richmond, Va., who married Nancy Coupland. Isham Randolph was the second son and child of Thomas Isham Randolph, of Dungeness, Goochland Co., Va. (See Randolph.) Julianna Randolph was the sister of Fannie P. Randolph, the wife of William N. Page. (See North End.)

Thomas N. Page and Julianna Randolph, his wife, had only one surviving child, viz.:

MANN PAGE, OF LOWER BRANDON, on James River, Prince George Co., Va., unmarried. He was born at Shelly, 21st April, 1835, a few months before his father's death. Being the eldest son of the eldest son, etc., he is the representative of the Page Family in Virginia. Should he die without issue, the eldest son of Major Francis N. Page comes next in order, and after his family, that of Dr. John R. Page, of Birmingham, Ala.

VII. MANN PAGE, of Greenland, Gloucester Co., Va., fifth child and third son of Mann Page, of Shelly, same county, Va., and Elizabeth Nelson, his wife, was born at the second-named place, 9th June, 1794, and died in January, 1841, aged 47 years.

He was among those who were appointed marshals, with power to select as many assistants as they might deem necessary, whose duty it was to form the procession and preserve order, on the 18th and 19th October, 1824, at Yorktown, York Co., Va., during the visit of General Lafayette (whose full name was Marie Jean Paul Roch Yves Gilbert Motier Marquis de Lafayette).

Mann Page married, first, in 1819, Judith, daughter of Francis Nelson, of Mont Air, Hanover Co., Va., fourth son and child of

Gov. Thomas Nelson, of Yorktown, Va. The wife of Francis Nelson was Lucy, youngest child of Hon. John Page, of North End, Gloucester (now Matthews) Co., Va., and Jane Byrd, his wife. (See North End.)

Judith Nelson, first wife of Mann Page, was the sister of Philip Nelson, of Mont Air, Hanover Co., Va., second husband of Jane Crease, widow of Rev. George W. Nelson, of the Episcopal Church. She was also the sister of Jane Nelson, who married, 1819, John Page, of North End, Clarke Co., Va., and was his first wife.

The children of Mann Page and Judith Nelson, his first wife, were as follows:

1. Francis Nelson Page, eldest, born at Greenland, Gloucester Co., Va., 28th October, 1820. Was educated at West Point Military Academy, and became a Major in the U. S. Army. Married, 25th February, 1851, Susan Duval, of Florida.
2. Powhatan Robertson Page (called Posie), born at Greenland, about 1822, and died 17th June, 1864, aged about 42 years. He served through the Mexican War as captain of a company in the 14th Regiment Infantry, U. S. Army, and was a gallant officer and soldier. He married, 1853, Elizabeth (called Lizzie), daughter of Dr. Samuel Scollay, of Smithfield, Jefferson Co., W. Va. He died in 1864, leaving a widow and one child, Sally Scollay Page, who removed with her mother to Clarksburgh, Harrison Co., W. Va. Mrs. Elizabeth Scollay Page was the half-sister of Mary Nelson Scollay who married Rev. G. W. Nelson of the Episcopal Church. Dr. Samuel Scollay was a native of Massachusetts and was born 21st January, 1781. He graduated at Harvard College in 1808, and in medicine at the University of Pennsylvania in 1876. He removed to Smithfield, and married Harriet Lowndes, who was his first wife; she was the granddaughter of Gov. Edward Lloyd, of Maryland, who married Elizabeth Tayloe of Mount Airy, Spottsylvania Co., Va., the sister of Mary Tayloe, who was the wife of Mann Page, Jr., who was the half-brother of Gov. John Page, of Virginia.

Mann Page, of Greenland, Gloucester Co., Va., married, secondly, in 1829, Anne Page Jones, of same county, Va. Their children were as follows:

1. John Randolph Page, eldest, physician, of Birmingham Ala., was born at Greenland, Gloucester Co., Va., in 1830. He married, 30th October, 1856, at Eagle Point, Gloucester Co., Va., Delia, eldest daughter of John Randolph Bryan, of Carysbrook, Fluvana Co., Va., and Elizabeth Coalter, his wife, who was the daughter of Judge Coalter, and the

favorite niece of John Randolph, of Roanoke. Dr. John R. Page and Delia, his wife, had nine children, as follows: (1) Mann Page, of Denver, Col., married Hattie Robbins, and has two children, (*a*) Mann, and (*b*) Winthrop; (2) Dr. Charles C. Page, of New York; (3) Anne Page, married 17th March, 1884, her cousin, Walter Taylor Page, of Omaha, Neb., and has one child, Nannie; (4) Delia Page; (5) Ada S. Page; (6) Joseph B. Page; and (7) John Randolph Page, Jr. The two first born, not mentioned (Randolph Bryan Page and Elizabeth Page), died infants.

2. Martha T. Page, born at Greenland, Gloucester Co., Va., about 1834; married, about 1864, H. W. Vandergrift, of Alexandria, Virginia, and had Kate and Annie.
3. Elizabeth N. Page (called Betty), born about 1840; married, about 1857, James Goggin, of Hempstead, Texas.
4. Richard M. Page, born at same place, about 1838; resides in Gloucester County, Va. Married, about 1878, Kate, daughter of the late Jacob Wray, of Hampton, Elizabeth City Co., Va. One child, Thomas Nelson.
5. Peyton N. Page, born at same place, about 1840, lawyer and Commonwealth's Attorney for Gloucester County, Va.; married, about 1875, Emily, daughter of Wyndham Kemp, of same county, and Anna Louise Perin, his wife. He died; no surviving issue.

VII. Captain Thomas Jefferson Page, U. S. Navy, eighth son and fourteenth child of Mann Page, of Shelly, Gloucester Co., Va., and Elizabeth Nelson, his wife, was born at Shelly, 8th January, 1808.

He married at Washington, D. C., in 1838, Benjamina, daughter of Benjamin Price, of Loudon County, Va. They both reside at Florence, Italy.

Thomas Jefferson Page entered the U. S. Navy in October, 1827, as midshipman. He was promoted to the rank of lieutenant in June, 1833, and to that of captain, in 1855. In the early part of his service he was employed, for a time, on the U. S. Coast Survey. In 1853 he was appointed to the command of an expedition for the exploration of the tributaries of the River La Plata, and adjacent countries, from which he returned in May, 1856, after an absence of three years and four months. His narrative of this expedition was published in 1859, 8vo, New York.

In 1857 Congress made a further appropriation to complete the exploration of the Parana and tributaries of the Paraguay Rivers. Commander Page was assigned to this service, which was finished in December, 1860.

The children of Capt. T. J. Page and Benjamina Price, his wife, were as follows:

CAPT. THOMAS JEFFERSON PAGE, U.S.N.,
FLORENCE, ITALY, 1892.
At the age of 84.

1. Thomas Jefferson Page, Jr., born in New Jersey, 15th February, 1839; died unmarried, at Florence, Italy, 16th June, 1864, aged 25 years. He was buried in the English cemetery there.
2. John Page, born at Washington, D. C., 29th November, 1840; removed to Estancia San Carlos, Bragado, Buenos Ayres, South America. Married, 1863, Julia Lowry, of Buenos Ayres, S. A. He was captain in Argentine S.A. Navy, and was killed by savages, in 1890, while exploring the river Pilcomayo.
3. Lilly Page, born at Washington, D. C., 1842, married, October, 1866, the Marquis Spinola, of Florence, Italy. He died, leaving her a widow with no surviving issue.
4. Philip N. Page, born at Washington, D. C., 2d May, 1847; also removed to Buenos Ayres, South America.
5. Mary Bell Page, born at Washington, D. C., 1848; died at Florence, Italy, 1870.
6. Frederick M. Page, born at Washington, D. C., 18th April, 1852; married, 28th October, 1880, Sadie Byrd, daughter of A. M. Chichester, of Loudon County, Va.
7. George C. Page, born at Washington, D. C., 28th September, 1857. He resides at Rome, Italy.

VIII. MAJOR FRANCIS NELSON PAGE, U. S. ARMY, eldest son and child of Mann Page, of Greenland, Gloucester Co., Va., and Judith Nelson, his first wife, was born there 28th October, 1820, and died at Fort Smith, Ark., 25th March, 1860, aged 40 years.

He graduated at the West Point Military Academy, in 1841, and served as lieutenant of infantry in the closing of the Florida War. He afterward served through the Mexican War with great gallantry. From an old U. S. Army Register we copy the following: "Francis Nelson Page (Virginia), Cadet, Sept., 1836; Bvt. Sec. Lieut. 7th Infantry, July, 1841; Adjutant 1845 to 1847; Brevet First Lieutenant for gallant conduct in defence of Fort Brown, 9th May, 1846; First Lieut. Aug., 1846; Assistant Adjutant-General (rank of Captain) May, 1847; Brevet Major for gallant and meritorious conduct in the battles of Contreras and Cherubusco, 20 Aug., 1847; distinguished and wounded in the battle of Chapultepec; relinquished rank in line, Aug., 1851."

After the war with Mexico, the Legislature of the State of Virginia presented him with a sword in consideration of his brilliant services. This sword and others, together with the pistols of General (also Governor) Thomas Nelson, of Yorktown, Va., were in the possession of Major Page's eldest son.

Major Francis N. Page married, 25th February, 1851, Susan, daughter of Col. William Duval, of Florida, who was afterward Indian Agent for the Indian Territory, at Fort Smith, Ark., and nephew of Judge Gabriel Duval, of Washington, D.C. The widow of Major Francis N. Page removed to St. Louis, Mo. Their children were:

1. Francis Nelson Page, Jr., eldest, born at Fort Smith, Ark., 21st February, 1852.
2. Lucy Nelson Page, born at Jefferson Barracks, Mo., 29th August, 1853. Married, 8th January, 1877, Dr. William A. Hardaway, of St. Louis, Mo.
3. Powhatan Randolph Page, born at last-named place, 8th December, 1854.
4. Kate Rector Page, born at Fort Brooke, Florida, 7th February, 1857. Married, 1883, Mr. Lawrence of Las Vegas, New Mexico.
5. Elias Rector Page, born at Fort Smith, Ark., 9th November, 1858. Died there, 1859, infant.

IV. John Page, of North End, situated on North River, Gloucester (now Matthews) Co., Va., second son of Hon. Mann Page, of Rosewell, same county, Va., and Judith Carter, his second wife (by whom alone he had surviving male issue), second and only surviving child of Hon. Matthew Page, of same place, and Mary Mann, his wife, second son (and only one having male issue), of Col. John Page, of England, and Williamsburg, James City Co., Va., progenitor of the Page family in Virginia, and Alice Luckin, his wife, was born at the second above-named place about the year 1720, and died about 1780, aged about 60 years. He is also mentioned as John Page of North River.

He married, in 1746, Jane Byrd, who was one of the younger children of Col. William E. Byrd, of Westover, on James River, Charles City Co., Va., and Maria Taylor, of Kensington, England, his second wife.

The following is a certificate from Mrs. Byrd regarding the entry in the old Byrd family Bible relating to Jane Byrd, of Westover:

69 Park Avenue, New York City, U. S. A.
October 23d, 1888.

I do hereby certify that the following is a true copy from the family Bible of Col. William Byrd, of Westover, Va., now in my possession:

"He (Col. William Byrd) married his second wife on the 9th of May 1794, Mrs. Maria Taylor, eldest daughter and one of the Coheiresses of Thomas Taylor of Kensington Esqr. They came to this Colony in 1726."

"This Lady was born in England the 10th of Nov. 1698 and died Aug. 28th 1771."

"Jane their 3rd Daughter was born Oct 13th 1729 & married John Page Esqr of North River in 1746 by whom she has a numerous issue."

Lucy Carter Byrd.

Witness,
Mary Wyman Byrd.

According to Governor's Page's letter, extracts from which may be seen in Bishop Meade, *op. cit.*, Vol. I., p. 147, *note*, he was educated a lawyer, and was a member of the Colonial Council, in place of his elder brother, Mann

(From the original portrait by Bridges, Virginia, 1750.)

HON. JOHN PAGE,

NORTH END, GLOUCESTER (NOW MATTHEWS) CO., VA.

Member of the Virginia Colonial Council, 1776.

Page, of Rosewell. In this capacity we find the name of Hon. John Page, of North End, in the Virginia Almanac for 1776. He was, therefore, a member of the last Virginia Council of His Majesty George III.

He was also a visitor of the College of William and Mary—his name appearing as such in the catalogue of that institution in 1764—being the early part of the reign of His Majesty George III.

In regard to Col. William E. Byrd, father of the above-mentioned Jane Byrd, it may be stated that his first wife was Lucy, daughter of Col. Daniel Park, the British officer who brought the news of the victory at Blenheim to Queen Anne. The portrait of this officer and many other celebrities, including Lord Albemarle and the beautiful Evelyn Byrd, is at Lower Brandon on James River, Prince George Co., Va. Colonel Byrd had no sons by Lucy Park, his first wife, but there were two daughters, one of whom was the celebrated beauty, Evelyn Byrd. During a visit to England, she was introduced to William Pitt (Lord Chatham), who remarked that "he no longer wondered why young gentlemen were so fond of going to Virginia to study ornithology, since such beautiful *Byrds* were there!" Colonel Byrd married, secondly, 9th of May, 1794, Mrs. Maria Taylor, of Kensington, England. Her maiden name is not known. The following is copied from a book by Lizzie Nicholas, now in possession of Mrs. George Byrd, of New York City: "Col. Byrd made a second alliance with Mrs. Maria Taylor, eldest daughter and one of the co-heiresses of Thomas Taylor, of Kensington, and in 1726 they came to reside in this Colony" (Virginia). She was born in England, 10th November, 1698, and died 28th August, 1771.

Colonel Byrd had by Maria Taylor, his second wife, a son (from whom the Byrds are descended) and three daughters—the third of whom was Jane Byrd. She was born October 13th, 1729. Colonel Byrd was born in 1674 and died in 1744, aged 70 years. He was buried at Westover.

He was one of the surveyors for establishing the line between Virginia and North Carolina. The original MS., written by himself, is at Lower Brandon, Va. (For the names of the surveyors of other portions of this line, see WALKER.)

Hon. John Page and Jane Byrd, his wife, were, doubtless, buried at North End; but, strange to say, it is not positively known. There are no tombstones there, or anywhere else, erected to their memory. As tombstones were brought over from England in those days, it is probable that the war of the Revolution broke up the business; and, before anything was done in the matter, their graves became obliterated and forgotten.

The North End house was destroyed by fire during the war of the Revolution—probably during Arnold's raid in Virginia.

Hon. John Page and Jane Byrd, his wife, had fifteen children in all, four of whom died infants, their names being unknown. The eleven that survived were as follows:

1. Mann Page, eldest, born at North End, Gloucester (now Matthews) Co., Va., about 1747; removed to Fairfield, Clarke Co., Va. He married, about 1767, Mary Mason Selden, of Salvington, Stafford Co., Va.

(From the original portrait, by Bridges, Virginia, 1750.)

JANE BYRD, OF WESTOVER, VIRGINIA,
WIFE OF HON. JOHN PAGE, OF NORTH END.
Married, 1746.

2. John Page, born at North End, Gloucester (now Matthews) Co., Va., about 1749; removed to Caroline County, Va. He married, in 1764, Elizabeth (called Betty) Burwell.
3. Jane Page, born about 1751; married, about 1770, Dr. Nathaniel Nelson, second son and child of President William Nelson, of Yorktown, Va.
4. Dr. William Page, born at North End, about 1753; removed to Richmond, Va. He married, about 1778, Miss Jones.
5. Judith Page, born about 1755, married, about 1775, Col. Hugh Nelson, third son and child of President William Nelson, of Yorktown, Va.
6. Carter Page, born at North End, 1758; removed to Willis' Fork, Cumberland Co., Va. He married, first, in 1783, Mary Cary, and secondly, in 1799, Lucy, eighth child and third daughter of Gov. Thomas Nelson, of Yorktown, Va.
7. Robert Page, born in 1764; removed to Janeville, Clarke Co., Va. He married, in 1788, Sarah Page, of Broadneck, Hanover Co., Va. As four other children had died infants—names unknown—when Robert was born he was really the *eleventh* child, although the *seventh* survivor.
8. Maria (called Molly) Page, born about 1765; married, first, John Byrd; secondly, Archie Bolling; and thirdly, Peter Randolph; by none of whom had she any issue.
9. Matthew Page, born about 1767; died unmarried.
10. Thomas Page, born about 1773; married, about 1798, Mildred, daughter of Edmund Pendleton, father of Edmund Pendleton, who married Jane B. Page, daughter of the above-named John Page (No. 2) and Elizabeth Burwell, his wife. Of the children of Thomas Page and Mildred Pendleton, his wife, Mildred Page married Palmer. There were also Thomas, Henry, and Robert, of whom nothing at present is known.
11. Lucy Page, youngest, born about 1775; married, about 1792, Francis Nelson, of Mont Air, Hanover Co., Va., fourth son and child of Gov. Thomas Nelson, of Yorktown, Va.

V. Mann Page, of Fairfield, Clarke Co., Va., eldest son and child of Hon. John Page, of North End, Gloucester (now Matthews) Co., Va., and Jane Byrd, his wife, was born at the last-named place about 1742. It is not known when he died or where he was buried. He married, about 1767, Mary Mason, daughter of Samuel Seldon, of Salvington, Stafford Co., Va. There are two Salvingtons, viz., Upper Salvington, on Potomac Run, and Lower Salvington, on Potomac Creek. It is not known which of the two is meant here.

Their only known surviving children were as follows:

1. William Byrd Page, eldest, born about 1768; married, about 1793, Anne, daughter of Richard Henry Lee, and sister of General Henry Lee (Light Horse Harry).

2. Jane Byrd Page, born about 1770; married, about 1790, Major Thomas Swann, of Baltimore, Md., from whom the wealthy family in that city is descended.

V. John Page, of Caroline County, Va., second son and child of Hon. John Page of North End, Gloucester (now Matthews) Co., Va., and Jane Byrd, his wife, was born at the last-named place about 1743, and died in 1789, aged about 46 years. It is not known where he was buried.

He was one of the original members of the Phi Beta Kappa Society that was organized at Williamsburg, James City Co., Va., 15th December, 1776.

He married, in 1764, Elizabeth (called Betty), daughter of Lewis Burwell, of King's Mills (Kingsmel), York Co., Va. She was burned to death in the Richmond Theatre, Va., 26th December, 1811, and her name appears on the monument erected there (the present Monumental Church) to the memory of those who perished in the flames on that occasion. John Page and Elizabeth Burwell, his wife, had fifteen children. Of these, Robert, John, Byrd, and Carter died unmarried, and probably young. Six others died infants—their names being unknown. The five surviving children were as follows:

1. Octavius Augustine Page, eldest, Lieutenant United States Navy, born about 1765, and died, in Boston, Mass., June, 1813, of fever, during the war of 1812, aged about 48. He was an officer of the ship *Chesapeake*, and was sick in Boston when the memorable fight with the *Shannon* took place. The news of the British victory and the death of Captain Lawrence, no doubt, hastened his death. He was unmarried. In the "American Universal Cyclopædia" he is mentioned as the son of Gov. John Page—an evident mistake.
2. Jane Burwell Page, born about 1774, married, 23d August, 1794, Edmund Pendleton, Jr., of Caroline County, Va., and was his first wife. (See Pendleton.)
3. Peyton Randolph Page, born about 1776; married, about 1801, the widow Bryant. He died, age unknown, leaving four children, of whom nothing at present is known. He belonged to the United States Navy; rank unknown. He was captured by the British during the war of 1812, and had a hard struggle with some prisoners about a *rat*, that all claimed as food.
4. Lewis Burwell Page, born about 1778; was a sailing-master in the United States Navy, and died in Portsmouth, Va., September 16th, 1826,

aged about 48 years. He married, about 1803, the Widow Reade, of Philadelphia, and left one child, Elizabeth, who married Dr. John R. Chandler, United States Navy. They had five children: (1) Alice Lee, unmarried, died of yellow fever in Norfolk, Va., in 1854; (2) Margaret Riché, married Rev. T. J. Beard, of Birmingham, Ala., and had issue; (3) Augustus Page, unmarried, died of yellow fever; (4) Mary Imogen, married Bishop Wingfield, of California, and had one child, Page Wingfield; (5) William Lewis, married Georgia Pulling; they had four children, all of whom died young but Sarah Elizabeth.

The widow Reade had one child, a daughter, by her first husband, who married Mr. Dennison, who was related to the late Admiral Rodgers, United States Navy.

5. Hugh Nelson Page, Captain United States Navy; youngest, and fifth survivor, and fifteenth child, was born in 1788. He married, first, in 1838, Imogen Wheeler. No issue. He married, secondly, in 1848, Elizabeth P. Wilson, and had issue.

V. DR. WILLIAM PAGE, of Richmond, Va., about the fourth child and third son of Hon. John Page, of North End, Gloucester (now Matthews) Co., Va., and Jane Byrd, his wife, was born at the last-named place about 1753. It is not known when he died, or at what age. He marrried, about 1778, a Miss Jones. It is not known whose daughter she was. Their children, so far as known, were as follows:

1. Jane Byrd Page, born about 1779; married, about 1799, Dr. Henry W. Lockett. No issue known.
2. William Byrd Page, born about 1781; married, about 1806, Lucy Segar. Their children were:
   (1) John Carter Page, shoe dealer, Richmond, Va.; married Martha Goff.
   (2) Mary Jane Page; married George Bargamin. Nothing further known at present.
3. John Carter Page, born about 1783; married, about 1808, a Miss Segar—probably sister of Lucy, who was the wife of his brother William. No issue known at present.

There is much more in connection with this branch of the family, no doubt; but little is known at present. The following is copied from the Richmond (Va.) daily *State*, 20th June, 1881:

"Last night Mr. Willam H. Page, City Gas Inspector, died at the residence of Mrs. Bargamin, after a long illness. While his demise was not unlooked for, it will cause profound regret to a large circle of friends and acquaintances. Mr. Page was made City Gas Inspector at the time of the reorganization of the city government, in 1865, and he filled the office faithfully to the time of his death. As a citizen, he was energetic and public-spirited. Mr. Page always manifested a deep interest in the welfare of the city. He was one of the first members of the Konservative Kampaign Klub, and was, as long as his health remained to him, one of the most active members of his party. He was also a contributing member of the Howitzers. Mr. Page was in the 35th year of his age. His funeral will take place to-morrow evening at five o'clock, from the Second Baptist Church."

From the fact that Mrs. Bargamin's name is mentioned in the foregoing notice, it is probable that the said William H. Page belonged to the last-mentioned portion of the Page family, though it is not positively certain.

V. Carter Page, of Willis' Fork, Cumberland Co., Va., sixth surviving child, and about the fourth son of Hon. John Page, of North End, Gloucester (now Matthews) Co., Va., and Jane Byrd, his wife, was born at North End in 1758, and died in April, 1825, aged 67. He was buried at The Fork, with Lucy Nelson, his second wife. His residence was so named from its proximity to the fork of Willis River.

According to the Virginia *Historical Register*, his name appears in the list of students who left the College of William and Mary in 1776, to join the American army. He rose to the rank of Major, and served as aide-de-camp to General Lafayette during the campaign in Virginia against Cornwallis.

During the visit of Lafayette to the United States, in 1824, Governor Pleasants, of Virginia, 10th August, 1824, addressed a letter to him at New York, inviting him to be present at Yorktown, Va., on the 19th October following. Hon. James Lyons, of Richmond, Va., was deputed to bear the invitation to the General in New York. He replied on the 18th, accepting the invitation.

At a meeting of the Mayor, Recorder, and Senior Alderman of the city of Richmond, 31st of August, 1824, for the purpose of adopting such measures as might be most expedient and proper for the reception of General Lafayette in that city, it was ordered as follows:

1. That the polite offer of the Governor to afford apartments in the Governor's House for the reception of Major-General Lafayette, and his suite, be thankfully accepted, and that arrangements for furnishing the same be accordingly made. (This was afterward changed, and General Lafayette was quartered in what was at that time the Eagle Hotel.)

2. That as it would be a subject of high gratification to the citizens of Richmond that General Lafayette, during his residence in that city, should be attended by as many of the officers of the Revolutionary war as may be practicable to assemble, a correspondence be opended with General Robert Poters-

field, Major John Nelson, Major Carter Page, Commodore James Barron, Colonel Robert Randolph, Captain Thomas Price, and other Revolutionary soldiers of Virginia, now living, inviting their attendance in Richmond upon the arrival of their distinguished fellow-soldier.

3. That John Marshall be solicited to prepare an appropriate address for the occasion.

4. That Mr. Jefferson, Mr. Madison, and Mr. Monroe be invited to be present.

(Signed) JOHN ADAMS, *Mayor*.
W. H. FITZWHYLSONN, *Recorder*.
THOS. BROCKENBROUGH, *Senior Alderman*.

When General Lafayette arrived in Richmond, Va., October 27th, 1824, it is said that the introduction of the Revolutionary officers here, as well as at Yorktown, was, perhaps, the most interesting and affecting scene of all. These aged and venerable men, amounting to forty in number, were presented to their old companion-in-arms in the spacious drawing-room appropriated to his use, on Tuesday evening, October 27th, 1824, very soon after his arrival. He received them in the most cordial and affectionate manner, evincing the deepest sympathy with them in the recollection of their hardships and dangers through which they had mutually passed, and the proud result of their joint labors.

At 5 o'clock P.M. the General sat down to dinner with his suite, the gentlemen who had attended him from Norfolk, the officers of the Revolutionary army, the officers of the Federal, State, and City Governments, and the members of the Committee of Arrangements.

Benjamin Watkins Leigh acted as president of one table, and Dr. John Brockenbrough of the other, assisted by Messrs. Fitzwhylsonn, Thomas Brockenbrough, R. G. Scott, and W. H. Roane, as vice-presidents, General Lafayette, the Chief Justice, and Mr. Calhoun at the right of Mr. Leigh, the Governor and Judge Brooke at his left; and on both sides and in front were stationed the Revolutionary officers.

Toasts were given by General Lafayette, Governor Pleasants, Chief Justice Marshall, Mr. Calhoun, and many others, including Major Carter Page, who gave the following: "The memory of Baron Viomenil, who gallantly stormed one of the British redoubts at Yorktown."

The name of Major Carter Page was inscribed with the names of other Revolutionary patriots on the west front of the obelisk temporarily erected for the occasion on the west of the principal entrance into the Capitol Square, at Richmond, Va.

While the author was in Richmond, Va., in July, 1861, in the barber shop of Lomax Smith, Richmond's great negro barber, under the Exchange Hotel, a street band struck up the Marseillaise Hymn. "Dey could play no more 'propriate chune den dat now," remarked Mr. Smith; "'minds me of Gineral Lafayette. I used to shave him and fix his har when he was in Richmond." Major Carter Page, like Gov. John Page, his first cousin, and Gov. Thomas Nelson, of Yorktown, Va., whose daughter Lucy was his second wife, probably spent his money freely in the Revolutionary cause, and like them (but unlike Washington) kept no account of it. Consequently it was impossible for Congress to reimburse him.

In regard to the Cary family, it may be said that Col. Miles Cary, the first of his family in Virginia, was the son of John Cary, of Bristol, England, whose younger brother, James Cary, emigrated to New England.

The said Col. Miles Cary was born in Bristol, England, A.D. 1620, and emigrated to Warwick County, Va., in 1640. He died there in 1677. He was the Royal Naval Officer for James River, and was a member of the Colonial Council, under Berkeley. He was a lineal descendant of Henry Cary, Lord Hunsdon, and was, at the time of his death, the heir apparent of the barony.

He married Ann, daughter of Captain Thomas Taylor, and by her had four sons. Of these only two are known to the writer at present, viz.:

1. Col. Miles Cary, Jr., probably the eldest, married Mary, daughter of Col. William Wilson, of Hampton, Va.
2. Henry Cary, probably one of the younger sons—the father of Col. Archibald Cary, of Ampthill, Chesterfield Co., Va.

Col. Miles Cary, Jr., and Mary Wilson, his wife, had an only surviving married son, viz.: Col. Wilson Cary, who was the grandfather of Wilson Jefferson Cary, of Carysbrooke, Fluvanna Co., Va. The latter married, in 1805, Virginia Randolph, and was the ancestor of the Carys of Baltimore, Md. (See Thomas Mann Randolph, of Tuckahoe.)

Mary Cary (called Polly), the first wife of Major Carter Page, was the daughter of Col. Archibald Cary, of Ampthill, Chesterfield Co., Va., and Mary Randolph, his wife, who was the daughter of Richard Randolph, of Curl's Neck, on James River, Henrico Co., Va., and Jane Bolling, his wife. The latter was fourth in descent from Pocahontas, as follows: John Rolfe married Pocahontas, in 1616; Thomas Rolfe, their son, married Miss Poythress; Jane Rolfe, their daughter, married Robert Bolling; John Bolling, their son, married Mary Kennon; and Jane Bolling, their daughter, married Richard Randolph. Pocahontas died at Gravesend, England, and

POCAHONTAS.
(From Barnes' Centennial History.)

is said to have been buried in the northwest corner of the churchyard there.

Col. Archibald Cary was born 24th January, 1721, O. S., or 4th February, 1721, N. S., and died on Tuesday, 26th February, 1787, in the 67th year of his age. His will was dated 21st February, 1787. He was a sterling patriot of the Revolution, and was a member of the Virginia Convention of 1776. He was called "Old Iron." He married, 31st May, 1744, Mary Randolph, of Curl's Neck, as we have already said. Their children were:

1. Anne Cary, born February, 1745; marrried, 18th November, 1761, Thomas Mann Randolph, of Tuckahoe, Goochland Co., Va., who was the father of Gov. Thomas Mann Randolph, of Edge Hill, Albemarle Co., Va. (See Randolph, of Tuckahoe.)
2. Mary Cary (No. 1), born July, 1747; died, August, 1748, infant.
3. Jane Cary, born 12th February, 1751; married, about 1768, Thomas Isham Randolph, of Dungeness, Goochland Co., Va.
4. Sarah Cary, born 23d February, 1753; married, about 1773, Mr. Bolling.

(From the original portrait.)

COL. ARCHIBALD CARY,

AMPTHILL, CHESTERFIELD CO., VA.

Died 26th February, 1787, aged 66.

5. Eliza Cary, born 9th April, 1755; died single, 2d August, 1775.
6. Henry Cary, only son, born 2d March, 1756; died, an infant, 17th May, 1758, aged about two years.
7. Mary Cary (No. 2), called Polly, first wife of Major Carter Page, of The Fork, Cumberland Co., Va.; born 4th December, 1766.
8. Elizabeth Cary (called Betsy), born about 1770; married, July, 1787, Robert Kincaid.

Major Carter Page married, first, 12th April, 1783, at Tuckahoe, Goochland Co., Va., Mary Cary (called Polly), daughter of Col. Archibald Cary, of Ampthill, Chesterfield Co., Va., and Mary Randolph, his wife. Mary Cary was born 4th December, 1766, and died 26th January, 1797, aged 31 years. She was buried at Presquisle, on James River, Va. Their children were as follows:

1. John Cary Page, eldest, born at The Fork, Cumberland Co., Va., 9th May, 1784; removed to Union Hill, same county; married, 12th October, 1808, Mary Anna Trent.
2. Henry Page, born at The Fork, 29th September, 1785; removed to Kentucky; married, 23d December, 1813, Jane B. Deane.
3. Carter Page, Jr. (No. 1), born 9th December, 1786; died 7th November, 1789, infant.
4. Lavinia Randolph Page, born 15th June, 1788; died 8th November, 1789, infant.
5. Carter Page, Jr. (No. 2), born 10th August, 1790; died 30th June, 1791, infant.
6. Dr. Mann Page, born at The Fork, 26th October, 1791; removed to Keswick (Turkey Hill), Albemarle Co., Va.; married, 12th December, 1815, Jane F. Walker.
7. William Page, born 21st August, 1793; died 26th December, 1793.
8. Mary Isham Page, born 30th December, 1794, was burned to death in the Richmond Theatre, Va., 26th December, 1811, aged 17. Her name is inscribed on the monument erected there (site of the present Monumental Church) to their memory.

Major Carter Page married, secondly, in 1799, Lucy, eighth child and third daughter of Gov. Thomas Nelson, of Yorktown, Va. After the death of her husband, in 1825, she became entitled to, and received, a pension from the United States Government, in consideration of his services as a soldier and an officer during the Revolutionary war. She was born 2d January, 1777, and died 5th January, 1863, aged 86 years. She was buried by the side of her husband at The Fork. Their children were as follows:

1. Thomas Nelson Page, born about 1800; died young.
2. Nelson Page, eldest survivor, born at The Fork, 8th November, 1801; died there in November, 1850, aged 49. He resided at The Fork, which he inherited. He married, first, in March, 1828, Lucia, daughter of Randolph Harrison, of Clifton, Cumberland Co., Va., and had:
   (1) Mary Randolph Page (called Polly), born about 1835; married Benjamin Harrison, son of William B. Harrison, of Upper Brandon, on James River, Va., and Mary Harrison, his wife, who was sister to Lucia, the wife of Nelson Page. Benjamin Harrison died in July, 1862. His widow resided at The Rowe, on James River, opposite Lower Brandon, Prince George Co., Va. She sold The Fork, her father's residence, about 1870. Their children were: (*a*) William Byrd; (*b*) Lucia, married, 1878, E. R. Cocke, of Cumberland County, Va.; (*c*) Nelson, died infant; and (*d*) Benjamin.
   (2) Lucius Cary Page, born about 1838; died young.

   Nelson Page married, secondly, Maria Hamilton. No issue.
3. William Nelson Page, born at The Fork, 28th February, 1803; removed to Ça Ira, Cumberland Co., Va.; married, 1827, Fannie P. Randolph, and had issue.
4. Lucy Jane Page, born at The Fork, 6th April, 1804; died 7th January, 1872, aged 68. She married, in 1827, Jonathan P. Cushing, of Massachusetts, who was President of Hampden Sidney College, Va. Their children were:
   (1) Lucy Cushing, born about 1830; married, about 1853, Francis D. Irving, of Cartersville, Cumberland Co., Va., and was his first wife. They had: (*a*) Robert, and (*b*) Lucius Cushing.
   (2) Bettie Cushing, born about 1835; married, about 1855, Rev. W. C. Meredith, of Winchester, Frederick Co., Va., and was his second wife. Their children were: (*a*) Jonathan Cushing, and (*b*) Lucy Page.
5. Robert Burwell Page, born at The Fork, 1806; died 1837, aged 31 years; married, November, 1829, Sarah H., daughter of Thomas May, of Buckingham County Court House, Va. Their children were:
   (1) Carter Page; died young.
   (2) Mary May Page, born about 1835; married, 1860, Francis D. Irving, and was his second wife. They removed to Farmville, Prince Edward Co., Va. She died in 1884. Children: (*a*) Dr. Paulus Irving, of Farmville, Pittsylvania Co., Va.; (*b*) Sarah May Irving, died single, 1883; (*c*) Francis D. Irving, and (*d*) Robert Page Irving.
   (3) Lucy Nelson Page, born about 1837; married Rev. James Grammar, of Ashland, Hanover Co., Va.
6. Thomas Page, born at The Fork, 8th June, 1807; removed to Locust Grove, Cumberland Co., Va.; he married, 5th November, 1839, Sally Page, of Clarke County, Va.
7. Mary Maria Page, born at The Fork in 1813; married, in 1835, Rev.

George W. Dame, of the Episcopal Church, Danville, Pittsylvania Co., Va. They were both alive in 1883. Children:

(1) Jonathan Cushing Dame.
(2) Lucy Carter Dame.
(3) Rev. William Meade Dame, of the Episcopal Church.
(4) Ellen Dame.
(5) Nelson Dame.
(6) Rev. George W. Dame, Jr., of the Episcopal Church.

The following is extracted from a letter from William N. Page, Esqr., of Ça Ira, Cumberland Co., Va., to Dr. R. C. M. Page, of New York City, dated 1st February, 1879:

"I have, as requested through my son, Dr. Isham Randolph Page, of Baltimore, Md., copied from the family Bible of Col. Archibald Cary the foregoing information, which is all that is accessible to me in regard to the first and second marriages of your grandfather (and my father), Major Carter Page. This gives the births, deaths, and ages of all the children of your grandfather by each of his wives. All the first have passed away, and of the second, my sister, Mrs. Mary Maria Page Dame, and myself, are the only survivors. I remain your only surviving (half) uncle—within a few days of 76 years. The family Bible of Col. Archibald Cary, which was kept at The Fork for some years after the death of Major Carter Page, afterwards passed into the family of John C. Page—the eldest son of the first wife, who resided at Union Hill, Cumberland Co., Va.

"The said Cary Family Bible is now in the possession of D. Coupland Randolph and Harriet Page, his wife, at Union Hill. This Bible does not at present contain the record of the marriage of Major Carter Page with Lucy Nelson, his second wife. After the death of Major Page, in April, 1825, his widow, under the law of Congress, became entitled to a pension, the legal claim to which could only be established by the evidence furnished in the record of her marriage with Major Carter Page, in the Cary Family Bible. The leaves containing the record of the fact were detached from the Bible and sent to the proper authorities at Washington, D. C. They availed in securing the pension, but were never sent back. This accounts for the non-appearance, at present, of Major Page's second marriage in its place in the Cary Family Bible."

Ça Ira is a French expression, signifying "that will go." It was a watchword during the French Revolution.

V. Robert Page, of Janeville, Clarke Co., Va., eleventh child and seventh survivor of Hon. John Page, of North End, Gloucester (now Matthews) Co., Va., and Jane Byrd, his wife, was born at the second-named place in 1764, and died at the first-named place, 1st January, 1840, aged 76 years.

According to the Virginia *Historical Register*, he was one of the students who left William and Mary College, in 1776, to join the American army. He rose to the rank of Captain, and was one of the Revolutionary officers who were invited to be present at the reception of General Lafayette, in Leesburg, Loudon Co., Va., 9th August, 1825, during the last visit of that distinguished officer to the United States. This occurred on the return of General Lafayette from Oakhill, Loudon Co., Va., the residence of President James Monroe, near Leesburg. According to Lanman's "Dictionary of Congress" Captain Robert Page was a Representative in the United States Congress, from Virginia, 1799–1801.

Hon. Robert Page married, in 1788, Sarah W. Page, who died 4th April, 1843, aged 67. She was the youngest surviving child of his uncle, Robert Page, of Broadneck, Hanover Co., Va., and was, therefore, his first cousin. (See BROADNECK.) Their children were as follows:

1. Jane Byrd Page, born at Janeville, Clarke Co., Va., in 1789; married, in 1812, John W. Page, of the same county.
2. John Page, eldest son, born at Janeville, Clarke Co., Va., 2d September, 1792; removed to North End, same county, Va. He married, first, in 1819, Jane Nelson, of Mont Air, Hanover Co., Va.; and, secondly, in 1836, Sarah Williamson, of Glenoker, Fauquier Co., Va. He had issue by both his wives.
3. Sarah Walker Page (called Sally), born at Janeville, 30th December, 1793; died unmarried.
4. Robert Page, born 23d June, 1795; died infant.
5. Judith Carter Page, born 25th April, 1800; died single.
6. Catherine Page, born 23d October, 1803; died infant.
7. Mary Mann Page, born 29th March, 1805; married, in 1832, Joseph A. Williamson, of Orange Court House, Va. She died in 1876, aged 70 years, and was buried at Tappahannock, Essex Co., Va. Their children were:
   (1) Robert Page Williamson, died single, 1854, aged 21 years.
   (2) Sally Page Williamson, ditto, 1872, aged 37 years.
   (3) Williams Williamson, ditto, 1858, aged 22 years.
   (4) Roberta Page Williamson, born in 1841; married, in 1862, Rev. John B. Newton, of the Episcopal Church, Richmond, Va., and has seven surviving children.
   (5) Joseph A. Williamson, Jr.; married, about 1868, Nellie, daughter of Dr. Thomas McGill, of Maryland, and has four children.
8. Robert Walker Page, born 17th April, 1807; died single.

VI. WILLIAM BYRD PAGE, of Fairfield, Clarke Co., Va., eldest son and child of Mann Page, of the same place, and Mary Mason Selden, his wife, eldest son of Hon. John Page, of North End,

Gloucester (now Matthews) Co., Va., and Jane Byrd, his wife, was born at the first-named place about 1768, and married, about 1793, Anne, daughter of ~~Richard~~ Henry Lee, and sister of General Lee (Light Horse Harry) of Revolutionary fame. Their children were as follows:

1. William Byrd Page, eldest, born about 1794; died single.
2. Mary Anne Page, born about 1796; died in December, 1873, aged about 77 years. She married, about 1816, General Roger Jones, Adjutant-General United States Army, and had twelve children, as follows:
   (1) William Page Jones, single, graduated at the West Point Military Academy, 1840; was killed same year by the falling of his horse.
   (2) Catesby ap Roger Jones; married Gertrude Tart, of Selma, Ala., and died there in June, 1877, leaving a widow and five children.
   (3) Letitia Corbin Jones; died, unmarried, in Georgetown, D. C., January, 1869.
   (4) Mary Jones; unmarried.
   (5) Dr. Eusebius Lee Jones, of New York City and California. He married, first, Julia Stewart, of King George County, Va., and had one child. He married, secondly, about 1873, Martha Moran, of New York City. Dr. Jones died in Oakland, Cal., in January, 1876.
   (6) Edmonia Page Jones; unmarried.
   (7) Roger Jones, Inspector-General United States Army, Washington, D. C. He graduated at West Point Military Academy in 1851, and married Frederica B. Jones, of New York. They have three children.
   (8) Walter Jones; died 1876. He married Miss Brooks, of Mobile, Ala., who died about 1873. They had three children.
   (9) Charles Lucian Jones; married Mary Anderson, of Wilmington, N. C., who died about 1871. No issue.
   (10) Thomas Skelton Jones; married in Nashville, Tenn.
   (11) Virginia Byrd Jones; unmarried.
   (12) Winfield Scott Jones; unmarried; banker in San Francisco, Cal.
3. Rev. Charles Henry Page, second son, and eldest to have issue, was born 1801. He married, 1827, Gabriella Crawford, of Amherst County, Va.
4. Mann Randolph Page, born about 1803; married Miss Beall, of Jefferson County, W. Va. His daughter, Jane Byrd Page, married, 11th May, 1854, Guerdon H. Pendleton, of Clarke County, Va. (See PENDLETON.) Mann R. Page died in 1872, leaving a large family. Those known at present are: (1) George R. Page, married, first, Miss Cabell, and, secondly, Miss Timberlake; (2) Jane Byrd Page, married Guerdon H. Pendleton, as already stated; (3) Mary Page, died single; (4) Anne Lee Page, single; (5) Margaret Byrd Page, married Charles S. Lee, of Jef-

ferson County, W. Va.; (6) Edmonia L. Page, single; (7) William Byrd Page, married Laura L. Lippitt and had two girls, Mary and Agnes.

5. Jane Byrd Page, born about 1805; unmarried.
6. Cary Selden Page, born about 1809; unmarried.
7. Captain Richard L. Page, United States Navy, born about 1811; resided at Norfolk, Va.; married, about 1832, Alexina Taylor, of same city. Their children are the following:
   (1) Fannie, married, about 1875, Captain Whittle, United States Navy, nephew of Bishop Whittle, of Virginia, and had issue.
   (2) William Byrd Page, mining engineer, married, about 1884, Louise Blow, of Norfolk, Va.
   (3) Alexina, died single.
   (4) Walter Taylor Page, analytical chemist, married at the University of Virginia, 17th March, 1884, Anne (called Nannie), daughter of Prof. John R. Page. Removed to Omaha, Neb.
8. Dr. Thomas S. Page, born about 1813; married Miss Joliff and died, leaving several children.
9. Edmonia Page, born about 1815; married, about the year 1833, Hall Neilson.

VI. Hugh Nelson Page, of Norfolk City, Va., Captain United States Navy, fifteenth and youngest child of John Page, of Caroline County, Va., and Elizabeth (called Betty) Burwell, his wife, second son and child of Hon. John Page, of North End, Gloucester (now Matthews) Co., Va., and Jane Byrd, his wife, was born at the second-named place in September, 1788, and died at the first-named place, 3d June, 1871, aged 82 years.

Hugh N. Page entered the United States Navy as midshipman, 1st September, 1811. In June, 1812, he was ordered to the gunboat squadron, stationed at Norfolk City, Va., for the protection of that harbor. On August 13th, same year, he was ordered to Commodore Chauncey's squadron, on Lake Ontario; but left this, and joined Commodore Perry, on Lake Erie—volunteers for this service having been called for. He was assigned to duty on board the schooner *Tigress*, Lieutenant Conklin, September 11th, 1811. He took an active part in the Battle of Lake Erie, which began at 12 m. and closed at 3 p.m., same day. In this action he behaved with great gallantry, and was wounded in the hand. He was placed in charge of the prisoners, and had the honor of bearing to General Harrison, who was then stationed at the mouth of Sandusky River, the immortal dispatch from Commodore Perry, "We have met the enemy and they are ours."

For his brilliant services on this occasion, young Page was voted a sword by the United States Congress, and one by the State of Virginia also.

He was next ordered to the *Niagara*, which, with others of the squadron, conveyed General Harrison's army to Malden, to attack General Procter, but the latter fled at the approach of the fleet.

In the spring of 1814, he went, under Commodore Sinclair, to Detroit, to convey Major Crogan's force to retake Mackinaw. Crogan was defeated, and his force was taken on board again. After destroying an English fort on Saginaw River, and burning a large schooner loaded with provisions, he proceeded to Erie, to winter there. After a leave of absence of three years, he was promoted to the rank of Lieutenant in 1818. He was ordered to the flagship *John Adams*, Commodore Perry, with whom he sailed to South America. On this voyage Commodore Perry died at Trinidad. In 1834 he took out the *Boxer*, with the United States *Chargé d'Affaires*, to Valparaiso, Chili.

In 1838 he was promoted to Commander, and in 1843 he was ordered to the Levant. Taking on board, at Norfolk City, Va., HENRY A. WISE, United States *Chargé d'Affaires* to Brazil, he landed him at Rio. He afterward cruised on the Pacific coast.

When the war with Mexico broke out, he was ordered to Monterey, which was seized, and the United States flag hoisted. October, 1847, he was ordered to take command of the receiving ship *Pennsylvania*, at Norfolk, Va.

In 1849 he was promoted to the rank of Captain, United States Navy, and ordered to the Pacific to take command of the flagship *Savannah*. He was retired in 1855, on leave pay.

Captain Hugh N. Page married, in November, 1838, Imogen, daughter of Guy Wheeler Esq., of Nansemond County, Va. She died in 1847, without issue. He married, secondly, 13th July, 1848, Elizabeth P., daughter of Holt Wilson, Esq., of Portsmouth, Va. Their children were as follows:

1. Mary Elizabeth Page, born in Portsmouth, Va., 19th June, 1850; died, unmarried, at the same place, 25th February, 1879, aged 28 years.
2. Hugh Nelson Page, Jr., born at Portsmouth, Va., 17th July, 1852; removed to Norfolk City, Va., and married, 23d October, 1878, Sallie, only surviving child of Dr. Thomas Newton, of the last-named place, and Miss Darragh, his wife. (The latter was descended from Lydia Darragh.) No known issue at present.
3. Holt Wilson Page, born at Portsmouth, Va., October 28th, 1853; married, 22d January, 1878, Hattie W., eldest daughter of Marshall Parks, of Norfolk City, Va. There were two children, viz.:
   (1) Marshall Park Page, born 29th October, 1878.
   (2) Bettie Burwell Page, born 30th January, 1880.
4. Carter Bruce Page, born at Portsmouth, Va., 24th May, 1855.
5. Edmund John Rutter Page, born at Portsmouth, Va., 22d November, 1857.

VI. John Cary Page, of Union Hill, Cumberland Co., Va., eldest son and child of Major Carter Page, of Willis Fork, same county, Va., and Mary Cary, his first wife, was born at the last-named place, 9th May, 1784, and died at Union Hill, 14th May, 1853, aged 69 years.

He was a very handsome man, of powerful frame and fine proportions, standing six feet four inches in height. In his face and expression he very much resembled his grandfather, Col. Archibald Cary. Even in his later years there was a strong family resemblance in his face to Colonel Cary's portrait. He was a man of great energy and fine judgment, and was wonderfully acute in discerning the characters and motives of others. Though he commenced life at 14 years of age, as a poor office boy in a store in Richmond, Va., he accumulated a large fortune before his death.

He was very successful in his last years as a farmer, having retired to his farm at Union Hill, some time before his death. He attributed his success to the correct business habits he had formed while a bookkeeper in Richmond, Va.

All his children were born at Locust Grove, Cumberland Co., Va. It is about one mile from The Fork. To his two daughters, Mrs. Fisher and Mrs. Hobson, he gave the Locust Grove property, and it was bought from them about 1840, by Thomas Page, their half-uncle.

John C. Page married, 12th October, 1808, Mary Anna, daughter of Dr. Alexander Trent, of Barley Hill, Cumberland Co., Va. She died 10th January, 1877, aged 86. Their children were as follows:

1. Lavinia Anderson Page, born at Locust Grove, Cumberland Co., Va., 20th June, 1809. Married, in 1832, Dr. Edward Fisher, Superintendent of the Insane Asylum at Staunton, Va. Children:
   (1) George Fisher, married, 1864, Miss Woodfin, of Powhatan County, Va.
   (2) John Page Fisher, called Pat, of Haxall's Flouring Mill, Richmond, Va., died single, in 1863.
   (3) Nannie Ambler Fisher, married, 1858, William H. Kennon, of Richmond, Va. She died, 1866, leaving several children.
   (4) Eliza Page Fisher, died single, 1867, aged 29.
   (5) Charles Fisher.
   (6) Edward Fisher.
2. Mary Anna Page, born 26th May, 1811; married, 1845, John Daniel, Esq., of Broomfield, Cumberland Co., Va.; died 1884. He died, 1850. They had two children:
   (1) Lucy Daniel, married, 1869, Francis Kinckel, of Lynchburg, Va., and has several children.

(2) Anna Daniel, married, 1870, M. Lewis Randolph, of Edge Hill, Albemarle Co., Va.

3. Virginia Randolph Page, born 17th August, 1813; married, 1833, Thomas Hobson, of Powhatan County, Va., who died in 1850. Children:
   (1) Mary Anna Hobson, married, 1854, Mann Page, of Albemarle County, Va., who died leaving one surviving child, Charlotte, who married Smith. One child, Mann Page Smith.
   (2) Caroline Hobson, called Caddy; unmarried.
   (3) Joseph Hobson: unmarried.
   (4) Virginia Page Hobson, married, 1863, Richard Archer, of Powhatan County, Va., and had three children.
   (5) Thomas Hobson, Jr., died single, 1864.
   (6) Ellen Hobson, married George N. Guthrie, of Gallatin, Sumner Co., Tenn.
   (7) Clara Hobson, married Nash, and had issue.
   (8) Alexander Hobson. (9) Cary Hobson.
4. Eliza Trent Page, born 19th October, 1815; died single, 16th September, 1838, aged 20 years.
5. Ellen Cary Page, born 19th June, 1817; died single, 19th May, 1837, aged 20 years.
6. Alexander Trent Page, eldest son, of Cumberland County, Va., born 21st November, 1819; died April 4th, 1845, aged 26. Married, in 1840, Martha Henderson, of Northfield, same county, and had one child, viz.: Martha Henderson Page, married, 1867, Mr. Stewart, of Alexandria, Va. She died in 1870, leaving two sons.
7. Maria Willis Page, born 18th January, 1822; died 1862, aged 40. She married, 1843, Rev. William H. Kinckel, of the Episcopal Church, Lynchburg, Va., and had:
   (1) Francis Kinckel, called Frank, married, 1869, Lucy Daniel, and has several children.
   (2) Anna Kinckel, married, about 1870, J. P. Williams, of Lynchburg, Va. (3) William Kinckel. (4) Maria Kinckel. (5) John P. Kinckel. (6) J. Carrington Kinckel. (7) Alexander Gilmer Kinckel. (8) Frederick Kinckel.
8. Archibald Cary Page, second son, and eldest to have male issue, born 22d April, 1824; died in 1871, at Spring Hill, Goochland Co., Va., aged 47. He married, in 1846, Lucy, daughter of Dr. John Trent, of Trenton, Cumberland Co., Va., and had two sons, viz.:
   (1) William H. Page, eldest, born about 1845, and
   (2) John C. Page.

   He married, secondly, about 1853, Lizzie Trent, sister of Lucy, the first wife, and had one child, viz.:
   (1) Archibald Cary Page, Jr.

   He married, thirdly, in 1869, Eliza Harrison, of Richmond, Va. No issue.
9. Carter Page, born 25th March, 1826; died 31st May, 1826, infant.
10. Harriet Randolph Page, born 15th April, 1827, married, 1857, D. Coup-

land Randolph, of Richmond, Va., son of Isham Randolph, of that city. They removed to Union Hill about 1865. She died 1884. Children:
(1) Mary A. Randolph. (2) D. C. Randolph, Jr. (3) B. Heath Randolph.

11. John Cary Page, Jr., born at Locust Grove, Cumberland Co., Va, 22d February, 1830; removed to Auburn, same county. He married, first, 1858, Nellie, daughter of Dr. Willie J. Eppes, of Millbrook, Buckingham Co., Va. Children:
(1) Willie J. Page, eldest, born 1859. (2) Mary A. Page. (3) Martha Burke Page.

Mrs. Nellie Eppes Page died about 1878, and John C. Page, Jr., removed to Clay Bank, Cumberland Co., Va: He married, secondly, about 1882, Julia Trent, widow of John Taylor Gray, Esq., of the firm of Adie & Gray, druggists, Richmond, Va.

12. Edward Trent Page, youngest, born 20th May, 1833; removed to Halfway Branch, Cumberland Co., Va. He married, in 1854, Bettie, daughter of J. S. Nicholas, of Seven Islands, same county. Children:
(1) Nannie Nicholas Page, married in Lynchburg.
(2) Mary Byrd Page.
(3) John Nicholas Page.
(4) Edward Trent Page, Jr.
(5) Bessie Coupland Page.

VI. Henry Page, of Todd County, Ky., second son and child of Major Carter Page, of The Fork, Cumberland Co., Va., and Mary Cary, his first wife, was born at the last-named place, 29th September, 1785, and died in Kentucky, in 1845, aged 60 years.

He was educated at William and Mary College, Williamsburg, James City Co., Va., in the catalogue of which institution his name appears in the alumni list for 1804. He lived, first, near Ça Ira, Cumberland Co., Va., where all his children were born. He removed to Kentucky about the year 1841.

He married, 23d December, 1813, Jane B. Deane, and their children were as follows:

1. Mary Cary Page, called Polly, born at Ça Ira, Cumberland Co., Va., 27th October, 1814, and married, 23d December, 1840, Rev. George McPhail, of the Presbyterian Church. He died about 1870, while President of Davidson College, North Carolina. Their children were:
(1) Jane McPhail, died single.
(2) Mary McPhail, married Rev. Mr. Davis, of the Presbyterian Church, and died.
(3) Henry McPhail, married, and resides in Norfolk City, Va.

(4) Lillian McPhail, married Rev. Mr. Irving, of the Presbyterian Church, and died.

2. Thomas Deane Page, eldest son, born at Ça Ira, Cumberland Co., Va., 27th July, 1816; removed to Henry County, Mo., where he died, 31st January, 1864, aged 48. He married, 1846, Isabella Catlett, of Todd County, Ky., and their children were:

(1) Fannie Catlett Page, married 28th October, 1874, William McCown, who died 1875.

(2) Henry Page, born 27th December, 1849; married 9th January, 1878, Maude G. Crews.

(3) Jane Deane Page, born about 1851; died 8th July, 1855.

(4) Thomas Deane Page, Jr., born 20th October, 1853.

(5) Calmere Catlett Page, born 24th April, 1856.

(6) Carter Page, died 30th August, 1876, aged 16 years.

(7) Isabella Page, born 22d April, 1859.

(8) John Cary Page, born 12th February, 1861.

One of the girls married Rev. Octavius Parker, of the Episcopal Church, in Selma, Fresno Co., Cal.

3. Carter Page, of Chillicothe, Mo., born at Ça Ira, Cumberland Co., Va., 4th May, 1818; married first, 14th December, 1843, Betty Byers, who died soon after, leaving one child, Henry Cary Page, who also died infant. He married secondly, 6th January, 1853, Sarah Bell Miller, of Cynthiana, Ky., and had:

(1) Elizabeth Deane Page, born 10th September, 1854.

(2) Henry Page, born 1st October, 1856; dentist in Chillicothe, Mo.

(3) Isaac Newton Page, born February, 1858.

(4) Eglantine Page, born 1860.

(5) James Page, born 1862.

(6) Virginia Lee Page, born 1865, and died infant.

(7) Catherine Page, born 1867, and died infant.

4. Eliza Wallace Page, born at Ça Ira, Cumberland Co., Va., 2d July, 1820; married, 1851, Jonathan Clarke Temple, of Logan County, Ky. He lived only a few weeks, but she never married again, and died 30th June, 1872, in Chillicothe, Mo., aged 52, leaving no issue.

5. Rev. James Jellis Page, born at Ça Ira, Cumberland Co., Va., 7th July, 1822; was educated at the Theological Seminary, Fairfax County, Va., and entered the Episcopal ministry. He married, 16th December, 1851, Virginia, daughter of E. W. Newton, of Charleston, W. Va. Mr. Newton was a native of Vermont, and a graduate of Dartmouth College. The wife of Mr. Newton belonged to the Nicholas family, who are descended from a Colonial minister of the Church of England. Children:

(1) Wood Newton Page, born 13th November, 1852.

(2) Rev. Henry Deane Page, born 2d November, 1854. He was educated for the Episcopal Church at the Theological Seminary, Fairfax County, Va. Married and has several children. For many years

he has been missionary to Japan and resides at 38 Tsukiji, Tokyo, Japan. One of his children, born October, 1892, is named after the author.

(3) Sarah Bell Page, born 28th July, 1856.

(4) Rev. Thomas Carter Page, of the Episcopal Church, born 8th December, 1858. Married and at present has charge of Bruton Parish, Williamsburg, Va.

(5) Mary Wallace Page, born 17th November, 1860.

(6) Lilla Leigh Page, born 7th May, 1868.

6. Anne Catharine Page, born at Ça Ira, Cumberland Co., Va., 13th January, 1825; married, 1850, Dr. Charles A. Williams, of Chillicothe, Mo. She died 1878, aged 53, and left four children, viz.:

(1) Jane Clark Williams, born 14th August, 1852; married 1st January, 1874, Henry M. Hatton, of Chillicothe, Mo., and had two children, of whom Hubert McPhail, born 18th September, 1877, was the second, and alone survived.

(2) Lucy Washington Williams, born 22d December, 1855.

(3) Henry Page Williams, died young.

(4) Charles Williams, born 3d February, 1866.

7. Martha Bell Page, youngest of Henry Page, and Jane B. Deane, his wife, was born at Ça Ira, Cumberland Co., Va., 17th February, 1827. Unmarried.

DR. MANN PAGE, of Keswick (also called Turkey Hill), Albemarle Co., Va., sixth child and third surviving son of Major Carter Page, of The Fork, Cumberland Co., Va., and Mary Cary, his first wife, was born at the last-named place, 26th October, 1791, and died at the first-named place, 15th May, 1850, aged 58 years and 7 months.

He was educated at Hampden Sidney College, Va., and afterward graduated in medicine at Philadelphia, in 1813.

The following is an exact copy of his Medical Diploma, now in the possession of his youngest son, Dr. R. Channing M. Page, of New York City:

OMNIBUS AD QUOS PRÆSENTES LITERÆ PERVENERINT SALUTEM: CUM GRADUS UNIVERSITATIS instituti fuerint, ut Viri de Literarum Republica bene meriti, seu nostræ Almæ Matris Gremio educati, seu bonarum artium Disciplinis aliunde eruditi, a Literatorum Vulgo secernerentur. SCIATIS QUOD NOS PRÆFECTUS, VICE PRÆFECTUS, ET PROFESSORES UNIVERSITATIS PENNSYLVANIENSIS GRADU DOCTORIS in Arte Medica libenter concesso TESTAMUR quanti fecimus Virum Probum MANN PAGE in Artis Medicæ Scientia plenius instructum, cujus Mores benevoli cum omnibus iis Artibus quæ optimum quemque ornant, nos illi devinxerint, Eundem idcirco virum honorabilem et ornatum MANN PAGE omnium Suffragiis DOCTOREM IN ARTE MEDICA creavimus et constituimus, eique hujus Diplomatis virtute, singula Jura Honores et Privilegia ad illum Gradum inter nos. IN CUJUS REI TESTIMONIUM, Sigillum Universitatis majus hisce Præsentibus apponi fecimus, Nominaque subscripsimus.

DATUM PHILADELPHIÆ Die Mensis Aprilis primo Annoque Salutis humanæ Millesimo Octingentessimo, et decimo tertio.

BENJ'N RUSH, M.D., Inst: et prax: med: et clin: Prof'r.
CASPARUS WISTAR, M.D., Anatomiæ Professor.
BENJAMIN SMITH BARTON, M.D., Mat. Med. Hist. Nat. Sc. Prof.
PHILIPPUS SYNG PHYSICK, M.D., Chirurgiæ Prof'r.
JOHANNES SYNG DORSEY, M.D., Chirurgiæ Prof'r adjunctus.
JOHANNES REDMAN COXE, M.D., Chem. Prof'r.
THO. C. JAMES, M.D., Art. Obstet. Prof'r.
JOHANNES ANDREWS, D.D., Præfectus.
ROBERTUS PATTERSON, A.M., Vice Præfectus.

The Seal consists of seven books piled upon each other, and bearing the following inscriptions from top to bottom respectively: "THEOLOG., ASTRONOM., PHILOS. NAT., MATHEMAT., LOGICA, RHETTORICA, GRAMMATICA." On the circumference of the Seal is the inscription: "SIGILLUM ACADEMIÆ PHILADEL. IN PENNSYLVANIA." Inside of this is the motto, "SINE MORIBUS VANÆ."

Dr. Mann Page commenced the practice of medicine in Richmond, Va., but after his marriage he retired to his wife's estate, called Turkey Hill, near Cobham, Albemarle Co., Va. The estate, consisting of 3,700 acres of land, was a part of the Castle Hill estate, owned by Hon. Francis Walker, but which originally belonged to Meriwether. (See Walker.)

On Friday, November 5th, 1824, a dinner was given to General Lafayette in the rotunda of the University of Virginia, by ex-President Thomas Jefferson. The General's son, George W. Lafayette, was also present. Ex-President James Madison, who was present, responded to the regular toast, "James Madison, the ablest expositor of the Constitution," and ended by proposing the following toast: "Liberty, which has virtue for its guest and gratitude for its feast." Volunteer toasts were proposed by Thomas J. Randolph, W. C. Rives, Th. Walker Gilmer, Dr. Mann Page, Wm. F. Gordon, V. W. Southall, N. P. Trist, Colonel S. Carr, Richard Duke, and others. Mr. Southall presided with great dignity, and none who were present will ever forget the enthusiasm of this reception.

Dr. Mann Page was, as we have already stated, the grandson of Col. Archibald Cary, who was descended from the Carys of Cockington and Torr Abbey, England. In regard to a certain decree, said to have been made in the Court of Chancery, England, respecting the property of the Carys of Cockington, Dr. Mann Page wrote to Francis R. Rives, Esq., Secretary of the American Legation, in London, under date of 22d February, 1843. Edward Everett was at that time the American Minister to England. In reply, Mr. Rives wrote from London, 27th March, 1843:

MY DEAR UNCLE: Immediately after the receipt of your letter, I addressed a note to H. J. Perry, Esq., the principal Secretary to the Lord High Chancellor, asking for the desired information, which, he wrote me, it was not in his power to give, unless some clue is furnished whereby the name of the suit in court can be ascertained. A copy of his reply I herewith transmit you. I then addressed myself to George Stanley Cary, Esq., the present representative of the Carys of Follaton House, who is ignorant of the Chancery decree in question. That gentleman forwarded a copy of my letter to the widow of his late cousin, the proprietor of Torr Abbey; and she turned the letter over to her cousin, Mr. Browne, who says they are not aware of any decree having been made in the Court of Chancery respecting the property of the Carys of Cockington (who are the ancestors of the Carys of Torr Abbey and of the Carys of Follaton House), nor have the family any recollection of any such matter. Entire copies of the letters of Messrs. Cary and Browne I likewise inclose you. These circumstances, it seems to me, furnish ample proof of the erroneous character of the information you have received respecting this affair. . . .

The following is a copy of the reply of George Stanley Cary, Esq., of Follaton House, to Mr. Francis R. Rives:

FOLLATON HOUSE, 22d March, 1843.

SIR: I beg to acknowledge the receipt of your letter this morning. I beg to state that I am totally unacquainted with any circumstance relative to the decree in Chancery that your correspondent in the United States alludes to. I have forwarded by this day's post a copy of your letter to the widow of my late cousin—the proprietor of Torr Abbey, where the family has resided the last 170 years.

I have, Sir, the honor to be your most ob't servant,

GEORGE STANLEY CARY.

TO FRANCIS R. RIVES, ESQ.

P.S.—Should any further information be sought for, relative to the Cary family, it will be most cheerfully given by Mrs. J. Cary, who resides at No. 16 Park Road, Regent's Park.

Mr. John Cary, of Cockington and Torr Abbey, residing in Vienna, Austria, heard, through Mr. Everett, of this letter from

Dr. Mann Page to Francis R. Rives, Esq., in regard to the Cary property, and wrote as follows:

VIENNA, March 14th, 1846.

DR. MANN PAGE, Albemarle County, Va., U. S. America.

MY DEAR SIR: On the 18th of June last, 1845, I availed myself of the pleasure of addressing you. Obtaining unfortunately no answer up to this day, I much fear that the said inclosure has, on account of special reasons, been mislaid. Allow me consequently to trouble you again with these lines, at the same time inclosing herewith a repetition of the letter in question, under date of 18th June last, 1845.

VIENNA, June 18th, 1845.

MY DEAR SIR: Informed at last, unfortunately but of late, of your address, through the medium of Mr. Everett, the American Minister at London, I venture to avail myself of the pleasure of inclosing you these lines on a most important subject regarding my family. I am apprised, my dear Sir, that you are the gentleman who addressed Mr. Everett, during the spring of 1843, an inclosure imparting to him information that you had received from England, to the effect that, according to a recent decree of English Chancery, a considerable amount of property had accrued to the heirs of Sir Henry Cary, of Cockington, in Devonshire. My much-lamented father, Mr. John Cary, of Cockington and Torr Abbey, in Devonshire, was directly descended from Sir Henry Cary, who was the son of Sir George Cary, of Cockington, Sheriff of Devonshire in the 18th of Charles I. After that monarch's fallen fortunes, Sir Henry Cary emigrated, with his family, to Virginia; which event is well known to me from records in English History, as more so from various important documents regarding my family; copies of which have been in my possession since my infancy. As a member of the family, being my father's youngest son, and as a father, as well as in behalf of my innumerable brothers and sisters, I shall feel myself, my dear Sir, much and much indebted to your extreme kindness in favoring me in short, if possible, with a few lines, informing me from what source in England you gained this intelligence.

I have resided on the Continent for many years, and here in Germany for sixteen years. I was formerly in the Austrian service, and at present retain the character of an Austrian officer. My brothers are dispersed in all parts of the world; which fate, my dear Sir, I do not doubt you are aware, befalls the younger sons in England. By chance, unfortunately but of late, I heard indirectly of the above-stated important communication. The amount of property in question, and said to be in the Court of English Chancery, is possibly leasehold property now falling in; and if this be the case, the same, instead of reverting to the present representative of my family, namely, to my nephew, Robert Cary, eldest son of my sister-in-law, Mrs. Cary, of Torr Abbey, in Devonshire, on his obtaining his majority of twenty-one years, the same must evidently, after having been sold, be equally divided among us brothers and sisters.

I repeat again and again, my dear Sir, how much and much I shall feel myself indebted to your extreme kindness if you will impart to me the source in England from which you gained your information regarding the matter, and also whether the property in question is personal or leasehold now falling in.

I gained information of this important event in the spring of 1833. My sister, who is at present married in Hungary, was on a visit to us here in Vienna, at that time. One day, during the month of April, 1833, she received from my mother-in-law, Mrs. John Cary, a letter which by chance fell into my hands.

In this letter she stated that my sister-in-law, Mrs. Cary, of Torr Abbey, had received, some days since, a most strange letter from the American Minister in London, stating that a member of the Cary family in the United States had heard that, by a late decree of English Chancery, a large amount of property had accrued to the heirs of Sir Henry Cary (son of Sir George Cary, of Cockington), and that the said property was leasehold property then falling in. Subsequently I addressed a letter on the subject to Mr. Edward Everett, American Minister in London, and he confirmed the statement communicated to my sister by my mother-in-law. Moreover, Mr. Everett addressed a letter on the subject to my sister-in-law, Mrs. Cary, of Torr Abbey, and he intimated to me her answer, stating that she was not aware of the existence of any such property, nor could she obtain any information respecting it, unless the date and the name of the decree in question were known.

I repeat again and again, my dear Sir, that I shall feel myself truly much indebted to your extreme kindness in forwarding to me as soon as possible information regarding this important subject. At the same time I should feel myself much obliged to you if you could forward to me the addresses of certain members of my family, residing in the State of Virginia, who are descendants of Sir Henry Cary, of Cockington and Torr Abbey, in Devonshire.

Trusting on the speedy answer, I remain my dear Sir, your most sincere and thankful friend,

JOHN CARY, of Cockington and Torr Abbey.

The origin of the statement that there had been a decree in the English Court of Chancery regarding the Cary property is unauthenticated. No such decree has been heard of by those who were certainly in a position to have known it, had it really ever been made. There is strong reason to suspect that it was merely a quack advertisement in some newspaper, by a so-called law firm which made a business of swindling credulous people about such matters. Not long since the author read an article in the London *Times* regarding the arrest and imprisonment of two men engaged in this business, in which a fee in advance is always required. The article concluded with a warning to people to put no confidence in such statements, as they invariably were mere baits for swindling the credulous.

The following is copied from a tablet in Grace Church, Walker's Parish, Albemarle Co., Va.:

IN MEMORIAM

MANN PAGE ESQ[RE] M. D.

born 26th Oct. 1791,
died 15th May 1850.
SON OF MAJOR CARTER PAGE, OF
THE AMERICAN REVOLUTIONARY ARMY,
AND OF MARY CARY HIS FIRST WIFE.
By his death, his family was
deprived of the protection and
guidance of a Christian husband
and father, and this church
of one of its founders.

HIS BELOVED WIFE,

JANE FRANCES WALKER.

born 17th Feb. 1799,
died 7th Feb. 1873:
WAS ENDEARED TO ALL WHO KNEW HER.
She was the eldest child of the
Hon. FRANCIS WALKER of Castle Hill,
and of JANE BYRD NELSON his wife,
of Yorktown Virginia.

Ex dono Ricardi Channing Moore Page filii eorum octavi
de Nov. Ebor. M.D. et auctoritate curatorum
MDCCCLXXXIX.

JANE FRANCES WALKER, the wife of Dr. Mann Page, was born in the Nelson House, at Yorktown, Va., 17th February, 1799, and died at Turkey Hill, 7th February, 1873, aged 74 years. She was married in the old Virginia Tavern near the west entrance to the Capitol square at Richmond, Va., and just opposite St. Paul's Church. Mammy Suky, then a girl and her waiting-maid, was present at the marriage and said that "Missis was a mighty pretty girl. She gim me the dress she got married in. It wuz blue and stuffy." Upon asking her what she meant by "stuffy" she said, "quilted-like." She may possibly have had reference to a quilted blue satin petticoat. The Virginia Tavern, the aristocratic hotel in Richmond in those days, was kept by Mrs. Col.

Hugh Nelson (Judith Page, of North End), called Big Mamma by the children, as she was very tall and stately in appearance. It subsequently passed into the hands of Capt. Thomas Nelson, who afterward removed to Oakland, Hanover Co., Va. From this tavern could be seen the reflection of the fire that destroyed the Richmond Theatre in 1811, some of the boarders having been victims. Mammy Suky, who accompanied Jane Frances Walker and her sister Judith to Mr. Fremont's school, died in 1890, aged 95.

Jane Frances Walker was descended on her mother's side from the Nelsons of Yorktown, Va., as follows: Thomas Nelson, of Yorktown, Va., first of his family in Virginia, and called Scotch Tom, married, 1710, Margaret Reid; their son, William Nelson, of the same place, and known as President Nelson, married, 1738, Elizabeth (called Betty) Burwell; their son, Col. Hugh Nelson, of the same place, married, 1775, Judith Page; their daughter, Jane Byrd Nelson, married, in 1798, Hon. Francis Walker, of Castle Hill, Albemarle Co., Va., and was the mother of Jane Frances Walker, the wife of Dr. Mann Page. On her father's side she was descended from the Washington family as follows: Col. John Washington and his brother Lawrence emigrated from England to Westmoreland County, Va., and became the progenitors of the Washington family in that State. Col. John Washington married, about 1650, Anne Pope, who was his second wife; their son, Lawrence, married, about 1675, Mildred Warner; they were the grandparents, through their son Augustine, of Gen. George Washington and his brother, Col. Samuel Washington (who married five times); and their daughter, Mildred, sister of Augustine Washington, and aunt of Gen. George Washington, married, about 1701, Roger Gregory; their three daughters married three brothers Thornton, Elizabeth Gregory marrying, about 1720, Reuben Thornton; their daughter, Mildred Thornton, married, first, Nicholas Meriwether, and secondly, Dr. Thomas Walker, of Castle Hill, Albemarle Co., Va.; their son, Hon. Francis Walker, married, 1798, Jane Byrd Nelson, of Yorktown, Va., and their eldest child was Jane Frances Walker, the wife of Dr. Mann Page. (See Nelson, also Walker.) Jane Frances Walker and Judith Page Walker, her younger sister, who married Hon. William C. Rives, United States Senator from Virginia, studied the French language in Richmond, Va., under M. Fremont, the father of the late Gen. John C. Fremont.

Dr. Mann Page married, 12th December, 1815, at Richmond, Va., Jane Frances, eldest child of Hon. Francis Walker, of Castle Hill, Albemarle Co., Va., and Jane Byrd Nelson, of Yorktown, Va., his wife. Children:

1. Maria Page, born in Richmond, Va., 14th December, 1816, died unmarried, at Turkey Hill, 15th June, 1837, aged 21 years.
2. Ella Page, born at Castle Hill, Albemarle Co., Va., 18th September, 1818; died unmarried, at Turkey Hill, 14th November, 1882, aged 64 years.

3. Francis Walker Page, eldest son, born at Turkey Hill, 17th November, 1820. Removed to Cobham Grove, Albemarle Co., Va., and died there 12th July, 1846, aged 26 years. He was buried at Turkey Hill. He married, 4th September, 1844, Anna E., daughter of Benjamin F. Cheesman and Maria S. Whittemore, his wife, both of New York City. Mrs. Cheesman is the daughter of Thomas Whittemore and Lucy Snow, his wife. Mr. Whittemore was born in Leicester, Mass., and removed to New York City, where he became a prominent and wealthy merchant. He died in 1829. He was sixth in descent from Thomas Whittemore, of Malden, Mass., who emigrated to America with Governor Winthrop, of that State, in the year 1635. Anna E. Cheesman was the niece of the late distinguished physician and surgeon, Dr. John S. Cheesman, of New York City, who was a contemporary of the late Prof. Valentine Mott, of that city. She died at Cobham Grove, April 7th, 1881, leaving one son, Francis Walker Page, Jr., born 20th July, 1845. Resides at Staunton, Va., unmarried.
4. Carter Henry Page, second son, born at Turkey Hill, Albemarle Co., Va., 21st November, 1822; removed first to Eldon, near Cobham, and secondly to 521 North First Street, Charlottesville, same county. He married, 24th November, 1857, Leila, daughter of Capt. William Graham, of Baltimore, Md. Children:
   (1) Leila Graham Page, born 21st December, 1858. Resides at Charlottesville.
   (2) William Graham Page, eldest son, born 31st August, 1860, lawyer; resides at Charlottesville, Va.
   (3) Carter H. Page, Jr., engineer, born 4th September, 1864. Travelled in Europe during the summer of 1882, with his uncle, Dr. R. C. M. Page, of New York. While in Paris he visited the grave of Lafayette in the *Cimetière Historique, No. 35 Rue Picpus, près de la barrière du Trône,* and placed a wreath of *immortelles* on the tombstone, as his great-grandfather, Major Carter Page, of The Fork, Cumberland Co., Va., had served as Aid-de-Camp to General Lafayette during the campaign in Virginia against Cornwallis, in 1781. Married, 30th April, 1891, Elizabeth H. Roberts, and has a son, born 6th Oct., 1892, and named after the author. At present they reside in Philadelphia.
   (4) Mary Bowdoin Page, born 26th June, 1866; married, 1st March, 1892, Gilbert Bonham Bird, of England.
5. John Cary Page, born 9th January, 1824; died infant, 16th April, 1826.
6. Frederick Winslow Page, born at Turkey Hill, 20th November, 1826; librarian University of Virginia, Albemarle County, Va. He married, 24th December, 1850, Anne Kinloch, daughter of Dr. Thomas W. Meriwether, of Kinloch, Albemarle Co., Va., and Anne Carter Nelson, his wife, who was a granddaughter of Gov. Thomas Nelson, of Yorktown, Va. Mrs. Anne Kinloch Meriwether Page died in the spring of 1867. He

married, secondly, 15th November, 1883, Lucy Cook Beale, the widow Brent. No issue. Children by the first marriage:

(1) Jane Walker Page, born at Lynchburg, Va., 22d September, 1851; married, 13th January, 1875, Thomas Walker Lewis, of Castalia, Albemarle Co., Va. They removed to Airslie, near by, in the same county, and have several children.

(2) Eliza M. Page, born 1st August, 1853; died single, 14th March, 1873.

(3) Annie Nelson Page, born 15th September, 1855; married, 13th January, 1875, Nathaniel Coleman, of News Ferry, Halifax Co., Va., and has issue. Annie bore a strong resemblance to the portrait of her ancestress, Jane Byrd, of Westover, on James River, Charles City Co., Va., who was the wife of Hon. John Page, of North End, Gloucester (now Matthews) Co., Va.

(4) Frederick K. Page, of Millwood, Albemarle Co., Va., born 24th July, 1857. He married, 20th November, 1878, Flora Temple, daughter of William Lewis, of same county. Children:

(*a*) William Douglas Page—August 30th, 1879.
(*b*) Evelyn Mabry Page—December 17th, 1881.
(*c*) Frederick Byrd Page—September 22d, 1883.
(*d*) Fannie Campbell Page—September 20th, 1886.
(*e*) Robert Shackleford Page—September 14th, 1888.

(5) William Douglas Page, born 11th June, 1859; died 14th April, 1878, aged 20 years, unmarried. He was buried in the Nelson Cemetery at Belvoir.

(6) Evelyn Byrd Page, born 21st September, 1862; married, 19th July, 1882, John M. Coleman, of Halifax County, Va., and has issue.

(7) Mildred Nelson Page, born 27th June, 1865. Resides with her uncle, Dr. R. C. M. Page, of New York City.

7. Jane Walker Page, born 18th October, 1828; died unmarried, 29th January, 1845, aged 17. Regarding this brilliant young lady who unfortunately died so young, Mrs. Judge Roger A. Pryor thus writes to the author: "I knew your father and mother, your sister Ella, and *well* did I know and love the brilliant sister who died so young—Jane—my classmate in music under the eccentric genius, Meerbach. And I feel deeply gratified that you permit me to aid in preserving from oblivion that pure, bright spirit whose hand clasped mine for a little way on the long journey of my life. Of her beauty of character and brilliant genius I cannot say too much."

8. Mann Page, Jr., born at Turkey Hill, Albemarle Co., Va., 1st May, 1831; removed to Mansfield, same county. He died in November, 1864, aged about 33 years, and was buried at Turkey Hill. He married, 15th May, 1855, Mary Anna Hobson, of Powhatan County, Va., and left one surviving child, viz., Charlotte Nelson Page, born 10th November, 1859, who married, 31st October, 1883, William Ed. Smith, of North Carolina, and has one son, Mann Page Smith.

9. Charlotte Nelson Page, born at Turkey Hill, Albemarle Co., Va., 25th March, 1832; died at Kinloch, same county, 1849, unmarried. She was buried at Turkey Hill.
10. William Wilmer Page, born 31st March, 1835; died of typhoid fever, 6th November, 1857, aged 22 years.
11. Thomas Walker Page, born at Turkey Hill, Albemarle Co., Va., 18th April, 1837; resided at same place, and died there 5th June, 1887, aged 50. He married 10th May, 1861, Nannie Watson, daughter of James Morris, of Sylvania, Green Springs, Louisa Co., Va., and Caroline Smith, his wife. Children:
    (1) Ella Rives Page, born 16th April, 1862.
    (2) James Morris Page, A.M , Ph.D., born 4th March, 1864. He originated and is the principal of The Keswick School.
    (3) Thomas Walker Page, Jr., A.M., born 4th December, 1866. Assistant in The Keswick School.
    (4) Constance Morris Page, born 17th April, 1869.
    (5) Mann Page, born 29th March, 1871.
    (6) Susan Rose Morris Page, born 30th August, 1878.
12. Dr. Richard Channing Moore Page, born 2d January, 1841, at Turkey Hill, Albemarle Co., Va.; removed to New York City in 1867. He married, 30th April, 1874, in the Memorial Episcopal Church, at Westport, Conn., Mary Elizabeth Fitch, widow of the Hon. Richard Henry Winslow, of that place.

Mary Elizabeth Fitch was the second daughter and youngest child of Stephen Fitch, Esq., of Norwich, New London Co., Conn., and Mary Ingraham Rogers, his wife. She first married Hon. Richard Henry Winslow, of Westport, Fairfield Co., Conn., who was the founder of the banking firm of Winslow, Lanier & Co., of New York City. He was a Connecticut State Senator, and was the Democratic candidate for Governor of that State in 1861. A short time before his death, which occurred 14th February, 1861, he commenced to build a beautiful granite church at Westport. This church is of the Protestant Episcopal denomination, and was subsequently completed by his widow. The interior is very handsome, and is finished off with carved oak and chestnut. Some of the frescoes on the walls so perfectly resemble statuary that they remind one of Dewitt's celebrated frescoes in the Royal Palace at Amsterdam, Holland. The windows are of stained glass—the memorial window in the rear of the chancel being one of the most beautiful in America. The organ, made by Hall & La Baugh, of New York City, cost five thousand dollars, and was presented by Mrs. Mary E. Fitch Winslow. The bell was cast by Naylor, of Troy, N. Y. Within the base of the tower is a well of excellent water, out of which Gen. George Washington drank in September, 1780, when stopping at the old tavern that formerly stood here. In the vestibule of the church is a mural tablet bearing the following inscription:

MEMORIAL CHURCH OF THE HOLY TRINITY, WESTPORT.

The CHURCH
OF THE HOLY TRINITY
was incorporated April 14, 1860;
REV. JOHN PURVES, Rector.
The corner-stone of this edifice was laid,
September 19, 1860,
By RT. REV. JOHN WILLIAMS, D.D., Assistant Bishop
In grateful commemoration of

RICHARD HENRY WINSLOW,

who bought the site and began the erection of this structure;
and of his widow,

MARY FITCH WINSLOW,

who completed it.
The Society, February 17, 1862,
adopted the corporate name it now bears.
The Church, first opened for divine service
February 23, 1862,
was solemnly consecrated to the worship of God
June 30, 1863,
according to the order of the Protestant Episcopal Church
in the United States of America.
In perpetual memory of these events
This tablet has been inscribed and is now set up by order of
WILLIAM HENRY BENJAMIN, Rector.
JOHN CLEAVELAND and WILLIAM H. MARVIN, Wardens.

William Wood,
John F. Buckley,
Elijah S. Downes,
John H. Gray,
Charles J. Ketchum,
George Jelliffe,
Henry Taylor, } *Vestrymen.*

The following is copied from a letter received from a former Rector of Memorial Church:

WESTPORT, Fairfield Co., Conn., 19th June, 1883.

DR. R. C. M. PAGE, New York City.

MY DEAR SIR: I send you the names of the first class confirmed in Memorial Church. They were confirmed by Assistant Bishop John Williams (Bishop Brownell being too old and infirm), of Connecticut, May 8th, 1860, and were as follows: Elizabeth I. Townsend, Jane Howel Townsend, M. A. Perring, James Frederick Perring, Laura Sophia Perring. It is impossible to find out who was confirmed first. The first person baptized (and consequently the first person made a member of the church) was William Payne, baptized June 24th, 1860, by the Rev. John Purves. The first marriage in the parish was that of Henry Augustus Ogden to Abbie Jane Coley, May 16th, 1860, also by Rev. John Purves. The first marriage in the church was that of William Kirk to Miss Smith, March 10th, 1863, by the Rev. Rufus Emery, of Southport, Conn. The first burial in the parish was that of the founder, Hon. Richard Henry Winslow, February 18th, 1861.

Yours truly,

ALONZO NORTON LEWIS, D.D., Rector.

The present Rector is Rev. Kenneth Mackenzie, who was formerly Assistant Rector of the Church of the Holy Trinity, Madison Ave., cor. 42d Street, New York. He is very popular and has a large and flourishing congregation.

"In May, 1860, the second Episcopal Society, in the town of Westport, purchased the property corner of East Church Street and Myrtle Avenue, known as the 'Wakeman Lot,' for the sum of two thousand dollars. R. H. Winslow, Francis Burritt, and Daniel J. Townsend were appointed a committee, with power, to build a stone church edifice and chapel upon the 'Wakeman Lot,' and to complete and furnish the same upon such plan, and in such mode and manner in all respects, as they may deem proper or expedient. The committee were instructed to make all contracts necessary, in order to carry into effect, and fully to exercise, the power delegated to them. In February, 1861, the society met with a great loss in the decease of Mr. Richard H. Winslow, and, in the following April, the decease of Mr. Francis Burritt. The church edifice, which had been commenced by Mr. Winslow, was, after his death, finished by his widow, Mary Fitch Winslow, who tendered its use to the society of the 'Holy Trinity.' The name of the society was shortly afterward changed to that of 'The Memorial Church of the Holy Trinity.'

"The site on which Memorial Church is built was the 'Wakeman Place,' formerly an old inn. Gen. George Washington passed a night at this tavern, in September, 1780, while returning from Hartford, where he had been to meet Count Rochambeau. During the demolition of the ancient edifice there was found among the *débris* a French crown-piece of an early date in the eighteenth century, in excellent preservation." ("Hist. of Fairfield County, Connecticut," p. 826. J. W. Lewis & Co., Philadelphia, 1881.)

MEMORIAL CHURCH OF THE HOLY TRINITY.—WESTPORT CONN.
BEGUN IN 1860 BY HON RICHARD HENRY WINSLOW, AND COMPLETED IN 1862 BY MARY FITCH WINSLOW.

Mary Elizabeth Fitch, the widow of Hon. Richard H. Winslow, and wife of Dr. R. Channing M. Page, of New York City, was descended on her mother's side from Sarah Wilson, of Boston, Mass., who married Edward Cowell, of England, the legal heir to all the property now included in the city of Leeds as follows: Joseph Wilson, of Boston, Mass., died in 1680, leaving the daughter, Sarah Wilson, who married Edward Cowell, of England, who removed to Boston, Mass. Their daughter, Sarah Wilson Cowell, married Timothy Ingraham, of Rhode Island. Solomon Ingraham, their son, married Lydia Vail, and had two children, viz.: (1) Capt. Solomon Ingraham, died unmarried; and (2) Mary Ingraham, who married Ebenezer Rogers. Their daughter, Mary Ingraham Rogers, married Stephen Fitch, of Norwich, New London Co., Conn. Their second daughter and youngest child was, as we have seen, Mary Elizabeth Fitch.

A stock company of gentlemen, composed of the descendants of Edward Cowell and Sarah Wilson, his wife, have, for some years past, been searching in the United States and England for the will of Edward Cowell, but so far have not succeeded in finding it. Capt. Solomon Ingraham had a copy of the original will. This copy was put away in a tin box in Boston, Mass., whence there is strong evidence that it was stolen by a lawyer. It is supposed that he sold it to interested parties in England, with a view to destroying an evidence of claim to the property, as well as preventing the discovery of the original will.

Regarding the present Keswick School, it is in a flourishing condition and is attended by about thirty pupils. The principal is James M. Page, A.M., Ph.D., the first assistant being his brother, Thomas W. Page, A.M. Several buildings have been recently erected on account of the increased number of scholars. In former years there was a school here or in the neighborhood for teaching the children of the various families, as follows:

1831–32. William W. Hawkins taught for a short time at the old Bentivoglio Tavern, which was kept at that time by Mr. Joseph Campbell. The school was then removed to a log house in the woods near by, called the Tick Hill Academy. Among the pupils were Frank W. Page, Carter H. Page, James Farish and John T. Farish, twin brothers, Reuben Gordon, William F. Gordon, Jr., Lewis Miller, and others. Mr. John T. Farish died in New York a few years ago a millionaire.

The old Bentivoglio Tavern, called old Benti for short, stood on the south side of the public road about a quarter of a mile east of the mouth of the Turkey Sag. The latter is the name of the public road that runs northwest over the mountains, along Feather-Bed Lane, across Turkey Run and through Turkey Gap. The tavern was originally built by Hon. Francis Walker, of Castle Hill, for the accommodation of travellers in those days. It has long since gone to ruin, and nothing but a depression in the ground now remains

(From a portrait by Healy, Corcoran Gallery, Washington, D. C.)

MRS. MARY ELIZABETH FITCH WINSLOW,

Wife of Dr. R. C. M. Page.

Married 30th April, 1874.

to mark the original site. The post-office at Lindsay's turnout on the railway, some two miles distant, is known as Bentivoglio. This and other beautiful Italian names for places in the neighborhood, such as Modena and Monticello, were doubtless given by Italian laborers imported in early times by Thomas Jefferson for the purpose of introducing grape culture.

1832–33. Mr. Crawford taught at the same place with the same scholars. Crawford was an exhorter in the Baptist Church and used the hickory freely. The boys were much afraid of him. Sometimes he would be absent the whole day preaching, and the boys would be afraid to go home. In the evening he would return, and the whole school, drawn up in line in the public road, would be put through a course of spelling.

1833–34. James L. Gordon taught at Edgeworth, the residence of his father, Gen. William F. Gordon, with much the same scholars.

1834–35. William W. Hawkins rented Bentivoglio Tavern and taught school again, Mr. Campbell having left. The scholars were nearly the same.

1835–36. Mr. Provost, a graduate of Princeton, N. J., taught at Castle Hill, the residence of Hon. William C. Rives. There were a limited number of pupils, among whom were Frank W. Page, Carter H. Page, Frederick W. Page, Francis R. Rives, and William C. Rives, Jr. Provost was one of the best teachers. He also courted all the marriageable girls in the neighborhood.

1836–37. Edwin Hall, of Maine, a pupil of the poet Longfellow and a graduate of Bowdoin, taught at Bentivoglio. Among the pupils were Frank W. Page, Carter H. Page, Frederick W. Page, Reuben Gordon, William Gordon, Henry Michie, Johnson Michie, and Lewis Miller.

1837–38. Giles Waldo, a graduate of Yale, taught at Bentivoglio. The scholars were the same with the addition of William Anderson and Richard Anderson, of Richmond, Va., as boarders.

1838–39. Mr. Janes, of Burlington, Vt., taught at Bentivoglio, and among the scholars were Robert W. Nelson, W. Douglas Meriwether, William C. Rives, Jr., Lewis Miller, William Lewis (Colonel), the brothers William, Richard, and Jack Anderson, and Carter and Frederick Page.

1839–40. Jacob Belville, of Princeton, taught at Bentivoglio, with the same scholars except R. W. Nelson and William and Richard Anderson.

1840–41–42. James Chisholm, of Harvard, taught at Keswick in the old school-house down in the lot. Among the scholars were Frederick W. Page, Mann Page, Jr., Wilmer Page, Lindsay Walker, George and Charles Gordon, twin brothers, Alexander Gordon, and Alfred Rives.

1842–43. Thomas W. Cattell, of New Jersey, graduate of Princeton. He taught at the same place, and the scholars were Frederick, Mann, Wilmer, and Thomas Page, George, Charles, Churchill, and Alexander Gordon, and William C. Cattell.

1843–44. George Jeffery, of Cambridge, England, taught at the same place with the same scholars except Frederick W. Page. It was about this time that F. W. Meerbach, a famous German pianist, gave music lessons to young ladies in the neighborhood. Mr. Jeffery was a very eccentric man, and the two had a quarrel, resulting in Mr. Jeffery's going next session to Edgeworth.

1844–45. George Jeffery taught at Edgeworth, the residence of Gen. William F. Gordon. The same boys except William C. Cattell.

1845–46. Mr. Taylor, a Princeton man, taught at Edgeworth with the same scholars.

1846–47–48. Frederick W. Page taught at Keswick in the old school-house in the lot. The scholars were Frank Hopkins, Churchill and Alexander Gordon, Mann, Wilmer, Thomas, and Channing Page. The latter wore a check apron, much to his annoyance.

1848–49. Calvin S. Maupin, of North Carolina, taught at Edgeworth, with the same boys except Channing, who was too young to walk there. Mr. Maupin was not a very literary man nor did he much enjoy conversation at meals, being usually blessed with a ravenous appetite. Thus while General Gordon was telling some anecdote about President Jackson, while he was a member of Congress, Mr. Maupin interrupted him in the middle at the most interesting part by remarking, "General, you got my bread!"

1849–50. Mann Page taught at Keswick. The scholars were Churchill, Alexander, and Mason Gordon, Henry Lewis, and Wilmer, Thomas, and Channing Page.

1850–51. Dabney C. T. Davis taught at Keswick. He was a graduate of the University of Virginia. The scholars were John and Hugh Nelson, twin brothers and boarders at Keswick, Wilmer, Thomas, and Channing Page, Churchill, Alexander, and Mason Gordon, and John and Rice McGhee, also twin brothers.

1851–52. Samuel S. Carr, of the University of Virginia, taught at Keswick. The scholars were the same except Churchill Gordon, who was absent. Lewis McGhee, brother of John and Rice, was a scholar this year. They came from Bedford County, Va., and boarded at Logan, the residence of Capt. M. Lewis Walker.

After that there were so few boys left in the neighborhood that there was no occasion for a school. Mason Gordon and Channing Page were sent to academies before going to college, and it was not until within a few years past that the present school was established.

VI. William Nelson Page, of Ça Ira, Cumberland Co., Va., third son and second surviving child (and eldest having surviving male issue) of Major Carter Page, of The Fork, same county, Va., and Lucy Nelson, his second wife, was born at The Fork, 28th February, 1803. He married, in 1827, Fannie P., daughter of Isham Randolph, of Richmond, Va., and had the following children:

1. Dr. Isham Randolph Page, eldest, born about 1834; removed to Baltimore, Md. He married, first, in 1863, Virginia Barton, of Lexington, Rockbridge Co., Va. She died, leaving one child, viz.: Virginia Bar-

ton Page, born 1864. He married, secondly, October 30th, 1866, Charlotte Stevens, of Baltimore, Md., and had two children, viz. :
(1) Frances McHenry Page, born about 1867.
(2) Robert Stevens Page, born about 1869.

2. Anne Randolph Page, called Nannie, died, 8 years old.
3. Philip Nelson Page, born about 1838, died young.
4. William Nelson Page, Jr., died 21st July, 1861, aged 20.
5. Rev. Coupland Randolph Page, of the Episcopal Church, born about 1842; married, 1876, Ellen Baker, of Winchester, Frederick Co., Va., and had several children.
6. Lucia Harrison Page, born about 1844, died young.
7. Fannie Randolph Page, born about 1846; married, 1873, Rev. W. C. Meredith, of the Episcopal Church. He resided at Winchester, Frederick Co., Va., and died about 1875, leaving her a widow with one child, viz., Fannie Randolph Meredith. Fannie R. Page was the third and last wife of Rev. W. C. Meredith, his second wife having been Bettie Cushing, of The Fork, by whom he had Jonathan Cushing Meredith, lawyer, removed to Kansas City, and Lucy Page Meredith.

VI. THOMAS PAGE, of Locust Grove, Cumberland Co., Va., sixth child and fifth son and survivor of Major Carter Page, of The Fork, same county, Va., and Lucy Nelson, his second wife, was born at the last-named place, 8th June, 1807, and died at the first-named place, 4th July, 1874, aged 67.

He married, 5th November, 1839, Sally, daughter of John W. Page (see Broadneck), of White Hall, Clarke Co., Va., and Jane Byrd Page, daughter of Hon. Robert Page, of Janeville, same county, Va. Mrs. Sally Page was born August, 1818, and died 27th November, 1872, aged 54 years. Their children were as follows:

1. Dr. Robert Page, eldest, born 12th January, 1842, and removed to Staunton, Augusta Co., Va. He married, 18th December, 1878, Anna, daughter of Willis W. Hobson, of same county, and Arabella Bolling, of Petersburg, Va., his wife. There are several children.
2. Carter Page, born about 1844; teacher.
3. Lucy Nelson Page, born 17th January, 1852; married, September 5th, 1877, W. T. Johnson, of Powhatan County, Va., and had one child—Sally P. Johnson.
4. James Chisholm Page, born 1855.
5. Thomas Nelson Page, born 6th June, 1860.
6. Willianna Page, born 27th October, 1864.

Four other children died infants—names unknown.

VI. John Page, of North End, Clarke Co., Va., second child and eldest son of Hon. Robert Page, of Janeville, same county, Va., and Sarah Walker Page, his wife (and first cousin), was born at the last-named place, 2d September, 1792.

He married, first, in 1819, Jane, daughter of Francis Nelson, of Mt. Air, Hanover Co., Va., and Lucy Page, his wife, who was the youngest child of Hon. John Page, of North End, Gloucester (now Matthews) Co., Va. Jane Nelson was the sister of Judith, who married, in 1819, Mann Page, of Greenland, Gloucester Co., Va., and was his first wife. (See Rosewell.) They were granddaughters of Gov. Thomas Nelson, of Yorktown, Va. The children of John Page, by the first marriage, were:

1. Robert Francis Page, born about 1820; removed to Campbell County, Va. He married, 1847, Lavinia Sullivan, daughter of James Christian, of New Kent County, Va. Children:
   (1) Edwin Randolph Page, born 19th September, 1849, at West Point, King William Co., Va. He married, about 1874, Olivia McDaniel, of Jones County, N. C.
   (2) Francis Nelson Page, born at Campbell Co., Va., 29th January, 1855; removed to California.
   (3) Roberta Frances Page, born at Campbell Court House, Va., 14th May, 1857; removed to Richmond, Va.
2. Edwin Randolph Page, born about 1822; also removed to Campbell County, Va. He married, 1850, the widow, Olivia Cam, daughter of John Alexander, of the same county, Va. Children:
   (1) Mary Mann Page, married Stephen M. Taylor and had issue.
   (2) William Nelson Page, of Powellton, Fayette Co., W. Va. Married, 7th February, 1882, Emma, daughter of Col. William Gilham, of the Virginia Military Institute, and Miss Hayden, of New York, his wife. Children: Delia, Hayden, Edwin Randolph, Josephine, and Evan Powell.
   (3) Edmonia Randolph Page; married, 1878, Thomas A. Bledsoe, of Augusta County, Va.
3. Judith Carter Page, born about 1824; died unmarried.
4. Lucy Nelson Page, born about 1828; married, 1860, James Madison Sublett, of Powhatan County, Va., and had:
   (1) Octavia Page Sublett.
   (2) Mary Carter Sublett.
   (3) Florence Sublett.
   (4) Lucy Nelson Sublett.
   (5) Olivia Byrd Sublett.
5. Thomas Mann Page, born about 1830; removed to Bedford County, Va.,

and married, 1854, Rosalie, daughter of James Brown, of Buckingham County, Va. Their only child is William Nelson Page, born about 1855.

John Page, of North End, Clarke Co., Va., married secondly, in 1836, Sarah Williamson, of Glenoker, Fauquier Co., Va. She was sister to Joseph A. Williamson, of Orange Court House, who married Mary Mann Page, daughter of Hon. Robert Page, of Janeville, Clarke Co., Va. The children by the second marriage were:

1. Helen Page, born 1839, and died single, 1859, aged 20.
2. Rev. William Williamson Page, of the Presbyterian Church, born 1841; removed to New York City; he married, 1877, Lizzie M., daughter of Rev. Nathaniel Pierson, of Baltimore, Md. She died about 1880, leaving one child—Surry Kent Page.

VII. Rev. Charles Henry Page, of the Episcopal Church, third child and second son (being also the eldest to have issue) of William Byrd Page, of Fairfield, Clarke Co., Va., and Anne Lee, his wife (who was sister to General Light Horse Harry Lee, of Revolutionary fame), eldest surviving son and child of Mann Page, of the same place, and Mary Mason Selden, his wife, eldest son and child of Hon. John Page, of North End, Gloucester (now Matthews) Co., Va., and Jane Byrd, his wife, was born at the first-named place in 1801, and died at Georgetown, D. C., in 1876, aged 75 years. He married, in 1827, Gabriella, daughter of Judge Crawford, of Amherst County, Va., who was a brother of William H. Crawford, of Georgia, one of the candidates for President of the United States in 1825. Their children were:

1. Jane Byrd Page, born about 1828; married, about 1848, Thomas Barbour Bryan, of Alexandria, Va. Children:
   (1) Charles Page Bryan.
   (2) Jeannie Byrd Bryan.
2. Elizabeth Spooner Page, born about 1833; married, about 1853, Dr. Glover Perin, Surgeon United States Army, and had:
   (1) Gabriel Perin; married Col. Henry Prout.
   (2) Mary Byrd Perin.
   (3) Lucy Legh Perin.
   (4) Charles Page Perin.
   (5) Betty Page Perin.
   (6) Sophia Perin.

(7) Virginia Langdon Perin.
(8) Glover Fitzhugh Perin.

3. Legh Richmond Page, eldest son, born about 1835; married, 1863, Page Waller, of Richmond, Va., and has issue.
4. William Wilmer Page, born about 1837; married, about 1865, Victoria Amiraux, of Canada. Children:
   (1) Gabriella Page.
   (2) William Wilmer Page, Jr.
   (3) Thayer Page.
5. Roger Jones Page, born about 1839; removed to Louisville, Ky., and married, 1867, Mary, daughter of Hon. John Mitchell, the Irish patriot and late member of the British Parliament from Tipperary, Ireland. They had a son, named John Mitchell Page.
6. Sophia Perin Page, born about 1841; married, 1862, Prof. Nathaniel Shaler, of Cambridge, Mass. Two children, viz.:
   (1) Gabriella Shaler.
   (2) Anne Shaler.
7. Charles Henry Page, Jr., born about 1845; married, 1876, Annie Brown, of Oregon.
8. Lucy Fitzhugh Meade Page; unmarried.

VIII. Legh Richmond Page, of Richmond, Va., lawyer, third child and eldest son of Rev. Charles Henry Page and Gabriella Crawford, his wife; third child and second son (being the eldest to have issue) of William Byrd Page, of Fairfield, Clarke Co., Va., and Anne Lee, his wife (who was sister of General Light Horse Harry Lee, of Revolutionary fame), eldest surviving son and child of Mann Page, of the same place, and Mary Mason Selden, his wife, eldest son and child of Hon. John Page, of North End, Gloucester (now Matthews) Co., Va., progenitor of the North End branch of the Page family in Virginia, and Jane Byrd, his wife, was born about 1835. Being the eldest son of the eldest son, etc., in descent from Hon. John Page, of North End, he is the representative of that branch of the Page family.

He married, in 1863, Page, daughter of Logan Waller, of Richmond, Va. Their children are:

1. Mary Lee Page, born in Richmond, Va., about 1864.
2. Charles Henry Page, eldest son, born at same place, about 1866.
3. Legh Richmond Page, Jr., born at same place, about 1868.
4. Waller Page, ditto, about 1870.
5. Brooks Page, ditto, about 1872.
6. Gabriella Page, ditto, about 1874.

IV. Robert Page, of Broadneck, Hanover Co., Va., third and last surviving son and child of Hon. Mann Page, of Rosewell, Gloucester Co., Va., and Judith Carter, his second wife (by whom alone he had surviving male issue), second and only surviving child of Hon. Matthew Page, of the same place, and Mary Mann, his wife, second son (and only one having male issue) of Col. John Page, of England, and Williamsburg, James City Co., Va., progenitor of the Page family in Virginia, and Alice Luckin, his wife, was born at the second-named place about 1722, and died suddenly at the first-named place, upon returning from a ride on horseback, about the year 1768, aged 46. He founded the Broadneck House, Hanover Co., Va., about 1750. It was destroyed by fire during the war of the Revolution, his two sons, Robert and John, being youths at that time.

His son Robert probably rebuilt the house after the war, while others of the family removed to Clarke County, Va.

He married, 20th January, 1750, at the age of about 28 years, Sarah Walker, sister of Clara Walker, who married Allen. The portrait of Clara Walker is said to be at Clairmont, the Allen residence, on James River, Va. The two sisters Walker were co-heiresses and daughters of an English gentleman.

The children of Robert Page and Sarah Walker were:

1. Mann Page (No. 1), born at Broadneck, Hanover Co., Va., 26th October, 1750; died infant.
2. Robert Page, Jr., eldest survivor, born at the same place 15th June, 1752; married, in 1779, Mary Braxton, of Chericoke, King William Co., Va.
3. Mann Page (No. 2), born 1754; died infant.
4. Judith Page, born 15th October, 1756; married, 1st September, 1774, John (?) Waller, who was born 25th July, 1753, and was Clerk of Spottsylvania County, 1774–86, member of the House of Delegates, 1791. Removed to Enfield, King William Co., Va., the old family residence, which Judge Waller purchased from his elder brother. Children:
   (1) Sarah Waller; married, about 1806, Richard Byrd.

(2) Benjamin Waller; married, about 1814, Miss Travis.
(3) Martha H. Waller; married, first, about 1810, William Montague, and, secondly, Joseph H. Travis.
(4) John Waller; married, about 1818, Miss Greenhow.
(5) Dorothy Waller; died single.

5. Catharine Page, born 7th November, 1758; married, February, 1778, Benjamin Carter Waller, of Williamsburg, James City Co., Va., who was born 24th December, 1757. Justice of York County, 1796, member of the House of Delegates, 1798–1800, and afterward Clerk of James City County, Va. They died many years ago, leaving:
(1) Martha Waller; married, first, about 1800, George W. Holmes, and, secondly, Lawrence Meuse.
(2) Benjamin C. Waller; married Hattie Catlett.
(3) William Waller; married Mary Berkely Griffin. Their granddaughter, Mary Stuart Waller, married Louis G. Young, of Charleston, S. C.
(4) Dr. Robert Page Waller; married, first, about 1815, Eliza C. Griffin, and, secondly, Julia W. Mercer.
6. John Page, born at Broadneck, Hanover Co., Va., 29th January, 1760; removed to Pagebrook, Clarke Co., Va. He married, in 1784, Maria H. Byrd.
7. Matthew Page, born at Broadneck, 4th March, 1762; removed to Annefield, Clarke Co., Va. He married, about 1787, Anne, daughter of Richard K. Meade and sister of Bishop William Meade, of Virginia. Children:
(1) Sally Page, married, about 1808, Rev. Charles W. Andrews, of Shepherdstown, Jefferson Co., W. Va.
(2) Mary Frances Page; married, about 1810, John Byrd. She died leaving one child, who married Rev. J. R. Jones, of Clarke County, Va.
8. Walker Page; born 1764; died unmarried.
9. Sarah Walker Page, youngest, born at Broadneck, 16th February, 1766; married, in 1788, Hon. Robert Page, of Janeville, Clarke Co., Va. (See North End.)

V. Robert Page, Jr., of Broadneck, Hanover Co., Va., second and eldest surviving son and child of Robert Page, of same place, and Sarah Walker, his wife, was born there 15th June, 1752, and died there, aged 42, in 1794.

As already stated, he probably rebuilt the Broadneck House, which had been destroyed by fire during the Revolutionary war, he being a youth at that time. His son, Walker Y. Page, is recorded as an alumnus in the catalogue of the College of William and Mary, at Williamsburg, James City Co., Va., for the year 1810. He is there mentioned as the "son of Robert Page, of Broadneck, Hanover Co., Va."

He married, in 1779, Mary, daughter of Carter Braxton, of Chericoke, King William Co., Va., and their children were as follows:

1. Robert Page, eldest, born about 1780; died single.
2. Carter Braxton Page, born about 1782; married, about 1807, Eliza Nicholson. No issue.
3. Sally W. Page, born about 1784; married, about 1804, Humphrey Brooke, of Spottsylvania County, Va. Children:
   (1) Mary Brooke; married, about 1825, Mr. Helm, and died, leaving many children.
   (2) Elizabeth (called Betsey) Brooke; married Thomas Blackburn, of Clarke County, Va., and died, leaving children.
   (3) Anne Brooke; married, about 1830, Oliver A. Shaw, of Louisiana, and died, leaving Johanna, Eliza, Oliver, Herbert, Sally, Stephen, and Judith; all of whom removed to California.
   (4) Robert Brooke; married, about 1838, Eliza Smith, and had one child, viz., Robert Carter Brooke.
   (5) Sarah W. Brooke; married Samuel Williamson.
   (6) Hon. Walker Brooke, United States Senator from Mississippi, 1852–53; died at Vicksburg, Miss., 1870. He married Miss Eskridge.
4. John W. Page, third son and eldest having issue, was born at Broadneck, Hanover Co., Va., 1786, and removed to Clarke County, Va. He married, first, 1812, Jane Byrd Page, of Janeville, same county, and had issue. He married, secondly, in 1833, Emily Smith, of Winchester, Frederick Co., Va. No issue.
5. Judith Robinson Page, born about 1788; died unmarried.
6. Walker Y. Page, born about 1790, and mentioned in the catalogue of William and Mary College for 1810 as "son of Robert Page, of Broadneck, Hanover Co., Va.;" died unmarried.
7. Mattie Page, born about 1792; died unmarried.
8. Catherine Page, born about 1794; died unmarried.

V. John Page, of Pagebrook, Clarke Co., Va., second son and child of Robert Page, of Broadneck, Hanover Co., Va., and Sarah Walker, his wife, was born at the last-named place 29th June, 1760. He died 17th September, 1838, aged 78.

He married, in 1784, Maria Horsemander, daughter of Col. William E. Byrd, of Westover, on James River, Charles City Co., Va. She was probably the niece of Jane Byrd, of that place, who married, 1746, Hon. John Page, of North End, Gloucester (now

Matthews) Co., Va. The children of John Page and Maria H. Byrd were as follows:

1. Nancy Page, born about 1786; died infant.
2. Mary W. Page, born about 1788; married, 1816, Benjamin Harrison, of Berkeley (Harrison's Landing), Charles City Co., Va., and died in Richmond, 1865, aged 77. She was buried at Pagebrook, Clarke Co., Va. Children:
   (1) Lucy Harrison; unmarried; resided in Clarke County, Va.
   (2) Henry Harrison; married, about 1845, Fannie Tab Burwell, daughter of George H. Burwell, of Carter Hall, Clarke Co., Va., and had (*a*) Henry, married Margaret, daughter of Dr. William Byrd Page, of Philadelphia, Pa.; (*b*) Maria, married Dr. Philip Burwell; (*c*) George B., and (*d*) Agnes.
   (3) Benjamin Harrison, Jr.; married, 1858, Mattie, daughter of Dr. Matthew Page, of Clarke County, Va., and Polly Randolph, his wife, and had (*a*) Dr. Benjamin Harrison; (*b*) Mary Cary, married Archie Bevan, of England; and (*c*) Gwynn P. Dr. Matthew Page was the eldest son of Gwynn Page, of Kentucky, who was the fourth child of Mann Page, of Rosewell, and Anne Corbin Tayloe, his second wife. (See Rosewell.)
   (4) Maria Harrison; died single.
   (5) Evelyn Harrison, ditto.
3. William Byrd Page, eldest son; born about 1790; married, first, about 1813, Evelyn Byrd Nelson; and, secondly, Eliza M. Atkinson.
4. Sarah W. Page, born about 1792; married, in 1815, Major Thomas M. Nelson, of Mecklenburg County, Va., who was a grandson of Secretary Thomas Nelson, of Yorktown, Va. She died 1835, aged about 43. (See Nelson.)
5. Dr. Robert Powell Page, born 11th January, 1794; married, first, about 1819, Mary Francis; and, secondly, about 1839, Susan G. Randolph.
6. Judge John E. Page, born 11th March, 1796; married, 1823, Emily McGuire.
7. Abby B. Page, born August, 1798; married, about 1816, John Hopkins, of Winchester, Frederick Co., Va., whom she survived. Their children were:
   (1) William E. Hopkins, Commodore United States Navy; resides in San Francisco, Cal.
   (2) John Page Hopkins, Jr.; died unmarried.
   (3) Dr. St. George Hopkins; married, first, about 1859, Miss Brown, of Philadelphia, and had one child—a daughter. He married, secondly, about 1868, Miss Cunningham, of Baltimore, Md., and has three children. He removed, with his family, to California.
8. Dr. Matthew Page, youngest; born at Pagebrook, Clarke Co., Va., 1801; removed to Edenton, Chowan Co., N. C. He married, first, 1829, Mary

Matilda, daughter of Josiah Collins, of the last-named place. She died, leaving no surviving issue. He married, secondly, in 1848, Henrietta Elizabeth Collins, sister of his first wife, and had one surviving child, viz. :

(1) Herbert Henry Page; born 15th November, 1851; married, 1876, Mary Louise, daughter of Dr. John Herbert Claiborn, of Petersburg, Va. They had several children, viz. : (*a*) Herbert Claiborn, born 17th September, 1877; (*b*) Byrd Alston, born 30th July, 1879; (*c*) Weldon Bathurst, born 11th November, 1880; and perhaps others.

VI. John White Page, of White Hall, Clarke Co., Va., fourth child and third son (being the eldest to have issue) of Robert Page, Jr., of Broadneck, Hanover Co., Va., and Mary Braxton, his wife, second and eldest surviving child and son of Robert Page, of the same place, and Sarah Walker, his wife, was born at Broadneck in 1786, and died in Winchester, Frederick Co., Va., 19th October, 1861, aged 75. His name appears in the catalogue of William and Mary College as an alumnus for 1807.

He married, first, in 1812, Jane Byrd, eldest child of Hon. Robert Page, of Janeville, Clarke Co., Va., and Sarah W. Page, his wife. (See North End.) The latter was, as we have seen, the youngest child of Robert Page, of Broadneck, Hanover Co., Va., and Sarah Walker, his wife. Mrs. Jane Byrd Page Page died in Winchester, Va., 27th March, 1830, aged 38. Their children were:

1. Robert Matthew Page, eldest, born 14th May, 1814; died unmarried in Texas, in 1839.
2. Walker Yates Page, second son, and eldest having issue, was born at Janeville, Clarke Co., Va., 16th December, 1816; removed to Frederick City, Md., and married, 1st June, 1858, Nannie C. Tyler, by whom he had issue.
3. Sally Page, born 7th August, 1818; died November 27th, 1872; married, 5th November, 1839, Thomas Page, of Locust Grove, Cumberland Co., Va. (See North End.)
4. Nathaniel B. Page, born 1820; married, 15th November, 1848, Mary Anna Richardson. No issue. He died in Washington, D. C., 27th July, 1853, aged 33.
5. Mary B. Page, born 16th August, 1821; unmarried; removed to Baltimore, Md.
6. Jane Byrd Page, born 23d May, 1823; died 27th February, 1855, aged 32. She married, 10th August, 1847, Rev. James Chisholm, who died in Portsmouth, Va., in 1854, during the yellow fever epidemic. He left two sons, viz. :

(1) William B. Chisholm, born 20th September, 1848, editor of the Auburn (N. Y.) *Independent*. Married, in 1873, Jeannie Johnston, and had one son.
(2) John W. Chisholm, died infant.

7. John White Page, Jr., born 9th November, 1824, at White Hall, Clarke Co., Va.; removed to Petersville, Frederick Co., Md., and married, 14th November, 1855, Ellen, daughter of Dr. George W. West, of the same county, Maryland. Children:
   (1) Judith Robinson Page, born 8th June, 1857.
   (2) George West Page, born 31st January, 1860. Removed to New York.
   (3) William C. Page, born 28th April, 1862. Removed to New York. Married, 28th November, 1885, Rosalie B. Williams, of Baltimore.
   (4) Ellen West Page, born 3d March, 1866.
   (5) Eliza Byrd Page, born 18th May, 1869.
   (6) Jane Byrd Page, born 17th March, 1874.
8. Judith Robinson Page, born 7th March, 1826; died unmarried, 4th September, 1856, aged 30 years.
9. Carter Braxton Page, youngest, born at White Hall, Clarke Co., Va., 18th June, 1829; removed to Bladensburg, Prince George Co., Md., where he died 28th April, 1881, aged 52 years. He married, first, in 1853, Emily, daughter of Dr. William Armistead, of Fluvanna County, Va., by whom he had five children, only one of whom survived, viz., Robert Matthew Page, born 1858. He married, secondly, 1st November, 1867, Evelina, daughter of William Gray, of Caroline County, Va. No issue.

John W. Page, of White Hall, Clarke Co., Va., married, secondly, in February, 1833, Emily, daughter of Gen. Edward Smith, of Winchester, Frederick Co., Va., by whom he had no issue.

VI. William Byrd Page, of Pagebrook, Clarke Co., Va., eldest son and child of John Page, of the same place, and Maria H. Byrd, his wife, was born there about 1790, and died 1st September, 1828, aged about 38 years. After his death, his younger brother, Judge John E. Page, resided at Pagebrook.

He married, first, about 1813, at Westover, on James River, Charles City Co., Va., Evelyn Byrd, daughter of Judge William Nelson (a younger brother of Gov. Thomas Nelson, of Yorktown, Va.) and Abby Byrd, his wife. Their children were as follows:

1. Anne Willing Page, born about 1814; married, in 1835, Thomas Carter, of Annefield, Clarke Co., Va., who formerly lived in King William County, Va. She was his second wife. Children:

(1) Dr. Charles Shirley Carter, of Baltimore, Md.; married Miss Swann, of that city.

(2) Captain William Page Carter, of Clarke County, Va.; married Lucy, daughter of Dr. Robert Powell Page, of the same county, and Susan G. Randolph, his second wife.

They are half brothers of Col. Thomas H. Carter, of Pampatike, Manquin P. O., King William Co., Va.

2. Dr. William Byrd Page, eldest son, born about 1817; removed to Philadelphia, Pa. He married, about 1840, Celestine, daughter of Samuel Davis, of Louisiana. Children: (1) S. Davis Page, Comptroller of the city of Philadelphia and the father of (*a*) Howard; (*b*) Ethel; and (*c*) William Byrd, the champion high jumper of the world; (2) Margaret, married Henry Harrison and had issue as already stated.
3. John Page, of Longwood, Clarke Co., Va., born about 1820. He married, about 1845, Lucy Mann Burwell, daughter of George H. Burwell, of Carter Hall, same county, the sister of Mrs. Henry Harrison. Children: (1) Evelyn; (2) Celestine.

William Byrd Page, of Pagebrook, Clarke Co., Va., married, secondly, about 1822, Eliza Mayo, daughter of Robert Atkinson, of Mansfield, near Petersburg, Dinwiddie Co., Va., and had children as follows:

1. Evelyn Byrd Page, born about 1823; married, about 1841, Richard Henry Lee, of Grafton, Clarke Co., Va. Children: (1) Rev. William Lee; (2) Richard Henry Lee, Jr.; (3) Mary Lee; (4) Charles Lee.
2. Mary Page, born about 1825; married, about 1842, William Norborn, son of Major Thomas M. Nelson, of Mecklenburg County, Va., who was a grandson of Secretary Thomas Nelson, of Yorktown, Va. (See Secretary Nelson.)

VI. Dr. Robert Powell Page, of Briars, Clarke Co., Va., fourth child and second son of John Page, of Pagebrook, Clarke Co., Va., and Maria H. Byrd, his wife, was born at the last-named place, 11th January, 1794, and died at the first-named place in March, 1849, aged 55 years. He was buried at Pagebrook.

It is probable that the portrait in the house of Mrs. Abby Byrd Page Hopkins, at Winchester, Frederick Co., Va., is his likeness—according to a letter written by his brother, the late Judge John E. Page, of Pagebrook, Clarke Co., Va. He married, first, about 1819, Mary, daughter of Thomas Willing Francis, of Philadelphia, Pa. Their children were as follows:

1. Maria B. Page, born about 1820; married, about 1840, Mayhew Wainwright, of New York City, and had four children, viz.:
   (1) Elizabeth (called Lizzie) Wainwright; married, about 1875, Dr. John Page Burwell, of Clarke County, Va., and died, 1883, without issue.
   (2) Mayhew Wainwright, Jr., Lieutenant United States Navy, killed by pirates on the Pacific coast.
   (3) Robert Wainwright, Lieutenant of Cavalry, United States Army.
   (4) Maria Wainwright, born about 1855; married, first, about 1873, Henry Slaughter, of New York City, and had two children, and, secondly, Mr. James. She was an actress—her *nom-de-théâtre* being Fannie Louise Buckingham.
2. Dora W. Page, born about 1822; married, about 1842, Nathaniel Burwell, of Clarke County, Va. Children: (1) Dr. John P. Burwell; (2) Dr. William P. Burwell; (3) Susie, married Archie Randolph and has issue; and (4) Mary Willing Page, single.
3. Nancy F. Page, born about 1824; married, about 1844, Joseph Pleasants, of Philadelphia, Pa. Now resides in Europe.

Dr. Robert Powell Page, of Briars, Clarke Co., Va., married, secondly, about 1839, Susan Grymes, daughter of Archie Randolph, of the same county, and Susan Burwell, of Carter Hall, same county, his wife. Archie Randolph was the eldest son of Thomas Isham Randolph, of Dungeness, Goochland Co., Va. (See Randolph.) The children by the second marriage were:

1. Elizabeth B. Page, born about 1838; died, unmarried, at Cobham Park, Albemarle Co., Va., during the summer of 1863, aged about 25 years.
2. Mary Francis Page, born about 1840; married, in 1867, John Esten Cooke, author, of Clarke County, Va. She died in 1878, leaving three children: (1) Susie Randolph, born 11th July, 1868; (2) Edmund Pendleton, born 18th May, 1870; (3) Robert Powell Page, born 12th October, 1874. Their father, John Esten Cooke, died 27th September, 1886, at Briars.
3. Lucy B. Page, born in 1842; married, in 1867, Captain William P. Carter, of Clarke County, Va.
4. Robert Powell Page, Jr., of Saratoga, Clarke Co., Va., born about 1846. He married, about 1870, Agnes, daughter of George H. Burwell, of Carter Hall, same county, and Agnes Atkinson, his wife. Children: (1) Agnes; (2) Mary; (3) Robert P.; (4) George; (5) Nathaniel B.

VI. Judge John E. Page, of Pagebrook, Clarke Co., Va., fifth child and third son of John Page, of same place, and Maria H. Byrd, his wife, was born there 11th March, 1796, and died there 4th

March, 1881, aged 84 years. He resided at Pagebrook after the death of his brother, William Byrd Page, in 1828.

He was Circuit Court Judge for the counties of Clarke and Warren, Virginia, up to the time of his death. In 1863 he brought his family to Albemarle County, Va., and resided, for about a year, at Cobham Park, the residence of William C. Rives, Esq., of Newport, R. I. The four children of Dr. Robert Powell Page, by the second wife, were with him. It was during this time that three of them died.

Judge John E. Page married, in 1823, Emily, daughter of Col. William H. McGuire, of Harper's Ferry, Loudon Co., Va., who was an officer of much distinction in the United States Army. Their children, as far as known, were as follows:

1. John Y. Page, eldest survivor, two having died infants, born in Clarke County, Va., 24th July, 1827; removed to Ferguson, St. Louis Co., Mo., where he practised law; married, about 1859, Lizzie Wash.
2. Mary M. Page, born April, 1829, unmarried.
3. Emma Page, born at Pagebrook, August, 1833; married, in 1853, Philip Nelson, of Nelson, Nelson Co., Va., and was his first wife. She died in October, 1860, leaving two children—William and Emily. (See Nelson.)
4. Anne W. Page (called Nannie), born at Pagebrook, Clarke Co., Va., November, 1835; married, in 1864, Dr. William Douglas Meriwether, of Kinloch, Albemarle Co., Va. (See Nelson.) She died at Culpepper, Va., in 1875, leaving one child, viz., Evelyn Page Meriwether.
5. Dr. Robert P. Page, born at Pagebrook, Clarke Co., Va., 12th March, 1838; removed to Berryville, same county, and married, about 1864, Martha Turner (called Mattie), daughter of William Hardee, of Petersburg, Dinwiddie Co., Va. Children: William Hardee, drowned in Georgia, June, 1883, Evelyn Byrd, John Evelyn, Bettie, and Edward Douglas.
6. Jane McGuire Page, born March, 1840, unmarried.
7. Evelyn Byrd Page, born February, 1842; died single, August, 1863, at Cobham Park, Albemarle Co., Va., aged 21 years. She was buried in the old Nelson cemetery, at Belvoir, same county, Va.
8. Edward Charles Page, born 1844; died infant, 1848.
9. William Byrd Page, born 17th July, 1848; died March, 1864, at Kinloch (the residence of Dr. Meriwether), Albemarle Co., Va., and was buried in the Nelson cemetery, at Belvoir, with his sister.

VII. WALKER YATES PAGE, OF FREDERICK CITY, Frederick Co., Md., eldest surviving son and second child of John W. Page, of

White Hall, Clarke Co., Va., and Jane Byrd Page, his first wife; fourth child and third son (being the eldest to have issue) of Robert Page, Jr., of Broadneck, Hanover Co., Va., and Mary Braxton, his wife, eldest son and child of Robert Page, of the same place, progenitor of the Broadneck branch of the Page family in Virginia, and Sarah Walker, his wife, was born at the second-named place 16th December, 1816. He removed to Frederick City, Frederick Co., Md. Being the eldest son of the eldest son, etc., in descent from Robert Page, of Broadneck, he is the representative of that branch of the family.

He married, 1st June, 1858, Nannie C., daughter of Dr. William Tyler, of Frederick City, Md. Their children (two having died infants) are as follows:

1. Mary Addison Page, born in May, 1859; married, 1879, William Stiles, of Baltimore, and had issue.
2. Nannie Walker Page, born July, 1864; died single.
3. William Tyler Page, only surviving son, born 8th October, 1868; resides in Baltimore.

PART II.

NELSON FAMILY.

(From a water-color copy by C. H. Sherman, New York, 1883, from the original portrait by unknown artist.)

HON. WILLIAM NELSON, OF YORKTOWN, VIRGINIA,

PRESIDENT OF THE DOMINION OF VIRGINIA.

Died 19th November, 1772, aged 61.

NELSON COAT-OF-ARMS.

I. THOMAS NELSON, OF YORKTOWN, York Co., Va., progenitor of the Nelson Family in that State, was the son of Hugh Nelson, of Penrith, County of Cumberland, England, and Sarah, his wife, and was born at the last-named place 20th February, 1677. He emigrated to the Colony of Virginia about the year 1700, and became the progenitor of the Nelson Family in Virginia.

He died at Yorktown, Va., 7th October, 1745, aged 68 years, and was buried in the Episcopal churchyard there. He was popularly known as Scotch Tom, from the fact that his parents were from the North of England, near Scotland. Above is given an exact copy of the coat-of-arms found on his tombstone at Yorktown, Va. The engraving is made from a drawing copied from the original tombstone at Yorktown, Va., May, 1883, by C. H. Sherman, of New York City.

The correct tinctures of this coat-of-arms are not known, as none are represented on the tombstone. In outline the arms are identical with those of Nelson, of Yorkshire, England, and this fact is suggestive of the origin of the names of Yorktown and York County, Va. The following is probably a correct description of Scotch Tom Nelson's coat-of-arms:

ARMS.—Per pale argent and sable, a cheveron between three fleurs-de-lis counterchanged.

CREST.—A fleur-de-lis per pale argent and sable.

No motto is mentioned on the tombstone, but, in the United States of America, one of Lord Nelson's might, without impropriety, be adopted, viz.: "*Palmam qui meruit ferat.*"

The following is an exact copy of the inscription found on the tombstone of Scotch Tom Nelson, at Yorktown, York Co., Va.:

Hic jacet
Spe certa resurgendi in Christo
THOMAS NELSON, Generosus
Filius Hugonis et Sariæ Nelson
de Penrith in Comitatu Cumbriæ
Natus 20mo die Februarii Anno Domini 1677
Vitæ bene gestæ finem implevit
7mo die Octobris 1745. Ætatis suæ 68.

The translation of the above inscription is as follows: "Here lieth, in the certain hope of being raised up in Christ, Thomas Nelson, Gentleman. Son of Hugh and Sarah Nelson, of Penrith, in the County of Cumberland. Born on the 20th day of February, in the year of our Lord, 1677. He completed a well-spent life on the 7th day of October, 1745. Aged 68."

His only portrait, a very fine one, was destroyed by fire, in Richmond, Va., in 1864.

According to Bishop Meade, *op. cit.*, Vol. I., p. 205, he founded Yorktown in 1705. "A few venerable relics of the past," says Bishop Meade, "are all that may now be seen. The old York House is the most memorable. The corner-stone of it was laid by old President Nelson, when an infant, as it was designed for him. He was held by his nurse, and the brick laid in his apron and passed through his little hands." That statement is evidently erroneous, since the present Nelson House, at Yorktown, Va., was founded at a later date, by President Nelson, who was born in 1711.

The following is probably the correct account of the Nelson houses at Yorktown, Va.:

First. Thomas Nelson, known as Scotch Tom, founded Yorktown, Va., about 1705, and, as any other emigrant would do, he built a wooden house first. Second. He built, about 1715, the first brick house. All traces of this house have disappeared. It was situated not far from the present Nelson House, in a northwesterly direction from the latter, and on the opposite side of the road that runs in front of it. This house was afterward occupied by Col. Hugh Nelson, grandson of Scotch Tom. A portion of the wall was standing about 1840, with multiflora roses growing over it. Third. Scotch Tom, about 1725, built another brick house for Secretary Thomas Nelson, his youngest son and third child. This stood several hundred yards from the present Nelson House, in a southeasterly direction from the latter. Being much nearer the lines during the siege of York, October, 1781, it was so bombarded that it was never repaired. Not a vestige of it now remains. Secretary Thomas Nelson was in this house when the siege commenced. During the bombardment his butler was killed while serving dinner, waiter in hand. Then Secretary Nelson left the house under a flag of truce, and was escorted into the American lines by his three sons, who were officers under Washington.

Fourth. The present Nelson brick house, which was occupied by Lord Cornwallis as headquarters of the British Army, during the siege, October, 1781, was built as late as 1740–41, by President William Nelson, for his eldest son, Thomas, afterward signer of the Declaration of Independence, Governor of Virginia, and Major-General in the American Army. Governor Nelson was an infant in 1740–41, having been born 26th December, 1738, and it was through his little hands that the first brick was made to pass when the present Nelson House was founded. For a picture of this house see Bishop Meade, *op. cit.*, Vol. I., p. 204; Scribner's *Monthly Illustrated Magazine* (*The Century*), October, 1881, p. 803; and the *Magazine of American History,* A. S. Barnes & Co., July, 1881, p. 47.

The old Custom-House at Yorktown, Va., was doubtless built about 1715, the same year as the first Nelson brick house—or even before it. In either case it

OLD CUSTOM-HOUSE, YORKTOWN, VA.

would be the oldest brick house in that section of the country, as it is the oldest and first Custom-House in the United States of America. It escaped serious injury during the bombardment, in October, 1781.

The following is copied from a letter to Dr. R. C. M. Page, of New York City, from Col. William Nelson, of Oakland, Hanover Co., Va., under date of April 3d, 1883:

"I learned in my young days from my father and mother that the present Nelson House at Yorktown, Va. (the same, by the way, in which I was born), was built about the year 1740–41, by President William Nelson for his eldest son, Governor Thomas Nelson—then an infant in his nurse's arms—and the first brick was made to pass through his little hands. This occurred a few years before the death of his grandfather, Scotch Tom, who died 7th October, 1745. Bishop Meade was certainly inaccurate in his statement of the building of that house. As regards your account of the other Nelson houses at Yorktown, Va., I think that it is as nearly accurate as you can get it at this late day.

"Gov. Thomas Nelson died 4th January, 1789, at one of his farms in Hanover County, Va., and his body was carried down to York and buried in the old churchyard, immediately at the foot of his father's tomb; so that grandfather, father, and son (Scotch Tom, President Nelson, and Governor Nelson) were buried in a continuous line, the head of the second near the foot of the first, and the head of the third near the foot of the second.

"I make this statement that you may put it on record, so that it may be known by those who desire it."

In regard to the parents of Col. William Nelson, author of the foregoing letter, it may be stated that his mother was Judith, eleventh and youngest child and fifth daughter of Gov. Thomas Nelson, and that Col. William Nelson's father was Thomas, eldest son and third child of Col. Hugh Nelson, of Yorktown, Va. The place was formerly called York simply; only after the Revolution was it called Yorktown.

Thomas Nelson, the first of his family in Virginia, and known as Scotch Tom, married first, about 1710, Margaret Reid, and their children were as follows:

1. William Nelson, eldest, born at Yorktown, York Co., Va., in 1711; died there 19th November, 1772, aged 61. He was known as PRESIDENT NELSON. Married, February, 1738, Elizabeth (called Betty) Burwell.
2. Mary Nelson, born at Yorktown, Va., about 1713; married, about 1733, Col. Edmund Berkeley, of Barnelms, Middlesex Co., Va. Children:
   (1) Edmund Berkeley, Jr., of same place, married, first, Mary Judith Randolph, of Tuckahoe, and, secondly, Mary Burwell.
   (2) Nelson Berkeley, of Airwell, Hanover Co., Va., married Elizabeth Wormeley Carter, granddaughter of Hon. Robert (King) Carter, and had issue.
   (3) Mary (called Molly) Berkeley, married Dr. Corbin Griffin, and had one child, viz., Major Griffin.
   (4) Sally Berkeley, single.
   (5) Lucy Berkeley, single.
3. Thomas Nelson, youngest, born at Yorktown, Va., about 1716; died

there, in 1782, aged 66. He was known as SECRETARY NELSON; married, about 1745, Lucy Armistead.

Thomas Nelson, known as Scotch Tom, married, secondly, about 1721, Fanny Houston, the widow Tucker, of Bermuda Islands, by whom he had one child, viz.:

Sally Nelson, born at Yorktown, Va., about 1722; married, about 1742, Col. Robin Burwell, of Isle-of-Wight County, Va. He was a brother of Elizabeth (called Betty) Burwell, wife of President William Nelson. The children of Col. Burwell and Sally Nelson, his wife, were:

(1) Nathaniel Burwell, of Lancaster County, Va., married Miss Wormeley, of Middlesex County, Va.

(2) Frances Burwell (called Fannie), first wife of Gov. John Page. There were probably other children, but their names are not known.

As the Nelsons of Virginia are known as descendants of President Nelson and Secretary Nelson, we will consider each of these two branches separately.

II. WILLIAM NELSON, OF YORKTOWN, York Co., Va., President of the Dominion of Virginia, and known as PRESIDENT NELSON, eldest son and child of Thomas Nelson, known as Scotch Tom, of England and the same place, progenitor of the Nelson Family in Virginia, and Margaret Reid, his first wife, was born there in 1711, and died there 19th November, 1772, aged 61 years. He was buried in the Episcopal churchyard, at Yorktown, Va.

The following is the inscription copied from his tombstone:

"Here lies the body of the Honourable WILLIAM
NELSON Esquire
late President of His Majesty's Council in this
Dominion. In whom the love of man and the love
of God so restrained and enforced each other
and so invigorated the mental powers in general
as not only to defend him from the vices and follies
of his country but also to render it a matter
of difficult decision in what part of laudable
conduct he most excelled. Whether in the tender and
endearing accomplishments of domestic life
or in the more active duties of a wider circuit
As a neighbour, a gentleman or a magistrate
whether in the graces of hospitality, or in the possession
of piety. Reader if you feel the spirit of that
excellent ardour which aspires to the felicity
of conscious virtue animated by those consolations
and divine admonitions, perform the
task and expect the distinction of the
righteous man.
He died the 19th of November, Anno Domini 1772.
Aged 61."

From the above epitaph it appears that he was President of the Council a short time before, or at the time of, his death. He had also been President of the Dominion. According to Bishop Meade, *op. cit.*, Vol. I., p. 205, he was "called President Nelson, because so often President of the Council, and at one time President of the Colony." "His Majesty's Council," in the inscription, refers, of course, to the Colonial Council of His Majesty, George II. or George III.

His portrait, three-quarter length, is in the Nelson House, at Yorktown, Va.

President William Nelson married, in February, 1738, Elizabeth (called Betty), only daughter of Nathaniel Burwell, of Gloucester County, Va., and Elizabeth Carter, his wife. The latter was the second daughter of Robert (King) Carter and Judith Armistead, his first wife. The children of President William Nelson and Elizabeth (called Betty) Burwell, his wife, were as follows:

1. Thomas Nelson, eldest, signer of the Declaration of American Independence, Governor of Virginia, and Major-General in the American Army, born at Yorktown, Va., 26th December, 1738; died 4th January, 1789, aged 51; married, 29th July, 1762, Lucy Grymes.
2. Dr. Nathaniel Nelson, born at Yorktown, Va., about 1745; died of pulmonary consumption in Bermuda Islands; married, about 1770, Jane, eldest daughter and about third child of Hon. John Page, of North End, Gloucester (now Matthews) Co., Va., and Jane Byrd, his wife. (See Page Family, North End.) Their children were:
   (1) Elizabeth (called Betsey); married Burwell, of Saratoga, Clarke Co., Va. Mrs. John Page, of Oakland Hanover Co., Va., was named after her. (See Page Family, Rosewell.)
   (2) William Nelson; died single, 1802, aged 22 years.
3. Col. Hugh Nelson, born at Yorktown, Va., in 1750; died 13th October, 1800, aged 50; married, about 1775, Judith, second daughter and about the fifth child of Hon. John Page, of North End. She was the sister of Jane Page, wife of Dr. Nathaniel Nelson.
4. Robert Nelson, born at Yorktown, Va., about 1752; removed to MALVERN HILL, near James River, Charles City Co., Va. He married, first, about 1777, Mary, second daughter of Hon. Philip Grymes, of Middlesex County, Va., and Mary Randolph, his wife. Mary Grymes was the sister of Lucy, who married Gov. Thomas Nelson, the eldest son. By the first wife, Robert Nelson, of Malvern Hill, had one child, viz., Elizabeth (called Betsey) Nelson; died single.

   He married, secondly, about 1756, Susan, daughter of Speaker John Robinson, of the Virginia House of Burgesses. The latter was the father of Beverly Robinson, of New York, the loyalist, who married Susanna Phillipse. The children of Robert Nelson, by the second wife, were:
   (1) William Nelson.
   (2) Mary Nelson; married Prosser.
   (3) Robert Nelson.
   (4) Susan Nelson.
   (5) Dr. Peyton Randolph Nelson.
   (6) Nathaniel Nelson.
   (7) Chiswell Nelson.

(8) Lucy Nelson.
(9) Ethelia Nelson.
(10) Nancy Nelson; married Moore.
(11) Robinette Nelson.

5. Judge William Nelson, of the District Court, was born at Yorktown, Va., about 1754, and died in 1813, aged about 59, and was buried at Yorktown. He was the godfather of his granddaughter, Anne Willing Page, the second wife of Thomas Carter, of Annefield, Clarke Co., Va. (See Page Family, Broadneck.) He was known as Uncle Judge Billy, and Col. William Nelson, of Oakland, Hanover Co., Va., was named after him. Judge William Nelson married, first, about 1779, Miss Taliaferro, of James City County, Va., and had one child, viz., Elizabeth (called Betsey) Nelson, who married Edwards.

He married, secondly, Abby, daughter of Col. William E. Byrd, of Westover, on James River, Charles City Co., Va., and Mary Willing, of Philadelphia, Pa., his wife. Children:
(1) Mary Nelson; married Pickens, of South Carolina.
(2) Abby Byrd Nelson.
(3) Evelyn Byrd Nelson; married, 1813, Willam Byrd Page, of Pagebrook, Clarke Co., Va., and was his first wife. (See Page Family, Broadneck.)
(4) Lucy Nelson; married Harrison, of Berkeley (Harrison's Landing), on James River, Charles City Co., Va.
(5) Rosalie Nelson.

6. Elizabeth Nelson, only daughter of President Nelson, married Captain Thompson, of H. M. S. *Ripon*, when he came over with Lord Botetourt on board. She went back to England with her husband and lived there.

According to Bishop Meade, *op. cit.*, Vol. I., pp. 205, 206, "President Nelson had many daughters, but only one lived beyond the twelfth year. One of the sons (name not known) became an idiot from a fall from an upper-story window, and another was burned to death. These afflictions contributed to make Mrs. Nelson a woman of sorrowful spirit." President Nelson left landed estates to each of his five surviving sons. Of these, William and Robert were captured by British troopers under Tarleton, at Castle Hill, the residence of Dr. Thomas Walker, Albemarle County, Va., during the war of the American Revolution.

The following is the will of President William Nelson, copied from the records in the Clerk's office at Yorktown, Va.:

In the name of God, Amen. I, William Nelson, of the Town and County of York in the Colony of Virginia Esquire, being at present indisposed, tho- in my perfect senses, do make this my last Will and Testament. My precious and immortal soul, whenever it shall please God to call me hence, I most humbly resign into the hands of Almighty God, hoping through the merits and mediation of my blessed Saviour and Redeemer Jesus Christ, to receive a full pardon of my great and manifold sins, and to partake of the joyful resurrection at the last day—My Body I desire may be interred as my Executors shall think fit, in a decent but not pompous manner, and as to the worldly Estate with which it hath pleased God to bless me, so much above my desire, I dispose of the same (my just debts and funeral expenses being first paid) in the following manner. I give and bequath unto my dear and well beloved wife, Elizabeth Nelson, the sum of five thousand pounds sterling to be paid her within one year after my decease. I also give to my said well beloved wife, the sum of Two hundred and fifty pounds Sterling per annum during her natural life—the first payment to be made within one month after my decease. I also give to my said well beloved wife, her Watch, all her Jewells, Rings, Snuff Boxes Clothes and other ornaments of which she may be possessed at the time of my death. I also give to my well beloved wife, during her natural life, my House wherein I now live, with the Lotts and Gardens thereto belonging, including the Store Garden, but not the Storehouses, also my Stable and the Lott whereon it stands, the use of all my Household furniture, Plate, Coach, Chariot and Cart with all their Harness, my Town Horses and Town Cows, and the use of Ten House Servants, such as she shall Chuse: all these things I say I give her the use of during her natural life—I also give to my said well beloved wife all the Liquors and Provisions of every Kind that shall be in the House at the time of my death, and any Mederia Wine and Rum imported for the use of my family, which may be in my storehouses. I likewise give her all such Family goods and liquors as I may have wrote for. I also give to my said wife such new goods as she may Chuse out of my Store for herself and the use of my three younger Children to the amount of One hundred and fifty pounds Sterling, prime Cost. I further give to my dear wife, during her natural life, the use and profits of my Plantations in Warwick and James City Counties, commonly called Cheesecake Plantation, with the use of the Slaves and Stocks of every kind thereto belonging, and after her decease, I give and devise the said lands, Slaves and Stocks and every thing else belonging thereto, to my son Hugh and his heirs forever. I also give to my said dear wife, during the term of her life, the use of my Plantations near Yorktown, called Pennys and Tarrapin Point including my meadows with the Slaves, horses, Carts and Stocks of every kind thereto belonging with liberty of Cutting her fire wood off the said lands and also off a Tract called Dowsings. It is my will, and I do accordingly direct that, of the annuity hereby given to my dear wife, one hundred pounds Sterling shall be paid yearly by my son Thomas out of the residue of my estate given to him, and seventy five pounds sterling shall be paid by each of my sons Hugh and Robert yearly out of the estates I shall give to them. It is my farther will and desire that my dear wife shall be supplyed out of any part of my estate, with such Beef, Pork, Wheat and Corn as she shall require annually. After the decease of my dear wife, I give to my son Hugh, his heirs and assigns forever the House I now live in, the lots and gardens thereto belonging, together with the Store Garden, but not the Storehouses, also my Stable and the lott on which it stands, likewise all the furniture of my House, as it may remain at his mother's death, my Plate excepted . . . I do also give to my said son Hugh and his heirs forever my Mulatto woman named Aggy with all her Children and future increase. I give and devise to my sons Thomas and Hugh and their heirs forever, as tenants in common and not as joint Tenants, my Store Houses in Yorktown and at the waterside, having already by deeds, given to my son Hugh, all my lands and Slaves in the Counties of Frederick and Fauquier, I only give him a legacy in money of Two Thousand Pounds Sterling.

I give and devise to my son Robert and his heirs forever, all my lands in the County of Albemarle with the Slaves and Stocks of every kind thereto belonging, which lands, Slaves and Stocks are now in the possession and occupation of my son Thomas Nelson, but as I shall, by this Will, give my said son Thomas a much larger proportion of my estate, I do hereby order and direct that he shall give a Release to his Brother Robert and his heirs forever of all that whole Estate in the County of Albemarle upon which condition, he is to hold my lands and estate in the County of Hanover. I also give and bequath to my said son Robert the sum of Two Thousand pounds sterling. I give and devise to my two sons, Nathaniel and William and their heirs forever, all my share and interest in The Dismal Swamp Scheme and, if either of them should die before he comes of age, I give and devise the whole to the survivor and his heirs forever. I also give and bequath to my said sons. Nathaniel and William, to each of them, I say, the sum of five thousand pounds sterling. I desire that the Pecuniary Legacy given to my dear wife may be first paid, and that the other money Legacies to my Children may be Collected and paid according to their Seniority, and that the parts of my younger sons may be placed out on interest till they respectively come of age. After the death of my wife, I give to my son, Thomas, my best silver Cup and the rest of my Plate I desire may be divided—two third parts of which I give to my son, Thomas, and the other third part to my son, Hugh. I give to my son Thomas my Mulatto woman, Hannah with her Children and all her future increase, to him and his heirs forever, and after the death of my dear wife, I give the Ten House Servants with their Children and future increase of which she is to have the use for life, unto my son Hugh and his heirs forever. I give to my son Thomas, my Virginia Amathyst Seal set in gold, to my son Hugh, my gold watch, Chain and Cornelian seal, to my son Robert my gold Stock Buckle, to my son Nathaniel my Sword and Pistols, and to my son William I give my best Garnett Sleeve Buttons sett in Gold. I give to my dear sister, Mary Berkely, the sum of twenty five pounds sterling per annum during her life, to be paid to her by son Thomas out of the residue of my estate, and I do hereby remit and release to my said Sister any sum or sums of money she may owe me at the time of my death. I give and bequath to my Cousin Hephzibah Nelson Twenty Pounds Current Money a year to be paid her by my son Thomas, out of the residue of my Estate, during her natural life. I give and bequath to the Court of Directors appointed by Act of Assembly to errect and superintend the Public Hospital for the reception of Lunatics &c, the sum of One hundred pounds current money to be by them applyed towards the farther relief of such Patients as may be sent to the said

Hospital as they, in their discretion, may think fit, but not to the enlargement of the Building or to any other purposé. I give and bequath Fifty Pounds current money to the poor of the Parish of York Hampton to be distributed as my Executors shall think proper. I desire that my wearing Apparel of every kind may be disposed of in such manner as my dear wife and my two eldest sons may Chuse. All the rest and residue of my estate of what nature or quality soever, whether real or personal in Virginia or elsewhere, I give, devise and bequath to my son, Thomas Nelson, to him, his heirs and assigns for ever. I appoint my dear Brother, the Hon : Thomas Nelson Esquire, my dear friend Robert Carter Nicholas Esq[r] and my two sons, Thomas and Hugh, Executors of this my Will, and guardians of my younger children during their minority. I desire that my Estate may not be appraised, and that my Executors may not be obliged to give any security for their performance of the Trust hereby reposed in them. Lastly, I do hereby revoke and annul all former wills by me heretofore made, and declare this to be my only true last Will and Testament.

In Testimony whereof, I have hereunto set my hand and affixed my seal this sixth day of October in the year of Our Lord one thousand seven hundred and Seventy two

[L. S.] W[M] NELSON

Signed, sealed, published and declared by the Hon. William Nelson Esquire as and for his last Will and Testament in presence of us who at his request and in his presence do hereunto subscribe our names as witnesses.

DUDLEY DIGGES
DAVID JAMESON
LAWE SMITH, JUNR

At a Court held for York County
21st day of December 1772.

This Will was proved according to law by the oaths of Dudley Digges David Jameson and Lawrence Smith Jun[r], the witnesses thereto, and ordered to be recorded, and on the motion of the Hon. Thomas Nelson Esquire, Robert Carter Nicholas, Thomas Nelson and Hugh Nelson Esquires, the Executors therein named, who made oath thereto as the law directs, Certificate was granted them for obtaining a Probat in due form.

Exam[d]

Teste, THOS. EVERARD Ct Cur[r]

A Copy
Teste,
A. F. HUDGINS,
Clerk of York Co. Cts., Va.

VIRGINIA,
YORK COUNTY, to wit:

I, A. F. HUDGINS, Clerk of the County Court of York County, State of Virginia, do hereby certify that the foregoing is a true copy of the last Will and Testament of William Nelson as the same appears of record and on file in my office.

Witness my hand, and the seal of said Court affixed this the 20th day of May, A.D. 1884 in the 108th year of the Commonwealth of Va.

[L. S.]

A. F. HUDGINS, Clerk.

VIRGINIA:

I, H. B. WARREN, Judge of the County Court of York County, State of Va., do certify that A. F. Hudgins, who hath given the foregoing certificate, is Clerk of said Court, and that his said attestation is in due form. Given under my hand this the 24th day of May, A.D. 1884, in the 108th year of the Commonwealth of Virginia.

H. B. WARREN, Judge.

III. THOMAS NELSON, OF YORKTOWN, York Co., Va., SIGNER OF THE DECLARATION OF AMERICAN INDEPENDENCE, GOVERNOR OF THE STATE OF VIRGINIA, and MAJOR GENERAL IN THE AMERICAN ARMY, was born at Yorktown, Va., 26th December, 1738. He was the eldest son and child of President William Nelson, of the same place, and Elizabeth (called Betty) Burwell, his wife; and President William Nelson was the eldest son and child of Thomas Nelson, known as Scotch Tom, of England and the same place, progenitor of the Nelson family in Virginia, and Margaret Reid, his first wife.

Governor Nelson died during an attack of asthma, caused by exposure during the war of the Revolution, at Mt. Air, Hanover Co., Va., on the 4th January, 1789, aged 51 years. He was buried at the foot of President Nelson's grave, at Yorktown, Va., but there has never been, as yet, any tombstone placed there to his memory.

According to Bishop Meade, *op. cit.*, Vol. I., pp. 206, 207, he "was placed under the care of Rev. Mr. Yates, of Gloucester County, Va., afterward President of William and Mary College, in order to prepare him for an English university. At the age of fourteen—sooner than was intended—he was sent thither. The circumstance which hastened his going was the following: On one Sunday afternoon, as his father was walking on the outskirts of the village of Yorktown, he found him at play with some of the little negroes of the place. Feeling the evil of such associations, and the difficulty of preventing them, he determined to send him at once to England; and a vessel being ready to sail he was despatched the next day to the care of his friends—Mr. Hunt, of London, and Beilby Porteus, then Fellow of Cambridge University, and afterwards Bishop of London. He went for some time to the preparatory school of Dr. Newcome, at Hackney, and then to the especial care and tutorship of

Dr. Porteus. The letters of Mr. Nelson to Mr. Hunt and Dr. Porteus—copies of which I have, and the answers to which are acknowledged—evince deep anxiety for the improvement of his son in all things, but especially in morals and religion. He is evidently uneasy about the spirited character of his son, fearing lest it might lead him astray, and begs his friends to inform him if his son shows a disposition to idleness and pleasure. In order to avoid the temptations incident to young men during the vacation—especially such as are far away from friends—he requests Dr. Porteus to place him, during those seasons, with some eminent scientific agriculturist, and thus prepare him for dealing with the soils of America. After seven years he returns home—being delayed several months beyond the time he intended, by a circumstance which showed the religious character of his father. In a letter to his friend, Mr. Hunt, he alludes to the fact that two young Virginians, whose habits he feared were not good, were coming over in the ship in which he expected his son, and he must request that he be not sent with them; that he would rather his coming be postponed six months than have them as his companions, though they were sons of some of the first families of Virginia, and of those who were on terms of intimacy with his. His return was accordingly delayed for some months. On his arrival, Mr. Nelson writes to his friends in England, that he is much pleased with the general improvement of his son, but regrets to find that he has fallen into that bad practice which most of the young Virginians going to England adopt, of smoking tobacco—adding emphatically, '*filthy tobacco;*' also that 'eating and drinking, though not to inebriety, more than was conducive to health and long life.' Still, he was rejoiced to see him, such as he was, with good principles."

While young Nelson was on his voyage home from England, he was elected a member of the Virginia House of Burgesses, although he was at that time barely 21 years of age.

He was one of the members of the First Convention, which met at Williamsburg, James City Co., Va., in 1774, to consider the matter of taxation of the colonies in America, by the Home Government in England. He was again a member of the Provincial Convention, and in July, 1774, he was appointed Colonel of the 2d Virginia Regiment of Infantry.

He was a member of the Convention which met at Williamsburg, James City Co., Va., in May, 1776, to frame a constitution for Virginia; and was elected to offer the resolution instructing the Virginia delegates in Congress, at Philadelphia, Pa., to propose a Declaration of Independence. HE SIGNED THE DECLARATION OF INDEPENDENCE OF 4TH JULY, 1776. In May, 1777, he was obliged, by an indisposition affecting his head, to resign his seat in Congress; but in the following August, during the alarm occasioned by the entry of the British fleet, under Admiral Howe, within the capes of Virginia, he was appointed Commander-in-chief of the Virginia State forces; and soon after, in response to an appeal from Congress, he raised a troop of cavalry with which he repaired to Philadelphia. In June, 1781, he was chosen GOVERNOR OF THE STATE OF VIRGINIA, a position to which he was recommended by Thomas Jefferson, then retiring from office. He participated in the siege of

Yorktown, Va., October, 1781, as Commander of the Virginia Militia, with the rank of Major-General in the American Army. His force, about 3,000 strong, was raised and equipped at his own expense, and constituted the second or reserve line, and performed fatigue duty during the siege. As it was thought that Lord Cornwallis, Commander of the British Army, occupied his house (the present Nelson House) as headquarters, he ordered it to be bombarded, saying to General Lafayette: "Spare no particle of my property so long as it affords comfort or shelter to the enemies of my country." His services, and, as a matter of policy, those also of the militia whom he had collected, were highly commended in the General Orders of Gen. George Washington, the American Commander-in-chief, 20th October, 1781, being the day after the surrender of Lord Cornwallis with the British Army. His statue was one of the six selected to be placed around the Washington Monument, at Richmond, Va. The other five were Thomas Jefferson, Patrick Henry, Andrew Lewis, John Marshall, and George Mason.

Governor Nelson built the Offley House, in Hanover County, Va., during the Revolution, in order to send his family there to a place of safety. For a description of this wretched little place see mention of Chatellux's account of it in Bishop Meade, *op. cit.*, Vol. I., p. 211 Here it was that the Governor's son Robert (afterward of Malvern Hill) used to sing the hymn:

"Send comfort down from thy right hand
To cheer us in this barren land," etc.

The old Offley House is probably gone, but the pond—the Offley pond—that well-known source of chills and fever for the whole neighborhood, yet remains.

Governor Nelson had left to him by his father, President Nelson, landed property, including the present Nelson House, at Yorktown, Va., and £40,000 in hard cash. As one Virginia shilling was equal to 16⅔ cents of United States coin, and twenty shillings made a pound, the value of the latter was about three dollars and thirty-three and a third cents. Forty thousand pounds would therefore be equal to a little more than one hundred and thirty-three thousand dollars of present United States coin—which was a great deal of money for those days.

Nevertheless, he died poor—having given nearly all he had to the cause of liberty. Such nobility of soul and purity of motive form a combination in character rarely seen in the history of the world, and no doubt he was conscientious in the matter; yet how different from Washington! The latter, although he had no large family to support, "magnanimously refused any pay for his services, but merely asked Congress to reimburse him for his expenses, an accurate account of which he had kept." It is needless to say that Congress promptly paid him, having the detailed accounts with dates specified, to be guided by. Had Governor Nelson kept an accurate account of his expenses, no doubt Congress would have gladly paid him back also. But it appears that he had no account to present to Congress. Consequently his family had to be that much poorer. One may, therefore, here see the difference between a patriotic man, and a patriotic man who was also wise.

(From the original portrait by Chamberlin, London, 1754.)

GOV. THOMAS NELSON, AT THE AGE OF 16,

YORKTOWN, YORK CO., VA.

Signer of the Declaration of Independence, 4th July, 1776.

The only original portrait of Gov. Thomas Nelson was painted when he was a youth of 16 years of age, by Chamberlin, in London, 1754. This portrait, the canvas of which measures about 30x40 inches, formerly hung in the parlor, at Oakland, Hanover Co., Va., but was removed to Shelly, Gloucester Co., same State. It is a good painting, but much abused, having a hole in the canvas at the chin. The following is a copy of a letter written by the artist that was sent by Anderson, of Richmond, Va. (since removed to New York City), to Shelly, Gloucester Co., Va., to photograph the portrait of Governor Nelson there:

RICHMOND, VA., March 19th, 1878.

FRIEND BRADY: Your communication received this morning. The description of the portrait of Gen. Thomas Nelson, at Shelly, Gloucester Co., Va., is as follows:

Age—about 16.
Hair—light, color of Naples yellow in the light.
Eyes—blue, medium shade.
Complexion—ruddy, with plenty of warm color.
Coat—gray.
Collar of coat—gray velvet.
Necktie—white.
Vest—white in shadow.
Buttons—brass.
Ruffle on sleeve—white.
Hat under arm—black.

Hoping this may be satisfactory,

Yours respectfully,

WM. E. TRAHEM.

It is only a half-length portrait, hat under left arm, but the left hand does not appear. The white ruffle on the right sleeve and part of the right hand is seen, the fingers being concealed from view by the waistcoat, in which the right hand partly rests.

This portrait has been copied for the capitol at Richmond, Va., where it may be seen among the Governors in the State library. There is also a copy at Independence Hall, Philadelphia, Pa., in the room where the famous Declaration was signed. Since the death of Mrs. Cornelia Griffith it has become the property of Thomas Nelson Page, the author.

The family Bible of Governor Thomas Nelson is at present in the possession of the Goggin family, in Campbell County, Va. For the purpose of obtaining a copy of the record contained in that Bible, I applied to W. Steptoe Nelson, Esq., of Forest Depot, Bedford Co., Va. Mr. Nelson wrote to Mr. Goggin on the subject, and received the following reply:

LEESVILLE, CAMPBELL CO., VA.,
28th March, 1883.

W. STEPTOE NELSON, ESQ., Forest Depot.

DEAR FRIEND AND COUSIN: Your letter in regard to the Nelson family Bible was received this evening. Enclosed you will find all the information in it regarding the Nelson family. The record refers only to Governor Nelson's family, and is written on the title leaf between the Old and New Testaments, as there is no blank space for family record. Nothing is said of the Pages.

Affectionately yrs., S. C. GOGGIN.

The following is an exact copy of the record in the family Bible of Gov. Thomas Nelson referred to:

Thomas Nelson and Lucy Grymes were married the 29th July, 1762.
William Nelson, born August 9th, 1763.
Thomas Nelson, born December 27th, 1764.
Philip Nelson, born March 14th, 1766.
Francis Nelson, born June 25th, 1767.
Hugh Nelson, born Septem'r 30th, 1768.
Elizabeth Nelson, born December 26th, 1770.
Mary Nelson, born December 19th, 1774.
Lucy Nelson, born Jan'y 2d, 1777.
Robert Nelson, born October 14th, 1778.
Susanna Nelson, born October 3d, 1780.
Judith Nelson, born May 8th, 1782.

Gov. Thomas Nelson married, 29th July, 1762, Lucy, daughter of Philip Grymes, of Middlesex County, Va., and Mary Randolph, his wife, who was the daughter of Sir John Randolph, of Williamsburg, James City Co., Va., and Susanna Beverly, his wife.

Gov. Nelson's wife, Lucy Grymes, lived to be eighty years old, "leaving," says Bishop Meade, "twenty dollars to her minister, and freedom to her servant, the only one she had." She was not buried with her husband at Yorktown, but at the east end of Fork Church graveyard, Hanover County, Va. Their children were as follows:

1. William Nelson, eldest, born at Yorktown, Va., 9th August, 1763; married, about 1790, Sally Burwell, eldest daughter of Gov. John Page.
2. Thomas Nelson, Jr., born at Yorktown, Va., 27th December, 1764, second son, and eldest to have surviving male issue; married, in 1795, Frances, third daughter and seventh child of Gov. John Page.
3. Philip Nelson, born at Yorktown, Va., 4th March, 1766; removed to Clarke County, Va., and married, 1789, Sarah N. Burwell.

4. Francis Nelson, born at Yorktown, Va., 25th June, 1767; removed to Mont Air, Hanover Co., Va., and married, about 1792, Lucy, youngest daughter of Hon. John Page, of North End, Gloucester (now Matthews) Co., Va.
5. Hon. Hugh Nelson, born at Yorktown, Va., 30th September, 1768; removed to Belvoir, Albemarle Co., Va., and married, in 1799, Eliza, daughter of Francis Kinloch, of South Carolina.
6. Elizabeth Nelson, eldest daughter, born at Yorktown, Va., 26th December, 1770; married, 5th June, 1788, Mann Page, of Shelly, Gloucester Co., Va., eldest son of Gov. John Page. (See Page Family, Rosewell.)
7. Mary Nelson, born at Yorktown, Va., 19th December, 1774; married, about 1792, Robert Carter, of Shirley, on James River, Va., by whom she had Hill Carter, and others.
8. Lucy Nelson, born at Yorktown, Va., 2d January, 1777; married, in 1799, Major Carter Page, of Willis Fork, Cumberland Co., Va., and was his second wife. (See Page Family, North End.)
9. Robert Nelson, born at Yorktown, Va., 14th October, 1778; married, April, 1803, Judith Carter, youngest daughter and ninth surviving child of Gov. John Page by his first wife. (See Page Family, Rosewell.) He was called Chancellor Nelson, from having been Chancellor of William and Mary College. He died, 1819, at Williamsburg, James City Co., Va., aged about 40. He was professor of law in William and Mary College, and was also Equity Judge. He was a Presidential Elector in 1813. They had one surviving child, viz.:
    (1) Lucy Nelson, who married, about 1830, Hugh N. Pendleton, of Caroline County, Va., and was his first wife. She died, leaving one child, viz., Julia Pendleton, who married, about 1853, James Allen, of Bedford, who died August, 1862, leaving one child, viz., Hugh Allen, who is the sole surviving descendant of Chancellor Robert Nelson. Julia Pendleton, the wife of James Allen, of Bedford County, Va., died 1865.
10. Susanna (called Susan or Suky) Nelson, born at Yorktown, Va., 3d October, 1780; married, in 1806, Francis Page, of Rugswamp, Hanover Co., Va., eighth child and fifth son of Gov. John Page. (See Page Family, Rosewell.)
11. Judith Nelson, born at Yorktown, Va., 8th May, 1782; married, 1804, Captain Thomas Nelson, of Oakland, Hanover Co., Va.

It will be seen that five of the children above mentioned married five of Gov. John Page's children; and two of them married two of the children of Hon. John Page, of North End, Gloucester (now Matthews) Co., Va. Thus of the eleven children of Gov. Thomas Nelson, of Yorktown, Va., and Lucy Grymes, his wife, seven of them married Pages.

III. Col. Hugh Nelson, of Yorktown, York Co., Va., about the third son and child of President William Nelson, of the same place, and Elizabeth (called Betty) Burwell, his wife, was born there in 1750, and died there 3d October, 1800, aged 50 years. He married, about 1775, Judith, about the second daughter and fifth surviving child of Hon. John Page, of North End, Gloucester (now Matthews) Co., Va., and Jane Byrd, his wife. The portrait of Judith Page is at Oakland, Hanover Co., Va. Judith Page Walker, her granddaughter, of Castle Hill, Albemarle Co., Va., who married Hon. William C. Rives, was named after her. The children of Col. Hugh Nelson and Judith Page, his wife, were as follows:

1. Jane Byrd Nelson, born at Yorktown, Va., about 1776; married, 1798, Hon. Francis Walker, of Castle Hill, Albemarle Co., Va. (See Walker.)
2. Lucy Nelson, born at Yorktown, about 1778; married, 16th May, 1798, Edmund Pendleton, Jr., of Caroline County, Va., and was his second wife. (See Pendleton.)
3. Captain Thomas Nelson, eldest son, born at Yorktown, Va., 1780; removed to Oakland, Hanover Co., Va., and married, 1804, Judith, youngest child of Gov. Thomas Nelson, of Yorktown, Va.
4. Dr. Nathaniel Nelson, born at Yorktown, Va., about 1786; removed to The Lodge, Hanover Co., Va., and married, about 1811, Lucy Mann, eldest daughter of Mann Page, of Shelly, Gloucester Co., Va. (See Rosewell.) Dr. Nelson first lived at a place called *De la Salva*, Gloucester Co., Va., but the name was changed to *Snugly* by some people who bought it. Children:
   (1) Elizabeth (called Betsey) Mann Nelson; married, about 1830, Rev. John R. Lee, of the Episcopal Church, and had (*a*) Mary, died aged 18, and (*b*) Charles D.
   (2) Judith Carter Nelson; single; Richmond, Va.
   (3) Thomasia Nelson; single.
   (4) Judge Hugh Nelson, of Franklin County, Va.; married Miss Taliaferro and had several children.
   (5) Nancy Nelson; married, about 1838, Dr. Binford, of Henry County, Va.
5. Carter Nelson, born about 1788; died single.
6. Frances Edmonia Nelson, born about 1790; died single. She had a talent for drawing and was an artist.
7. Maria Nelson, youngest, born 1794; was burned to death in the Richmond (Va.) Theatre, December 26th, 1811, aged 17. Her body was identified by the watch of Hon. Francis Walker, her brother-in-law, of Castle Hill, Albemarle Co., Va. This watch was found on her body in a partially fused condition, but was easily identified. Dr. Robert W. Nelson, of Charlottesville, Albemarle Co., Va., had the watch, and a little diamond belonging to it was in possession of Dr. R. C. M. Page, of New York.

IV. WILLIAM NELSON, of Yorktown, York Co., Va., eldest son and child of Gov. Thomas Nelson, of the same place, and Lucy Grymes, his wife, eldest son and child of President William Nelson, of the same place, and Elizabeth (called Betty) Burwell, his wife, eldest son and child of Thomas Nelson, known as Scotch Tom, of England and the same place, progenitor of the Nelson Family in Virginia, and Margaret Reid, his wife, was born at Yorktown, Va., 9th August, 1763.

He married, about 1790, Sally Burwell, eldest daughter and fourth child of Gov. John Page, of Rosewell, Gloucester Co., Va., and Frances (called Fannie) Burwell, his first wife. (See Page Family, Rosewell.) Their children were:

1. Thomas Nelson, eldest, born at Yorktown, Va., about 1791; married, about 1815, Mary Lewis, the widow Peyton. No issue. She was probably the daughter of Warner Lewis, who married a daughter of Col. John Chiswell. He died probably young. Rebecca, the only child of the widow Peyton, married Edward Marshall, of Fauquier County, Va.
2. Elizabeth Nelson, born at Yorktown, Va., about 1793; married, about 1813, West, of Accomac County, Va., and had one child, Sarah, who married, about 1835, William Parker, of the same county, and had issue.
3. William Nelson, Jr., second son, and eldest to have issue, was born at Yorktown, York Co., Va., 1801. He married, first, in 1827, Mrs. Catherine Fox and had:
   (1) Lucy Thomas Nelson, married, about 1851, William Howard, of York County, Va., and had issue.
   (2) Sally Burwell Nelson, married, 1854, Felix B. Welton, of Morefield, Hardy Co., W. Va., and had issue.
   (3) Catharine Nelson, single.
   (4) Mary Berkeley Nelson.
   (5) Elizabeth Page Nelson, of New York City.

   William Nelson, Jr., of Yorktown, Va., married, secondly, about 1844, Mrs. Martha Whiting, who was a Miss Shield, of York County, Va., and had:
   (1) William Nelson, Jr., died 10th September, 1877, at St. Louis, Mo., aged 32. He left a widow, but no issue, and this branch became extinct.
   (2) Fannie Burwell Nelson, of Yorktown, Va., married, November, 1886, Corbin W. Mercer, 501 West Grace St., Richmond, Va. He is great-grandson of Gen. Hugh Mercer, who was killed at the battle of Princeton, N. J., in the American Revolution. Two children: (*a*) William Nelson, died infant, and (*b*) Waller Nelson, born 1881.

IV. THOMAS NELSON, JR., second son and child of Gov. Thomas Nelson, of Yorktown, York Co., Va., and Lucy Grymes, his wife, was born there 27th December, 1764, and married, 1795, Frances, third daughter and seventh surviving child of Gov. John Page and Frances (called Fannie) Burwell, his first wife. The name of his brother William's family having become extinct upon the death of William Nelson, Jr., 10th September, 1877, at St. Louis, Mo., without issue, the family of Thomas Nelson became representative of the family.

The children of Thomas Nelson and Frances Page, his wife, were:

1. Thomasia Nelson, born about 1796; married, 1821, Bishop William Meade, of the Episcopal Church, Virginia, and was his second wife. She was buried in The Fork Church graveyard, Hanover County, Va.
2. Fannie Nelson, born about 1798; died unmarried.
3. Thomas Nelson, born about 1800; died unmarried.
4. Rev. George Washington Nelson, born about 1805; married, about 1835, Jane Crease, of Alexandria, Va., and was her first husband.

Thomas Nelson died, date unknown, leaving his widow, who married, secondly, Dr. Carter Berkeley, of Edgewood, Hanover Co., Va. Their children were:

1. Carter Berkeley; married a sister of Bishop McIlvaine, of Ohio, and died leaving one child, who married Captain McCauley, United States Navy.
2. Catherine (called Kitty), who married Lucius Minor, of Edgewood, Hanover Co., Va., and was the mother of Charles L. C. Minor, C. N. Berkeley Minor, and others. Mrs. Lewis Willis Minor, 30 Holt St., Norfolk, Va., has copies of the Clere portraits of King Carter, Betty Landon, Charles Carter, Anne Byrd, and others.

IV. PHILIP NELSON, of Clarke County, Va., third son and child of Gov. Thomas Nelson, of Yorktown, York Co., Va., and Lucy Grymes, his wife, was born at the last-named place, March 14th, 1766, and married, 1789, Sarah N., daughter of Nathaniel Burwell, of Isle of Wight County, Va. Sarah was a niece of Gov. John Page's first wife. Their children were as follows:

1. Thomas Nelson, eldest, born in Clarke County, Va., about 1790; married, 1820, Mildred Nelson, of Belvoir, Albemarle Co., Va.
2. Mary Nelson, born about 1792; married, about 1812, Bishop William

Meade, of Virginia, and was his first wife. She was the first cousin of Thomasia Nelson, his second wife.

3. Dr. William Nelson, born in Clarke County, Va., about 1795, resided there. He married, 1834, Nancy Mitchell, of Charleston, S. C., and had:
   (1) Philip Nelson, eldest, born in Clarke County, Va., about 1835; removed to Oak Ridge (Mr. Richard Gamble's old place), Albemarle Co., Va. He married, about 1873, Emily, daughter of Rev. John P. McGuire, of Essex County, Va. She is the sister of Rev. Kinloch Nelson's wife.
   (2) Charlotte Nelson, single.
   (3) Annie Nelson, died single.
   (4) Selma Nelson, single. The two sisters, Charlotte and Selma, resided with their brother at Oak Ridge.

IV. Francis Nelson, of Mont Air, Hanover Co., Va., fourth son and child of Gov. Thomas Nelson, of Yorktown, York Co., Va., and Lucy Grymes, his wife, was born at the last-named place, 25th June, 1767, and married, about 1792, Lucy, youngest surviving and fifteenth child of Hon. John Page, of North End, Gloucester (now Matthews) Co., Va., and Jane Byrd, his wife.

Their children were as follows:

1. Thomas Nelson, eldest, born about 1793; died single.
2. Mann Nelson, born about 1795; married, first, about 1820, Amelia Washington, and, second, Lydia Kounstar.
3. Susan Nelson, born about 1796; died single.
4. Jane Nelson, born about 1798; married, in 1819, John Page, of North End, Clarke Co., Va., and was his first wife. (See Page Family, North End.)
5. Lucy Nelson, born about 1799; died single.
6. Judith Nelson, born about 1801; married, 1819, Mann Page, of Greenland, Gloucester Co., Va., and was his first wife. (See Page Family, Rosewell.)
7. Sally Page Nelson, born 10th December, 1801; married, 21st January, 1841, Dr. Samuel Scollay, of Smithfield, Jefferson Co., W. Va., and was his second wife. Children:
   (1) Francis Nelson Scollay, born 1841, died infant.
   (2) Harriet Lowndes Scollay, born 11th May, 1843; married Dr. Mason Evans, of Middleway, Jefferson Co., W. Va., and had issue.
   (3) Mary Nelson Scollay, born 15th October, 1844; married, 17th October, 1865, Rev. G. W. Nelson, and had issue.

   Elizabeth Scollay, wife of Capt. P. R. Page, U. S. A., was a daughter by the first marriage.

8. Maria Nelson, born about 1803; married, about 1823, John Redman, of Jefferson County, W. Va.
9. William Nelson, born about 1807; married, about 1832, Mary, daughter of Col. William Macon, of Mount Prospect, New Kent Co., Va. No issue. William Nelson at one time worked on the farm of Dr. Mann Page, at Turkey Hill, Albemarle Co., Va.
10. Francis Nelson, known as "one-arm Frank," born about 1809; married, about 1840, Letitia Prosser, of Bremo, Charles City Co., Va. He died, leaving a widow and six children.

 Francis Nelson at one time worked on the Belvoir farm, Albemarle County, Va. He afterward worked at Shirley, on James River, Va. At the latter place he lost his arm in some machinery.
11. Philip Nelson, born at Mont Air, Hanover Co., Va., about 1811; resided there. He married, in 1845, Jane Crease, widow of Rev. George W. Nelson, of the Episcopal Church, and was her second husband. Children:
 (1) Francis Nelson.
 (2) Caroline; died in 1876, aged 18.
 (3) William Nelson.
12. Hugh Nelson, born at Mont Air, Hanover Co., Va., about 1813; removed to Clarke County, Va. He married, 1836, Adelaide Holker, of Boston, Mass. He died at the former residence of K. S. Nelson, Albemarle County, Va., about 1863, and was buried at Belvoir, same county. Two children, viz.:
 (1) Hugh Nelson.
 (2) Nannie Nelson; died single.
13. Fannie Nelson, born about 1815; single.
14. Elizabeth (called Betsey) Nelson, born about 1817; married, 1835, Dr. James McCoughtry, and had issue.

IV. Hon. Hugh Nelson, of Belvoir, Albemarle Co., Va., fifth son and child of Gov. Thomas Nelson, of Yorktown, York Co., Va., and Lucy Grymes, his wife, was born at Yorktown, Va., 30th September, 1768, and died at Belvoir, 18th March, 1836, aged 68.

He was at one time Speaker of the House of Delegates of Virginia. He was afterward Judge of the Federal Court, and was sometimes called Judge Nelson; Presidential Elector in 1809; Representative in the United States Congress from Virginia, 1811–23; and immediately thereafter he was appointed Minister to Spain by President James Monroe, during the latter part of his administration.

He married, 1799, Eliza, only child of Francis Kinloch, of Charleston, S. C., and Mildred Walker, his first wife. (See Walker.) Their children were:

1. Francis Kinloch Nelson, eldest, born at Belvoir, Albemarle Co., Va., in 1800; removed, first, to Peachylorum, and then to Cloverfields (his second wife's residence), both in the county of Albemarle. It was at the latter place that he died, 1862, aged 62 years. Peachylorum was a part of the Walker estate, and was probably named after Peachy Walker, who was the twelfth and youngest child of Dr. Thomas Walker, of Castle Hill, same county.

Francis K. Nelson married, first, at Shelly, Gloucester Co., Va., 24th April, 1823, Anne (called Nancy) Page, of that place. (See Page Family, Rosewell.) Children:

(1) Isabella Nelson; married, 1856, Dr. John F. Gardener, and died, leaving Nancy (called Nina) and Francis.

(2) Hester Nelson; died unmarried.

Francis K. Nelson married, secondly, 1843, Margaret Douglas Meriwether, widow of Francis Meriwether, of Bedford County, Va., by whom she had two children—(*a*) Mary Walker Meriwether, married Thomas J. Randolph, Jr., of Edge Hill, Albemarle Co., Va., and (*b*) Charles Meriwether. She had no issue by her second husband, Francis K. Nelson. She was known as Aunt Peggy, and was the daughter of Capt. W. D. Meriwether, of Cloverfields, Albemarle Co., Va.

2. Mildred Nelson, born about 1802; married, in 1820, Thomas Nelson, of Clarke County, Va., who was her first cousin.

3. Anne Carter Nelson, born about 1804; married, 1824, Dr. Thomas Warner Meriwether, of Kinloch, Albemarle Co., Va. She died there in 1858, aged about 54. Dr. T. W. Meriwether died in 1862. Their children were:

(1) Dr. William Douglas Meriwether; died in Tennessee, 1880. He married, first, 1847, Phœbe Gardener, of Richmond, Va., and had: (*a*) Mary Gardener, who married Wallace, of Kentucky; (*b*) William Hunter; (*c*) Thomas Warner, of Norwalk, Conn., married, 1st September, 1886, Alice Emma Blandford, and has issue; and (*d*) Isabella.

Dr. W. D. Meriwether married, secondly, 1864, Anne W. (called Nannie) Page. (See Page Family, Broadneck.) She died at Culpepper, Va., in 1873, leaving one child, viz., Evelyn.

(2) Mildred Nelson Meriwether; married, 1856, George Macon, of Cloverfields, Albemarle Co., Va., who died a few years ago, and had: (*a*) Thomas; (*b*) Charlotte, married Frank M. Randolph; (*c*) Littleton; (*d*) George; and (*e*) Douglas.

(3) Anne Kinloch Meriwether, married, 24th December, 1850, Frederick W. Page, of Millwood, Albemarle Co., Va. (See Page Family, North End.)

(4) Eliza Meriwether; married, 1853, N. H. Massie, of Charlottesville, Va., and was his first wife. She died without issue.

(5) Charlotte Nelson Meriwether; married, 1865, Thomas Jefferson

(From a miniature in possession of Dr. Page.)

HON. HUGH NELSON,
BELVOIR, ALBEMARLE CO., VA.
Representative U. S. Congress, 1811-23.

Randolph, Jr., and was his second wife. She died, 1876, leaving one child, viz., Mary Walker.

(6) Thomas W. Meriwether, Jr. ; died single, 1862.

(7) Jane Meriwether; died infant.

4. Dr. Thomas Hugh Nelson, born at Belvoir, Albemarle Co., Va., 30th May, 1807; removed to Elk Hill, Bedford Co., Va., where he died, 11th November, 1861, in the 55th year of his age. He married, first, in June, 1833, Sarah A., daughter of John Alexander, Esq., of Campbell County, Va. Children:

(1) Charlotte Simmons Nelson, born 14th March, 1834; died single.

(2) John Alexander Nelson, born 9th January, 1836; died, single, 11th October, 1863, aged 27.

(3) Hugh Nelson, twin brother of John; died, single, 10th November, 1866, aged 30 years.

(4) William Steptoe Nelson, born 2d November, 1837.

(5) Eliza Kinloch Nelson, born 15th August, 1839; married, September, 1860, Dr. James H. Bowyer. She died 17th November, 1880, aged 41 years. She left three children: (*a*) Thomas Hugh, born 2d August, 1863; (*b*) Eddie Page, born 24th September, 1865; (*c*) Lulie Preston, born 1st May, 1867.

(6) Thomas Walker Nelson, born 9th March, 1841; married, 3d November, 1869, Lilia McDaniel, who died 6th April, 1870. No issue.

(7) Cleland Kinloch Nelson, born 2d September, 1842; married, 6th November, 1873, Ella Scott, of Lynchburg, Va. Children: (*a*) Charles, (*b*) Sallie, (*c*) Helen.

(8) Helen Lewis Nelson, born 15th July, 1844; married, April, 1875, J. N. Early, of Bedford County, Va. Children: (*a*) Lilia Page, (*b*) Susan Alexander, (*c*) Henry W., (*d*) Helen Kinloch.

Dr. Thomas Hugh Nelson married, secondly, 4th October, 1853, Mrs. Mary Ann Meem, of Lynchburg, Va. Her maiden name was Matthews. The children by the second marriage were:

(1) Emily G. Nelson, born 4th July, 1854; married, 31st October, 1877, W. H. Dabney, of Lynchburg, Va. Three children: (*a*) William B., born 15th September, 1878; (*b*) Thomas Hugh, born 18th August, 1881; (*c*) Mary C., born 2d March, 1883.

(2) Edwin M. Nelson, born 12th October, 1855.

(3) Frank W. Nelson, born 16th February, 1857.

(4) C. Page Nelson, born 16th December, 1859; married, 16th December, 1880, Charles T. Dabney, of Alexandria, Va., and has one child, Mary Norvell.

(5) Charles Keating Nelson, born 20th October, 1860.

All the members of this family live in Bedford County, Va., except Nos. (1) and (4) of the children by the second marriage.

5. Charlotte Nelson, born about 1808; died single.

6. Rev. Cleland K. Nelson, of the Episcopal Church, was born at Belvoir, Albemarle Co., Va., about 1814 (as two other children died infant),

and removed to Annapolis, Md. He died 30th October, 1890. He married, first, 1840, Mary A., daughter of John Marbury, of Georgetown, D. C. Children:

(1) Mary Cleland Nelson, married, 1868, Holmes E. Offley, banker, Washington, D. C., and has several children.

(2) John Nelson, married, resides in Baltimore, Md.

Rev. C. K. Nelson, married, secondly, Mary Hagner, of Washington, D. C., and has Fanny and Hugh.

7. Caroline Nelson, born 1816; died single, 1853, aged 36.

8. Keating Simmons Nelson, born 1819, at Belvoir, Albemarle Co., Va.; married, 1841, Julia, daughter of Thornton Rogers, of Keswick, Albemarle Co., Va. She died September, 1890. Children:

(1) Hugh Nelson, married, 1864, Rose Bentley, and has three sons.

(2) Francis K. Nelson, died 1864.

(3) Margaret Nelson, died young.

(4) Bettie H. Nelson, married, 1876, Beverly Mason, of Fairfax County, Va., and has several children.

(5) Celia R. Nelson, married, about 1870, Goolrick, of Fredericksburg, Va., and has several children.

(6) Rev. Cleland K. Nelson, Bishop of Georgia since November, 1891, to succeed Bishop Beckwith, deceased; married Miss Matthews, of Port Tobacco, Md.

(7) Keating S. Nelson, Jr.

(8) William M. Nelson.

9. Dr. Robert William Nelson, born 1822, at Belvoir, Albemarle Co., Va.; removed to Charlottesville, same county. He married, in 1844, his first cousin, Virginia L., daughter of Capt. Thomas Nelson, of Oakland, Hanover Co., Va. Children:

(1) Dr. Hugh Thomas Nelson, married, 1871, Mary (called Polly) Gilliam, and has several children.

(2) Nancy Nelson, died infant.

(3) Susan P. Nelson.

(4) Robert W. Nelson, Jr.

(5) William Nelson.

(6) Eliza Nelson. Two others died infants.

IV. CAPTAIN THOMAS NELSON, of Oakland, Hanover Co., Va., eldest son and third child of Col. Hugh Nelson, of Yorktown, York Co., Va., and Judith Page, his wife, was born at Yorktown, Va., 1780, and died at Oakland, in 1859, aged 79 years. He was buried at Fork Church, Hanover Co., Va. He lived in Richmond, Va., at one time, where he was the proprietor of the *Virginia Hotel* near the Capitol Square. He was Commissioner of Loans, a federal office held by him under the United States Government. He afterward retired to his farm at Oakland, Hanover Co., Va. He married, 1804, Judith, youngest child of Gov. Thomas Nelson, of Yorktown, York Co., Va., and Lucy Grymes, his wife. She was, therefore, his first cousin. She died, 1869, aged 87, and was buried at Fork Church. The two were known as Uncle Tom and Aunt Judy. Their children were as follows:

1. Hugh Thomas Nelson, eldest, born 1805, at Oakland, Hanover Co., Va.; died unmarried.
2. Mary Carter Nelson, born about 1805; died unmarried in 1861, aged 56 years.
3. Col. William Nelson, known as William Particular, born about 1807; resided, unmarried, at Oakland. He was named after Judge William Nelson, fifth son of President Nelson. He died 17th April, 1892.
4. Maria Nelson, born about 1809; died single.
5. Judith Nelson, born 1815; died 1832, single.
6. Lucy Nelson, born 1817; died single, 1872, aged 55.
7. Rev. Robert Nelson, of the Episcopal Church, born at Oakland, Hanover Co., Va., in 1819, was missionary to China for thirty years. Upon his return to America he took charge of the parish of Waterbury, Conn. Died at Oakland, Hanover Co., Va., 15th July, 1886, aged 68. He married, 1848, Rose, daughter of James Points, Esq., of Staunton, Augusta Co., Va. She died several years before he did. Children:
   (1) James P. Nelson, eldest, married, 4th February, 1873, Mary W., daughter of Edward W. Morris, of Hanover County, Va.
   (2) Thomas Nelson, married, 2d September, 1880, Mary Alice, daughter of Joseph House, Esq., of Virginia City, Placer Co., Cal.
   (3) Mary C. Nelson.
   (4) John Nelson.
   (5) Rosebud Nelson.
   (6) Emily Nelson.
   (7) Ruth Nelson.
8. Elizabeth (called Betsey) Burwell Nelson, born about 1824; married, 1847, John Page. (See Page Family, Rosewell.)
9. Virginia L. Nelson, born about 1826; married, 1844, Dr. Robert W. Nelson, of Charlottesville, Albemarle Co., Va., as we have already seen.

V. Rev. George Washington Nelson, of the Episcopal Church, fourth child and second son of Thomas Nelson, Jr., and Frances Page, his wife, second child and son (being also the eldest to have surviving male issue) of Gov. Thomas Nelson, of Yorktown, York Co., Va., and Lucy Grymes, his wife, eldest son of President William Nelson, of the same place, and Elizabeth (called Betty)

Burwell, his wife, eldest son of Thomas Nelson, known as Scotch Tom, of England and the same place, progenitor of the Nelson Family in Virginia, and Margaret Reid, his first wife, was born about 1805, and married, May, 1834, Jane Crease, of Alexandria, Va., and was her first husband. He died about 1840. His widow married, secondly, in 1845, Philip Nelson, of Mont Air, Hanover Co., Va., and had issue, as we have already seen. She died at Wytheville, Wythe Co., Va., in 1878, aged 62 years, and was buried there.

The children of Rev. G. W. Nelson and Jane Crease, his wife, were as follows:

1. Thomas Crease Nelson, eldest, born about 1836; died single, at Mont Air, Hanover Co., Va., November, 1857, aged about 21.
2. Jane Nelson, born about 1838; single.
3. Rev. George Washington Nelson, Jr., born in 1840; married, 17th October, 1865, Mary Nelson (called Mollie), daughter of Dr. Samuel Scollay, of Smithfield, Jefferson Co., W. Va., and Sally Page Nelson, his second wife. Being the eldest son of the eldest son, etc., he is the representative of the Nelson Family in Virginia. Children:
   (1) Sally Page Nelson, born 4th July, 1866.
   (2) Thomas Crease Nelson, born 7th January, 1868.
   (3) Harry Lee Nelson, born 5th October, 1869.
   (4) Charlotte Cazenove Nelson, born 16th September, 1871.
   (5) George W. Nelson, Jr., born 29th July, 1875.
   (6) Philip Nelson, born 21st September, 1878.
   (7) Samuel Scollay Nelson, born 20th July, 1880.
   (8) Caroline Peyton Nelson, born 26th May, 1882.
   One was born in 1873, but died infant.

V. Thomas Nelson, of Clarke County, Va., school-teacher, eldest son of Philip Nelson, of same county, and Sarah N. Burwell, his wife, third son of Gov. Thomas Nelson, of Yorktown, Va., and Lucy Grymes, his wife, was born in Clarke Co., Va., about 1790, and married, 1820, his first cousin, Mildred, daughter of Hon. Hugh Nelson, of Belvoir, Albemarle Co., Va. Their children were:

1. Dr. Robert Burwell Nelson, eldest, of Charlottesville, Va., born about 1823; died 1868, aged 45. He married, 1847, Mary S., daughter of John Price, of Fincastle, Botetourt Co., Va., where Dr. Nelson first practised his profession. Children:
   (1) Thomas F. Nelson, married, about 1874, Sophia Wormeley, who died leaving one son.
   (2) Dr. J. William Nelson, removed to Philadelphia.
   (3) Robert Nelson, died young.

2. Rev. William Meade Nelson, of the Episcopal Church, born 1825; died 1876, aged 51. He married, about 1850, Sarah W., daughter of Dr. Thomas Semmes, of Alexandria, Va., and left two daughters, Ann Sophia and Eliza Kinloch.
3. Philip Nelson, of Nelson, Nelson Co., Va., born about 1828; married, first, in 1853, Emily, daughter of Judge John E. Page, of Clarke County, Va. (See Page Family, Broadneck.) She died, leaving two children, William and Emily.

He married, secondly, Fannie Effenger, of Nelson County, Va., and had several children.

4. Eliza Kinloch Nelson, born in Clarke County, Va., about 1821; married, in 1856, Nathaniel H. Massie, of Charlottesville, Albemarle Co., Va., and was his second wife. They had several children.
5. Archie Nelson, born about 1832; was killed by a tree falling on him while at work, in 1868. Married, 1857, Eliza J., daughter of John Price, of Fincastle, Botetourt Co., Va., and Eliza his wife. Children:
   (1) Eliza, born 1858, died young.
   (2) Dr. John Price Nelson, born 11th November, 1860, resides in Lincoln, Neb.
   (3) Archie McGill Nelson, born 9th November, 1862.
   (4) Hugh Thomas Nelson, born 15th March, 1865.
6. Sallie Burwell Nelson, born in Clarke County, Va., about 1836: married, 1868, Thomas Williamson, of Leesburg, Loudon Co., Va. He was the son of Professor Williamson, of the Virginia Military Institute, at Lexington, Rockbridge Co., Va. Children:
   (1) Thomas Williamson.
   (2) Robert Williamson.
   (3) Garnet Williamson.
   (4) Nancy Williamson.
7. Mary Nelson, born in Clarke County, Va., about 1837; married Rev. Mr. Quimby, missionary to Japan, now dead.
8. Rev. Kinloch Nelson, of the Episcopal Church, youngest, born in Clarke County, Va., 1839; removed to the Episcopal Theological Seminary, Fairfax County, Va., and became Professor of Bible History in that institution. He married, in 1868, Fenton, daughter of Rev. John P. McGuire, of Essex County, Va. They have several children. His daughter Grace married Helfenstein.

II. THOMAS NELSON, of Yorktown, York Co., Va., Secretary of the Colonial Council of Virginia, and hence known as SECRETARY NELSON, second son and third child of Thomas Nelson, known as Scotch Tom, of England and the same place, progenitor of the Nelson Family in Virginia, and Margaret Reid, his first wife, was born at Yorktown, Va., in 1716, and died there in 1782, aged 66. He was buried there. There is no tombstone over his grave, and no, portrait of him exists.

He married, about 1745, Lucy Armistead, who was probably a younger relative of Judith Armistead, the first wife of Robert (King) Carter. The name of Armistead is said to have originated in Virginia, with William Armistead, or D'Armstadt, who emigrated from Hesse Darmstadt to Virginia in 1636, and settled in Elizabeth City County, in that State.

Secretary Nelson and Lucy Armistead, his wife, had no daughters, and only three surviving sons, all of whom were heroes in the Revolution, and became officers in the American army, under Washington. They were all present at the siege of Yorktown, in October, 1781, and brought their father into the American lines under flag of truce. They were as follows:

1. Col. William Nelson, of the American army, eldest, was born at Yorktown, Va., 17th June, 1746, and removed to The Dorrill, Hanover Co., Va.; married, 24th November, 1770, Lucy Chiswell.
2. Capt. Thomas Nelson, of the American army, was born about 1748, at Yorktown, York Co., Va., and removed to Bears Spring, Hanover Co., same State. He married, about 1775, Sally, daughter of Col. Wilson Cary, of Williamsburg, James City Co., Va. There was only one child so far as known, viz.:
   (1) Wilson Cary Nelson, born about 1776, at Bears Spring, Hanover Co., Va.; married, but the name of his wife is at present unknown. He had two daughters, viz.: (*a*) Catherine, who married, about 1831, Charles Page, of Hanovertown, Hanover Co., Va.; and (*b*) Lucy, who married, about 1833, John F. Page, of same place. (See Page Family, Rosewell.)

3. Major John Nelson, of the American army, was born at Yorktown, Va., about 1750, and removed to Oakhill, Mecklenburg Co., Va. He married, about 1772, Nancy Carter, of Williamsburg, Va.

III. Col. William Nelson, of The Dorrill, Hanover Co., Va., eldest son and child of Secretary Thomas Nelson, of Yorktown, York Co., Va., and Lucy Armistead, his wife, second son and third child of Thomas Nelson, known as Scotch Tom, of England and Yorktown, Hanover Co., Va., progenitor of the Nelson Family in Virginia, and Margaret Reid, his first wife, was born at Yorktown, Va., 17th June, 1746, and died 25th November, 1807, aged 61 years.

He was educated in England, with his first cousin, Gov. Thomas Nelson, of Yorktown, Va. He was present at the battles of Monmouth and Brandywine, and all the Northern battles in which Washington's army was engaged. He was also present at the siege of Yorktown, Va., in October, 1781, with the rank of Colonel of Infantry in the American army. He married, 24th November, 1770, Lucy, daughter of Col. John Chiswell and Elizabeth Randolph, his wife, who was a daughter of Councillor William Randolph, of Turkey Island, Henrico Co., Va. Lucy Chiswell was born 3d August, 1752, and died 14th April, 1810, aged 58 years. They had the following children:

1. Lucy Nelson, born at The Dorrill, Hanover Co., Va., 13th September, 1771; married, 13th November, 1809, William Meaux, of New Kent County, Va., and died without issue, 15th September, 1824.
2. Elizabeth Nelson, born 18th May, 1773; died single.
3. Caroline Nelson (No. 1), born 18th May, 1775; died 6th July, same year.
4. Norborne Thomas Nelson, eldest son, born at The Dorrill, Hanover Co., Va., 29th August, 1776; married, about 1801, his first cousin, Lucy, daughter of Major John Nelson, of Oakhill, Mecklenburg Co., Va., and had many children. One of these, Lucy Chiswell Nelson, married H. M. Robinson, of New Orleans, La., and was the mother of Norborne Thomas Nelson Robinson, of Washington, D.C., and others. Catherine Page Nelson, another daughter, married Collier, father of William Armistead Nelson Collier, of Memphis, Tenn. Other children removed to Kentucky. Norborne Thomas Nelson removed to Arkansas in 1836 and died there in 1844, aged 68.
5. Warner Lewis Nelson, born 28th December, 1777; died 29th April, 1785.
6. Sally Cary Nelson, born 6th April, 1780; married, first, 1799, Charles Page, of Hanovertown, Va. (See Page Family, Rosewell.) She married, secondly, Thomas Atkinson, of Mansfield, near Petersburg, Din-

widdie Co., Va., by whom she had no issue. She died, January, 1861, aged 81 years.

7. William Nelson, born 30th October, 1781; died infant, 2d April, 1782.
8. Mary Chiswell Nelson, born 20th March, 1783; married, about 1803, Mann Page, of Hanovertown, Va., brother of Charles. (See Page Family, Rosewell.)
9. Dr. William Randolph Nelson, born 9th October, 1784; died at Gould Hill, Hanover Co., Va., 1862, aged 78 years. He married, about 1809, the widow Lucy Oliver, whose maiden name was Tomlin. No surviving issue.
10. Caroline Nelson (No. 2), born 27th May, 1786; died 12th November, 1790, infant.
11. Fanny P. Nelson, born 23d December, 1787; married, 1807, John Spottswood Wellford, of Fredericksburg, Va. Children:
    (1) Jane Wellford; married, about 1828, James Park Corbin, of Moss Neck, Caroline Co., Va., and had: (*a*) S. Wellford Corbin, of Farley Vale, King George Co., Va.; (*b*) Mrs. John Dickinson, of Fredericksburg, Va.; (*c*) Kate Corbin; married, first, 1863, Alexander S. Pendleton, of Lexington, Rockbridge Co., Va., who died, 1864, with no surviving issue. She married, secondly, John Brooke, of Lexington, Va., and had several children; (*d*) James Park Corbin, Jr., married Miss Ficklin.
    (2) Dr. William Nelson Wellford, of Farley, Culpepper Co., Va., married, about 1835, Mrs. Farley Fauntleroy, whose maiden name was Corbin. He died in July, 1872, leaving: (*a*) Dr. William N. Wellford, Jr., of Campbell County, Va., who married and had several children; and (*b*) R. Corbin Wellford, died in Memphis, Tenn., about 1886, and others.
    (3) Mary C. Wellford; married, about 1837, Dr. George F. Carmichael, of Fredericksburg, Va. She died, leaving three sons: (*a*) James, (*b*) Spottswood, and (*c*) Charles Carter.
12. George R. Nelson, born 16th October, 1789; died 20th November, 1802, probably single. At his request, his portion of his father's estate was given to his eldest brother, Norborne Thomas Nelson.
13. Susan R. C. Nelson, born 18th May, 1791; married, first, 2d March, 1809, William Wellford, brother of J. Spottswood Wellford, of Fredericksburg, Va. William Wellford died, leaving one child, Lucy Nelson Wellford, who married, about 1830, Dr. Robert C. Randolph, of New Market, Clarke Co., Va. (See Randolph.) Susan R. Nelson, the widow Wellford, married, secondly, Philip Burwell, of Chapel Hill, Clarke Co., Va. He died 11th February, 1849, and she died 27th December, 1869, aged 78 years. In 1868 Mrs. Susan Wellford Burwell gave to N. T. N. Robinson, of New Orleans, La., a silver spoon bearing the arms of Col. John Chiswell.
16. Hugh Nelson (14 and 15 died infants, names unknown), born at The Dorrill, Hanover Co., Va.; married, in 1826, Elizabeth Harrison Minge.

He died, 1st April, 1862, aged 69. His wife was of Wyanoke, on James River, Charles City Co., Va. She was a great-niece of William Henry Harrison, President of the United States of America, and granddaughter of Benjamin Harrison, of Berkeley (Harrison's Landing), on James River, Va., who was one of the signers of the Declaration of Independence. Children:

(1) Sally Nelson; single.

(2) Lucy Nelson; single.

(3) Fanny Page Nelson, born at Petersburg, Va., 29th August, 1832; married, 25th April, 1861, Charles Carter, who resides at Hollyoak, near Shirley, on James River, Charles City Co., Va., and has: (*a*) Mary Randolph, born 14th February, 1862; (*b*) Lucy Nelson, born 14th July, 1866; (*c*) Charles Hill, born 1st May, 1868; (*d*) Elizabeth Minge, born 26th October, 1870; (*e*) Fanny Boykin, born 5th December, 1873.

(4) Hugh Nelson; married, about 1865, Maria, daughter of John Selden, near Westover, on James River, Charles City Co., Va., and had one child, viz.: William.

(5) Mary Nelson.

(6) William R. Nelson; removed to Selma, Alabama, and married, about 1867, Octavia Stevens, of Tennessee.

17. Armistead Nelson, youngest, born at The Dorrill, Hanover Co., Va., 11th February, 1795; became an officer in the United States navy, under Commodore Decatur. He afterward resigned, and became a merchant. He married, about 1820, Mary Henderson, of Fredericksburg, Va., and had one son, viz.:

(1) Dr. William A. Nelson, United States Navy; married, about 1846, Mary Moncure, of Stafford County, Va.

III. Major John Nelson, of Oak Hill, Mecklenburg Co., Va., third son and youngest child of Secretary Thomas Nelson, of Yorktown, York Co., Va., and Lucy Armistead, his wife, was born at Yorktown, Va., about 1748. When the war of the American Revolution commenced, he entered the American army, and rose to the rank of Major of Cavalry. He married, in 1780, Nancy, daughter of John Carter, a merchant, of Williamsburg, James City Co., Va. They are said to have had a large family; but the following names only are known:

1. Major Thomas M. Nelson, eldest, born 1782; married, 1815, Sarah W., daughter of John Page, of Pagebrook, Clarke Co., Va. (see Page Family, Broadneck), and had issue.

2. John Nelson, born about 1783 at Oak Hill, Mecklenburg Co., Va., and was unmarried.

3. Lucy Nelson, born about 1785; married, about 1801, as we have seen, her first cousin, Norborne Thomas Nelson, eldest son and fourth child of Col. William Nelson, of The Dorrill, Hanover Co., Va.
4. Robert Nelson, born 30th January, 1787, married, 10th January, 1809, Isabella Hopkins Wilson, and had issue.
5. William Nelson, married Martha Walker. Children: (1) Anna Matilda Nelson, married Dr. Jeffries; (2) Sallie Page Nelson, married Mr. Hughes; (3) John Nelson, unmarried; (4) Daughter, married Burwell; (5) Catharine Nelson; (6) Virginia Nelson; (7) William Nelson, married Mrs. Watkins; (8) Frank Nelson, removed to Texas. Catherine and Virginia were both married, but the names of their husbands are not known.
6. Nancy Nelson, married Erasmus Kennon.
7. Matilda Nelson, married John Lewis.
8. Hugh Nelson, born 17th August, 1827; removed to Missouri; married, 9th September, 1856, Harriet Bolling Archer, and had issue.

IV. MAJOR THOMAS M. NELSON, United States army, eldest son and child of Major John Nelson, of Oak Hill, Mecklenburg Co., Va., and Nancy Carter, his wife, second son and child of Secretary Thomas Nelson, of Yorktown, York Co., Va., and Lucy Armistead, his wife, was born at the first-named place in 1782, and removed to Columbus, Muscogee Co., Ga., where he died 10th November, 1853, aged 71 years. He served with distinction in the war of 1812, as Captain of Infantry. After the war he was promoted to the rank of Major. He soon after resigned, and was a representative in the United States Congress, from Virginia, 1816–19. He declined a re-election, and retired to private life. He was a Presidential Elector in 1829 and 1833.

He married, 1815, Sarah Walker Page, of Pagebrook, Clarke Co., Va., who was the daughter of John Page, of that place, and the sister of Judge John E. Page, also of the same place. (See Page Family, Broadneck.) Mrs. Sarah W. P. Nelson died, 1835, aged about 43. Their children were:

1. Evelyn Byrd Page Nelson, born 1819; married, about 1839, Robert Carter, of Columbus, Ga. Children: (1) Thomas Michelle Carter, born 1840, married Miss Chin, and had (*a*) Evelyn who married William Wooten, of Albany, Ga., and (*b*) Maria. (2) Robert E. Carter, born in 1842, married Eliza Redd—one child, William.
2. Hon. John P. Nelson, born 19th December, 1822; eldest son, and Representative in the U. S. Congress from Georgia; married Eliza Hern, of

Rahway, N. J. He died in 1848 without male issue, but left three daughters: (1) Anne Nelson, married C. Barghmann, of Jersey City, N. J.; (2) Rose Nelson, who married in New York, but has no surviving issue; and (3) Eliza Nelson, married Boughton, of Bainbridge, Ga. No issue known.

3. Col. William Nelson, of Millwood, Clarke Co., Va., born 24th July, 1824; married, 22d February, 1852, Mary A., daughter of William Byrd Page, of Pagebrook, Clarke Co., Va., and Eliza Atkinson, his second wife. Children: (1) Thomas M. Nelson, born 12th March, 1853; married, in 1877, Susie H. Atkinson, of Baltimore, and had (*a*) William Norborne, born November, 1878, and (*b*) Mann A., born 3d July, 1883. (2) Eliza A. Nelson, born 6th March, 1855; married, 1878, John C. Woolfolk, of Columbus, Ga., who died in 1890. They had (*a*) Mann N., born August, 1878, (*b*) Maria Page, (*c*) Rosa Gray, (*d*) John C., born 1887. (3) Evelyn Willing Nelson, born 14th June, 1861.
4. Maria B. Nelson, born 1826; married, in 1845, William G. Woolfolk of Columbus, Ga., and had (*a*) Thomas N., (*b*) William E., (*c*) John C., (*d*) Joseph W., (*e*) Rosa, married Robert Abee, of Baltimore, Md., (*f*) Arthur, (*g*) Henry, (*h*) Albert, (*i*) Robert, (*k*) Charles.
5. Rosalie Nelson, born 1828; married, in 1847, Dr. F. O. Ticknor, of Columbus, Ga. Children: (1) Dr. W. Douglas Ticknor; (2) George Ticknor. (3) Thomas M. Ticknor; (4) Frank A. Ticknor; (5) William Nelson Ticknor. All are married except Frank.
6. Col. Thomas M. Nelson, Jr., born 1833, died in Mississippi, 1863; he married, in 1863, Fannie, daughter of Nelson Tift, of Albany, Ga., and left one son, Thomas M. Nelson, Jr.

IV. Robert Nelson, of Oak Hill, Mecklenburg Co., Va., third son of Major John Nelson, of the same place, and Nancy Carter, his wife, third son and youngest child of Secretary Thomas Nelson, of Yorktown, York Co., Va., and Lucy Armistead, his wife, was born at the first-named place, 30th January, 1787, and married, 10th January, 1809, Isabella Hopkins Wilson. She was born in Mecklenburg County, Va., 6th April, 1793, and died in Belton, Tex., 20th March, 1877. He died 26th March, 1846, in the 60th year of his age. Children:

1. Nancy Carter Nelson, born 18th April, 1814; died in Belton, Tex., 30th May, 1873. She married, 6th November, 1833, Francis W. Venable, and had issue.
2. John Wilson Nelson, born at Petersburg, Va., 1st March, 1810; married, 24th September, 1833, Harriet Elizabeth Shore, and had issue.
3. Nathaniel Bacon Nelson, married, 31st October, 1833, Mary Speed, and had issue. He died in Texas in July, 1863.

4. Elizabeth Smith Nelson, married, 5th June, 1833, Robert Alexander Atkinson, of Dinwiddie County, Va.; removed to Gonzales, Tex., in 1857. Children: (1) Mary Isabella Atkinson. (2) Anne Eliza Atkinson, married, 22d December, 1857, Henry Clay Pleasants, of Mansfield, Gonzales Co., Tex., and had (*a*) Mary, married J. J. Cocke, who had Annie and James; (*b*) Robert, married Mary White, and had Aaron White; (*c*) Harriet Margaret, married Walter K. Bruden, and had Annie Pleasants and Paul Hamilton; (*d*) John James; (3) Robert Thomas Atkinson; (4) Mary Nelson Atkinson; (5) William Mayo Atkinson, lawyer, married Mary Lane, of Clinton, Tex., 17th January, 1870, and had (*a*) William Lane, (*b*) Cora Belle, (*c*) Lulu Lane, (*d*) Robert Alexander, (*e*) John Mayo Pleasants, (*f*) Samuel Winston, (*g*) Roger; (6) Dr. Roger Atkinson, of Gonzales, Tex., married 5th June, 1879, Alice Duval Brawnley, of King and Queen Co., Va., and had (*a*) Robert Brawnley, (*b*) Roger Nelson, (*c*) Lucy Pleasants, (*d*) Alice Elizabeth; (7) Jane Minge Atkinson; (8) Isabella Nelson Atkinson; (9) Elizabeth Nelson Atkinson; (10) Dr. John Joseph Atkinson, married, 20th April, 1887, Johanna Clara Eckhardt, of Yorktown, De Witt Co., Tex., and had (*a*) Elizabeth Nelson, (*b*) Helen Louisa, and (*c*) John Joseph.
5. Robert Carter Nelson, Jr., born about 1816; married, first, Mary Scott, daughter of Samuel Watkins, of Petersburg, Va., and secondly, Lucy Cunningham, of Mecklenburg County, Va. It is not known by which of the wives the children are descended. They are: (1) Watkins Nelson; (2) Louisa Nelson; (3) Isabella Nelson; (4) Annie Nelson; (5) John Nelson; (6) Bettie Nelson; (7) Mary Scott Nelson; (8) Robert Nelson.
6. Lucy Armistead Nelson, married, 1841, Rev. Thomas E. Locke, of Mount Holly, Lunenburg Co., Va., and had issue.
7. Mary Nelson, married E. H. Harrington, and had (1) Hugh Harrington and (2) Isabella Harrington.
8. Hugh Nelson.

IV. Hugh Nelson, youngest son and child of Major John Nelson, of Oak Hill, Mecklenburg Co., Va., and Nancy Carter, his wife, third son and youngest child of Secretary Thomas Nelson, of Yorktown, York Co., Va., and Lucy Armistead, his wife, was born in Halifax County, Va., 17th August, 1827, and removed to St. Charles County, Mo. He married, 9th September, 1856, Harriet Bolling Archer, who was born in Petersburg, Va., 23d October, 1839. Their children were:

1. Robert Carter Nelson, born in St. Charles County, Mo., 19th July, 1857. He married, 24th June, 1884, at Wenona, Ill., Jennie Emma Moulton, who was born 31st August, 1859. They had (1) Robert Moulton Nelson, born 24th May, 1885, at Fayetteville, Ark; (2) Nathaniel Archer

Nelson, born 26th June, 1887, in Wichita, Kan.; (3) Hugh McKay Nelson, born 22d September, 1889, at Fayetteville, Ark. They all now reside in St. Louis, Mo.

2. Mary Shore Nelson, born in St. Charles County, Mo., 8th April, 1859; married, at St. Louis, Mo., 11th September, 1889, James Thomas Tate, of Robinson, Tex. Children: (1) Harriet Nelson Tate, born at St. Louis, Mo., 3d August, 1890; (2) Mary Ruth Tate, born at same place, 29th August, 1892. They all reside in Robinson, Tex.
3. Edward Archer Nelson, born in St. Charles County, Mo., 6th October, 1860, unmarried.
4. John Wilson Nelson, born same place, 11th November, 1861, died infant, 2d December, 1863.
5. Nathaniel Bacon Nelson, died young.

6 and 7. Isabella and Harriet, twins, died young.

8 and 9. Rosalie Nelson and Henry Lee Nelson, twins, born 5th October, 1871.

The following is extracted from a letter from George E. Hunt, United States forecast official, Omaha, Neb., 3d December, 1892:

My mother was named Sarah Morduette Nelson; her father was Dr. Hugh Nelson, of Oak Hill, Roanoke, Va., whose father was named John, or John Carter Nelson. Beyond this, I know very little of my mother's family, but am under the impression, as you intimate, that we are descendants of the Secretary Nelson branch of the family. My father was Dr. A. D. Hunt, and he and my mother were distantly related; my grandmother, on the mother side, having been Miss Mary Hunt, also of Virginia.

V. John Wilson Nelson, eldest son of Robert Nelson, of Oak Hill, Mecklenburg Co., Va., and Isabella Hopkins Wilson, his wife, third son of Major John Nelson, of the same place, and Nancy Carter his wife, third son and youngest child of Secretary Thomas Nelson, of Yorktown, York Co., Va., and Lucy Armistead his wife, was born near Petersburg, Va., 1st March, 1810, and removed to St. Charles County, Mo. He died there, 4th April, 1860, in the 51st year of his age. He married 24th September, 1833, Harriet Elizabeth Shore, who was born at Petersburg, Va., 5th February, 1815. She died in Missouri, 18th August, 1873, in the 59th year of her age. Their children were:

1. Thomas Shore Nelson, born in Petersburg, Va., 12th August, 1834; died 9th June, 1866, aged 32. He married in Haywood County, Tenn., in the autumn of 1864, Elizabeth Kimbrough, who died in Meridian, Miss., 29th September, 1886. They had a daughter, Lula Shore Nelson, born in

Haywood County, Tenn., 13th September, 1865; married, 6th March, 1888, S. S. Granberry, of Meridian, Miss., and they have two children, (*a*) Laura, born 11th February, 1889, and (*b*) James Kimbrough, born in the spring of 1892. They all live in Meridian, Miss.

2. Anna Carter Nelson, born in Petersburg, Va., 1st July, 1841; married in Missouri, 1st March, 1859, Judge John T. Powell, who died 4th September, 1891. They had nine children, as follows: (1) Ben. T. Powell, died infant; (2) Mary Ann Powell, born 18th September, 1861; (3) John Nelson Powell, born 26th August, 1863; (4) Chester B. Powell, of Newburg, Mo., married 23d September, 1891, Lottie Nivens; (5) Harriet E. Powell, born 1st September, 1868; (6) Edward J. Powell, born 20th October, 1870; (7) Julius W. Powell, born 23d December, 1873; (8) Marion P. Powell, born 14th January, 1876; (9) Robert Carter Powell, born 18th August, 1879.
3. Elizabeth Smith Nelson, born in St. Louis, Mo., 9th January, 1844; married, 4th November, 1874, Judge William Walla Edwards, of St. Charles County, Mo., and had (1) Harriet E. Edwards, died infant; (2) William W. Edwards, jr., born 14th February, 1878; (3) Julius Carter Edwards, born 15th February, 1883.
4. Marion Preston Nelson, born in St. Louis, Mo., 24th December, 1845; married, 22d November, 1871, Julius Moulton, engineer, of St. Charles County, Mo. No surviving issue.
5. Robert Nelson, born in St. Louis, Mo., 27th July, 1848; married, August 6th, 1869, Harriet V. Pitzen, and had two children, died infants.

Four other children of John W. Nelson and Harriet E. Shore, his wife, died infants.

V. Nathaniel Bacon Nelson, second son of Robert Nelson, of Oak Hill, Mecklenburg Co., Va., and Isabella his wife, was born 22d January, 1812, and died in Texas, July, 1863. He married, 31st October, 1833, Mary Speed who died in Texas in February, 1881. Their children were:

1. George Nelson, born 21st August, 1834, died infant.
2. Mary Isabella Nelson, born 21st December, 1835; married, 1855, Peter Stokes, of Virginia, and had issue.
3. Harriet Nelson (called Hattie), born 23d April, 1837; married David S. Speed, and had issue.
4. Robert Nelson, born 2d March, 1839; married Bettie Rather, who died. Children: (1) William S. Nelson; (2) Mary Nelson; (3) Frank Nelson; (4) Bettie Nelson, and (5) Richard Nelson.
5. Anne Eliza Nelson, born 26th December, 1841, married, 11th December, 1866, William J. Venable.
6. William Fownes Nelson, born 15th April, 1843; married, 21st January, 1875, Alice Gee, and had (1) Willie Russell Nelson, died infant; (2)

Annie V. Nelson, born 20th November, 1876; (3) Hugh Edward Nelson, born 24th October, 1878; (4) Lily Belle Nelson; (5) Fletcher Gay Nelson, died infant; (6) Norborne Nelson, born 11th July, 1884; (7) Daisy Oliver Nelson, born 1st November, 1886.

7. Lucy Maria Nelson, born 12th April, 1846; married R. A. Buchanan, since died. They had issue.
8. Sallie Speed Nelson, born 26th December, 1849; married Lewis G. Sims, and had issue.
9. Edward Speed Nelson, born 2d June, 1852; married Laura Sims, and had (1) Bettie Nelson; (2) William Fownes Nelson; (3) Mary Nelson; (4) Cora Belle Nelson; (5) Frank V. Nelson; (6) Alice Nelson; (7) Hattie Nelson; (8) Nellie Nelson, died infant; (9) Edward Nelson, and (10) Nettie Nelson.

PART III.

WALKER FAMILY.

(From a water-color drawing by C. H. Sherman, New York, 1881.)

HON. FRANCIS WALKER,

CASTLE HILL, ALBEMARLE CO., VA.

Died 1806, aged 42.

WALKER FAMILY.

The WALKERS, OF VIRGINIA, came from Staffordshire, England, about 1650, at an early period in the history of the Colony of Virginia. The Walker Family Bible is in the possession of Dr. Bernard H. Walker, of Stevensville, King and Queen Co., Va., and was printed in 1589.

I. THOMAS WALKER, OF GLOUCESTER COUNTY, VA., progenitor of the Walker Family in Virginia, was a member of the Colonial Assembly in 1662, being at that time a Representative from the County of Gloucester. His wife and children are at present unknown to the writer, though his eldest son was probably named Thomas.

. . . .

III. THOMAS WALKER, OF KING AND QUEEN COUNTY, VA., was probably a grandson of the above-mentioned Thomas Walker, of Gloucester County, same State. The following is copied from a letter from Dr. Bernard H. Walker, of Stevensville, King and Queen Co., Va., to Dr. R. C. M. Page, of New York City, dated 30th October, 1880:

The old Walker Family Bible, in my possession, was printed in 1589, and the New Testament was attached in 1602. In this old Bible there is this memorandum: "September y[e] 24th, 1709. I went to Sant Clemones Church. (signed) Thomas Walker."

The next memorandum is this: "My dafter, Mary Peachy Walker, was born y[e] first oure of y[e] thirtieth day of Janevary, 1710, babtised the day follow[g] y[e] 31st." There are also in said Bible the following memoranda:

"John Walker borne y[e] 29 of April, at five, 1711.

"Tho[s] Walker borne Jan[y] y[e] 25, 1715.

"Mary Peachy Walker married May y[e] 13 in the year of our Lord, 1732.

"John Walker, married 9th Nov., 1735, Miss Baylor, of Essex County, Virginia, and had three children, viz: :

"1. Baylor Walker, a son.

"2. Susannah Walker.

"3. Elizabeth Walker."

Thomas Walker, of King and Queen County, Va., married, 29th September, 1709, at St. Clement's Church, in said county, Susanna, whose surname was probably PEACHY. Their children were as follows:

1. Mary Peachy Walker, born 1710; married, 13th May, 1732, Dr. George Gilmer, of Williamsburg, James City Co., Va., and had Dr. George Gilmer, of Pen Park, Albemarle Co., Va., who was the grandfather of Gov. Thomas Walker Gilmer.
2. John Walker, eldest son, born 29th April, 1711; married, but the names of his wife and children are at present unknown to the writer. His descendants live in King and Queen County, Va., of whom Dr. Bernard H. Walker, above-mentioned, is probably the representative. Dr. Walker A. Hawes, of New York City, formerly of Virginia, is also a descendant. The Baptist minister, Robert B. Semple, father of Baylor Semple, who was the Whig editor of the old Fredericksburg (Virginia) *News*, was his descendant by his daughter.
3. Dr. Thomas Walker, second son, born in King and Queen County, Va., 25th January, 1715; removed to Castle Hill, Albemarle Co., Va. He married, first, in 1741, Mildred Thornton, the widow Meriwether, by whom he had issue. He married, secondly, about 1781, Elizabeth Thornton, first cousin of his first wife and sister of Mildred Thornton, who was the second of the five wives of Col. Samuel Washington, brother of Gen. George Washington. Dr. Thomas Walker had no issue by his second wife.

IV. DR. THOMAS WALKER, OF CASTLE HILL, Albemarle Co., Va., third child and second son of Thomas Walker, of King and Queen County, Va., and Susanna [Peachy], his wife, grandson (?) of Thomas Walker, of Gloucester County, Va., progenitor of the Walker Family in Virginia, name of his wife unknown, was born at the second-named place, 25th January, 1715, and removed to the first-named place, where he died 9th November, 1794, aged 79 years and nearly 10 months.

He was probably the first white man that ever entered Kentucky, having gone there in 1750, or thirteen years before Daniel Boone. His diary from 16th March to 13th July, 1750, regarding one of his western expeditions was published, 1888, in Boston, at the instance of William C. Rives, Esq., of the American Historical Association. The missing portion of the original MS. is in the possession of the widow Thomas W. Page, of Albemarle County, Va. Dr. Walker's hatchet, with which he marked trees that formed the boundary lines of the lands purchased by him from the Indians, was found several years ago in Kentucky, where he had lost it. It was marked "T. W.," and is said to be now in a museum in Louisville, Ky.

Walker's Mountains, in Southwest Virginia, are probably named after Dr. Thomas Walker. On his way to Kentucky, about 1750, he gave the name to Cumberland Gap and Cumberland River, in honor of the Duke of Cumberland, who routed the rebels at the battle of Culloden about 1747.

On the 10th October, 1774, the Indians, under their chief, CORNSTALK, were defeated by the Colonial troops under the command of Andrew Lewis, at the BATTLE OF POINT PLEASANT. This place is situated on the right bank of the Great Kanawha River, at its junction with the Ohio River, in what is now called West Virginia.

The cause of this battle appears to have been disaffection on the part of the Indians with the TREATY OF LANCASTER, as well as others that were subsequently made in confirmation of it. The Treaty of Lancaster was made on the 2d July, 1744, between representatives of the Six Nations of Indians and Commissioners of His Majesty, George II. By this treaty the Indians agreed forever to abandon all claim to any territory within the Colony of Virginia. The Treaty of Lancaster, and several other documents, which are written on parchment, and were in the possession of Dr. Thomas Walker, are now in the possession of the widow of Thomas Walker Page, of Keswick (Turkey Hill), Albemarle Co., Va., they having come to him through his mother, Jane Frances Walker Page, the granddaughter of Dr. Thomas Walker. The following is a copy of the Treaty of Lancaster:

"To all people to whom these presents shall come.

Canasateego, Tachanoontia, Joneehat, Caxhayion, Torachdadon, Neecokanyhak, and Rociniwuchto, Sachems or chiefs of the nation of the Onondagas, Saquesonyunt, Gachiaddodon, Hucdsaly-akon, Rowanhohiso, Osochquah, and Seayenties, Sachems or chiefs of the nation of Cahugas, Swadany *alias* Stuckelimy Onechuaagua, Onoch-Kally dawy, *alias* Watsathua, Tohashwaniarorow, Amyhoctkhaw, and Tear-Haasuy, Sachems or chiefs of the nations of the Tuscaroras, Tanasanegoes, & Tanichuintees, Sachems or chiefs of the nation of the Senikers send Greeting.

WHEREAS the six United nations of Indians laying claim to some Lands in the Colony of Virginia, signified their Willingness to enter into a Treaty concerning the same, Whereupon Thomas Lee Esqr, a member in Ordinary of his Majesty's honourable Council of State and one of the Judges of the Supreme Court of Judicature in that Colony, and William Beverly Esqr, Colonel and County Lieutenant of the County of Orange, and one of the representatives of the people in the house of Burgesses of that Colony, were deputed by the Governor of the said Colony as Commissioners to Treat with the said Six nations or their Deputies, Sachems or chiefs as well of, and concerning the said claim as to renew their covenant chain between the said Colony and the said Six nations, and the said Commissioners, having met at Lancaster, in Lancaster County, and Province of Pensylvania, and as a foundation for a Stricter amity & Peace at their Juncture, agreed with the said Sachems or Chiefs of the said Six Nations, for a Disclaimer and Renunciation of all their Claim or Pretence of right whatsoever of the said Six Nations and an Acknowledgement of the Right of our Sovereign, the King of Great Britain, to all the Land in the Colony of Virginia. Now know ye that for and in consideration of the Sum of four hundred pounds current Money of Pensylvania paid and delivered to the abovenamed Sachems or Chiefs partly in Goods and partly in Gold Money by the said Commissioners, they the said Sachems or Chiefs on behalf of the said Six Nations do hereby renounce and disclaim not only all the Right of the said Six Nations, but also recognize and acknowledge the right and Title of our Sovereign, the King of Great Britain, to all the Lands within the said Colony as it is now or hereafter may be peopled and owned by his said Majesty, our Sovereign Lord, the King, his heirs and possessors. In Witness whereof the said Sachems or Chiefs for themselves and on behalf of the people of the Six Nations aforesaid, have hereunto put their hands and Seals the Second day of July, in the Eighteenth Year of the reign of our Sovereign Lord George the Second of Great Britain etc., and in the year of our Lord One thousand seven hundred and forty-four.

Signed Sealed and Delivered
In the Presence of

EWD. JENNINGS, CONRAD WEISOR, Interpreter

P. Thomas -- EDWD SMOUT

P. KING --- WILLIAM MARSHE.

THOS COLVIL		
JAMES HAMILTON		
RICHD PETERS	Tanickeinties	[L. S.]
WM LOGAN	Onucknaxgua	[L. S.]
JNO. TAYLOE JUNR	Shickelimy	[L. S.]
PHIL. LUD. LEE	Watsatuha	[L. S.]
PRESBY THORNTON	Tohasaangarrorons	[L. S.]
NAT. RIGBY	Anuchockin	[L. S.]

Witnesses	Signers	Mark	Seal
NAT. RIGBIE JUN[R]	Tiorhasuy		[L. S.]
BENEDICT CALVERT	Sidoceax		[L. S.]
JAMES PATTON	Attiuska		[L. S.]
JAMES LOGAN JUN[R]	Teewachadachgua		
THO[S] COOKSON	Thorntua Waggon		
THO[S] CRADDOCK	Canassatego		[L. S.]
ROB[T] BROOKE JUN[R]	Tochanoontia		[L. S.]
JAS. MADISON	Johnuas		[L. S.]
WILLIAM BLACK	Saxagan		[L. S.]
	Torachaadon		[L. S.]

Signer	Mark	Seal
HEECOHANYHAK	his mark	[L. S.]
POTIRAWUCHTA		[L. S.]
TAΓ AGHSACKGUA		[I]
SAGUCHSONYUNT		[L. S.]
GACHRADODON		[L. S.]
HATASLYAKEN		[L. S.]
ROWANHOHEISO		[L. S.]
O SOGHGUAH		[L. S.]
SEAYENTUS		[L. S.]
TANANANEGO		[L. S.]

VIRGINIA ss^{t}

At a General Court held at the Capitol the 25th day of October, 1744.

This Deed Poll was proved by the oaths of Edmund Jennings Esqr. Philip Lud. Lee, and William Black three of the Witnesses thereto and ordered to be Recorded.

Teste BEN. WALLER C. G C.

A Copy

Teste

PETER PELHAM JUN. &
BEN. WALLER C. G C.

The Capitol of Virginia in those days was at Williamsburg, James City County.

It appears from the foregoing Treaty of Lancaster that the claim to all lands in the Colony of Virginia was purchased from the Indians for the sum of four hundred pounds of Pennsylvania currency (between twelve and fifteen hundred dollars), to be paid "partly in Goods and partly in Gold Money," but especially "partly in Goods," no doubt, such as cheap whiskey, gunpowder, tobacco, and the like. This was, however, comparatively, a very large sum to pay for a sound title to all the land within the Colony of Virginia, when we consider the fact that Manhattan Island, upon which the city of New York now stands, was purchased from the Indians by the Dutch for the sum of twenty-four dollars! Sharp bargains these, all done up as they were in due form according to law, and not far behind similar jobs of the present day.

Some of the Sachems probably became dissatisfied with the Treaty of Lancaster (made 2d July, 1744), and it appears that, subsequently, other treaties were made from time to time, confirming the Treaty of Lancaster. For instance, a "powwow" was held, for this object, at Loggstown (Ohio) in 1752. The following is a copy of the parchment:

Whereas at the Treaty of Lancaster, in the County of Lancaster, and Province of Pensylvania, held between the Government of Virginia, and the Six United Nations of Indians in the Year of our Lord 1744, The hon.^{ble} Thomas Lee and William Beverly Esqr, being Commissioners, a Deed Recognizing and acknowledging the right and Title of his Majesty our Sovereing Lord, the King of Great Britain, to all the Lands within the Colony of Virginia, as it was then or might be hereafter peopled and bounded by his said Majesty our Sovereign Lord the King, his heirs and successors, was signed sealed and delivered by the Sachems and Chiefs of the Six United Nations then present as may more fully appear by the said Deed, reference thereto being had: We Conogareira, Chescaga, Cononsagret, Eaghnisance, Togrondoara, and Thornarissa, Sachems and Chiefs of the said Six Nations now inCouncil at Loggstown, do hereby Signify our Consent to & Confirmation of the said Deed in as full and ample a manner as if the same was here recited, and whereas his Majesty, the King of Great Britain, has at present a Design of making a Settlement or Settlements of British-Subjects on the Southern or Eastern parts of the River thus called otherwise Allegany, we in Council Joshua Fry, Lunsford Lomax, and James Patton Esq[re] being Commissioners on behalf of his Majesty, Do give our consent thereto and do further promise that the said Settlement or Settlements shall be unmolested by us, & that we will, as far as in our power, assist and Protect the British Subjects there inhabiting.

In Witness whereof we have hereunto put our hands and Seals this thirteenth day of June in the Year of our Lord 1752.

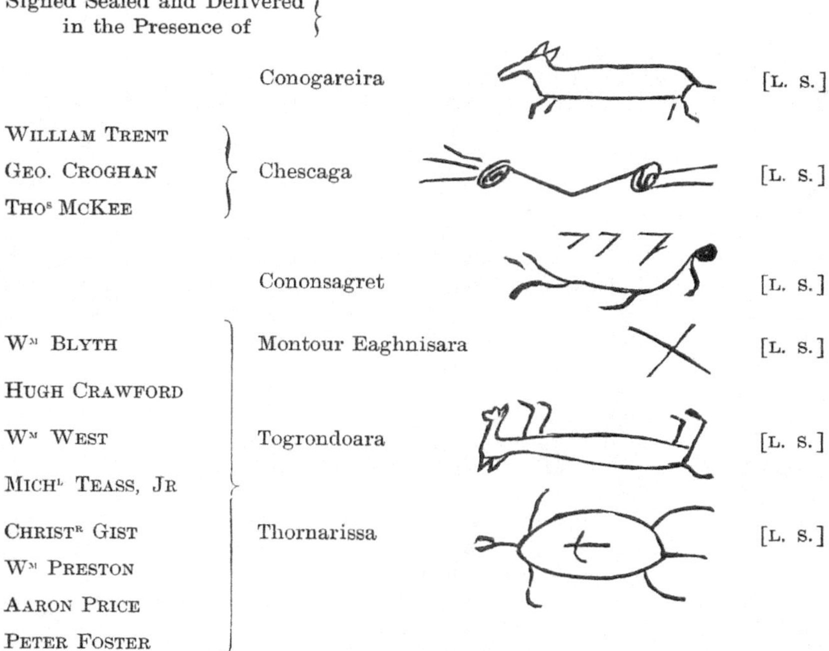
Signed Sealed and Delivered in the Presence of

Witnesses	Signer		Seal
	Conogareira		[L. S.]
William Trent Geo. Croghan Thos McKee	Chescaga		[L. S.]
	Cononsagret		[L. S.]
Wm Blyth Hugh Crawford Wm West Michl Teass, Jr Christr Gist Wm Preston Aaron Price Peter Foster	Montour Eaghnisara Togrondoara Thornarissa		[L. S.] [L. S.] [L. S.]

VIRGINIA, ss[t]

At a General Court held at the Court house in Williamsburg the 2d day of November 1752.

This Deed Poll was acknowledged by Montour Eaghnisara one of the Sachems within named and was proved to be the Act and Deed of the said Sachems also within named by the oath of William Trent, and William Preston, Witnesses thereto and Ordered to be Recorded.

Teste BEN. WALLER W. C W.

A Copy

Teste

PETER PELHAM, JUN^R &

BEN. WALLER C D G. Cur.

The following are copies of parchments which explain themselves. They have reference to the purchase of six millions of acres of land on the Ohio River by certain persons, among whom we find Dr. Thomas Walker and his two sons, John Walker and Thomas Walker, Jr.

THIS INDENTURE made this thirtieth day of July in the year of Our Lord One Thousand Seven hundred and Seventy Seven BETWEEN George Croghan Esqr, of Fort Pitt in the State of Virginia of the one part, and Thomas Walker, John Walker, Thomas Walker Junr, Nicholas Lewis, George Gilmer, Mathew Maury, Reuben Lindsay, of the County of Albemarle, Henry Fry, of the County of Culpepper and Joseph Hornsby, of the City of Williamsburg, in the State aforesaid, of the other part WITNESSETH. WHEREAS the aforementioned George Croghan Esq$_r$ did on the tenth day of July, Anno Domini One Thousand Seven hundred and Seventy five, purchase of the Chiefs or Sachems of the Six United Nations of Indians a Certain Tract or Parcel of land in fee marked by Certain Boundaries and Containing by Estimation Six Million of Acres, all which will fully appear by a true and Accurate Copy of the Deed of the aforesaid purchase hereto annexed, recourse being thereunto had. Now THIS INDENTURE WITNESSETH that the said George Croghan Esqr hath for and in Consideration of the Sum of five thousand Spanish Dollars, to him in hand paid, the Receipt whereof he doth hereby acknowledge, Bargained, Sold, Aliened, Enfeoffed and delivered, and by these Presents doth Bargain, Sell, Alien, Enfeoff and deliver unto the aforesaid Thomas Walker, John Walker, Thomas Walker Junr, Nicholas Lewis, George Gilmer, Mathew Maury, Reuben Lindsay, Henry Fry, and Joseph Hornsby, one Clear Eight and Fortieth part of the Tract or Parcel of Land of the Six United Nations of Indians purchased as heretofore-mentioned, and as by the annexed Deed described, to them, their Heirs and Assigns forever: not as Joint Tenants but Tenants in Common, in the Proportions hereafter to be mentioned, that is to say to the afores^d John Walker one full Sixth part of the land hereby Conveyed, to the aforesaid Thomas Walker Junr one full Seventh part of the Premises hereby Conveyed, to the aforesaid Thomas Walker one full Eighth part of the Land hereby Conveyed, and all the Rest and Residue of the Land hereby Conveyed after the deducting of the aforesaid three Shares to be divided among Thomas Walker, Nicholas Lewis, George Gilmer, Mathew

Maury, Reuben Lindsay, Henry Fry, and Joseph Hornsby, two Shares to the said Thomas Walker, and to the others one full share each, the land so to be laid off as to allow the afore-mentioned Grantees their Just proportion on the River, TO HAVE AND TO HOLD the aforesaid Land together with all and Singular, the Profits, Priviledges, Immunities and Hereditaments thereunto belonging or in any wise appertaining in the Proportions heretofore Specified, them the aforesaid Thomas Walker, John Walker, Thomas Walker Jun[r], Nicholas Lewis, George Gilmer, Mathew Maury, Reuben Lindsay, Henry Fry, and Joseph Hornsby, their Heirs and Assigns forever, not as Joint Tenants but as Tenants in Common according to the true intent and meaning of this Indenture. IN TESTIMONY whereof the aforesaid George Croghan hath hereunto set his hand and affixed his Seal the date first-above written.

Sealed and Delivered }
In the Presence of }
GEORGE ROOTES }
BARNARD GRATZ } WILLIAM COOPER
GEO. CROGHAN [SEAL]
STROTHER JONES }
THOMAS EDMONDSON JUN[R] } J. PEYTON JUN[R]

Received of John Walker Esq[r], one of the Grantees within mentioned, the within mentioned Consideration Money full this 30th day of July 1777.

GEO. CROGHAN.

Teste
GEO. ROOTES,
BARNARD GRATZ.

MEMORANDUM.

Livery and Seisin made at the dating and ensealing the within Presents

GEO. CROGHAN.

Teste
GEO. ROOTES
STROTHER JONES.
THOMAS EDMONDSON JUN[R]
WILLIAM COOPER
J. PEYTON JUN[R]

CROGHAN }
to } Deed.
WALKER & al. }

TO ALL PEOPLE to whom these Presents shall come GREETING:

KNOW YE that we Kayathsuda, Tiendenago, Guitogunt, Oquncequago, Tegurahogo and Saquonea, Chiefs and Sachems of the Six United Nations of Indians and being and effectually Representing all the Tribes of the said Six United Nations send Greeting. NOW KNOW YE THEREFORE that we the said Chiefs or Sachems of the Six United Nations in full Council at Fort Pitt assembled: for and in Consideration of the Sum of Twelve Thousand Spanish Dollars, or value thereof in merchandize to us in hand paid by George Croghan, the Receipt whereof we do hereby acknowledge: and for and in Consideration of the great Justice and Integrity of the said George Croghan, Used and Exercised by him towards the Six Nations and their Allies in all his Publick and Private Conduct and Transactions wherein they have been Concerned, HAVE Granted, Bargained, Sold, Aliened, Released, Enfeoffed, Ratified and fully Confirmed a Certain Tract or Parcel of Land BEGINNING at the Shore on the South side of the River Ohio, Opposite the mouth of French Creek or Beef River, thence down the said River Ohio on the South side thereof Opposite the mouth of Big Beaver Creek, thence on a straight or direct line, across the said River Ohio, to the mouth of the said Beaver Creek, thence along the said Beaver Creek on the northerly side of the same, to an Old Indian Town, known by the name of Kaskaskias, thence up a Branch of the said Beaver Creek, known by the name of Shinango, and on the northerly side of the same to the Head or Termination of the said Branch, thence on a Straight or direct line to the head of French Creek, or Beef River, thence down the said Creek or River, on the Southerly side of the same, to the mouth thereof, and from thence in a Straight or direct Line across the River Ohio to the place of Beginning, Containing, by Estimation, Six Millions of Acres, be the same more or less. And by these Presents do Grant, Bargain, Sell, Alien, Release, Enfeoff, Ratify and fully Confirm unto the Said George Croghan, his Heirs and Assigns all the above described Tract or Parcel of Land, Granted or intended to be Granted, and also the Mines, Minerals, Ores, Trees, Islands, Woods, Underwoods, Waters, Watercourses, Profits, Commodities, Advantages, Rights, Liberties, Priviledges, Hereditaments and Appurtenances whatsoever to the said Tract or Parcel of Land belonging or in anywise Appertaining, and also the Reversion and Reversions, Remainder and Remainders, Rents, Issues and Profits thereof, and all the Estate Right of Title, Interest, Use, Property, Possession, Claim and demand of us the said Kayathsuda, Tiendenago, Guitogunt, Oquncequago, Tegurahogo, and Saquonea, Chiefs or Sachems aforesaid, and of all and every Other Person and Persons whatsoever of or belonging to the said Nations of, in, to, and out of the Premises and every part and Parcel thereof TO HAVE AND TO HOLD the said Tract or Parcel of Land, and all and Singular the said Granted or Bargained Premises with the Appurtenances unto the said George Croghan, his Heirs and Assigns forever, and the said Kayathsuda, Tiendenago, Guitogunt, Oquncequago, Tegurahogo, and Saquonea, for themselves and for the Six United Nations and all and every Nation and Nations, and their and every one of their Posterities, the said Tract of Land and Premises and every part thereof against them the said Kayathsuda, Tiendenago, Guitogunt, Oquncequago, Tegurahogo, and Saquonea and against the Six United Nations and their Tributaries and Dependents and all and every one of their Posterities unto the said George Croghan, his Heirs and Assigns shall and will Warrant and forever defend by these Presents, PROVIDED always nevertheless, and it is the true intent and meaning of these Presents that the said George Croghan, his Heirs, Executors, Administrators and Assigns shall not make any Settlements on the above described or mentioned Tract or Parcel of Land for the term of Fifteen Years, unless the Indians settled in that part of the Country shall remove farther down the River Ohio to a better Hunting Country, any thing herein Contained to the Contrary thereof in anywise notwithstanding.

IN WITNESS whereof we the said Chiefs and Sachems in behalf of ourselves Respectively, and in behalf of the whole Six United Nations aforesaid, have hereunto set our hands and Seals in the Presence of the Persons subscribing as Witnesses hereunto, at a Congress held at Fort Pitt this tenth day of July in the year of our Lord, One Thousand Seven hundred and Seventy five.

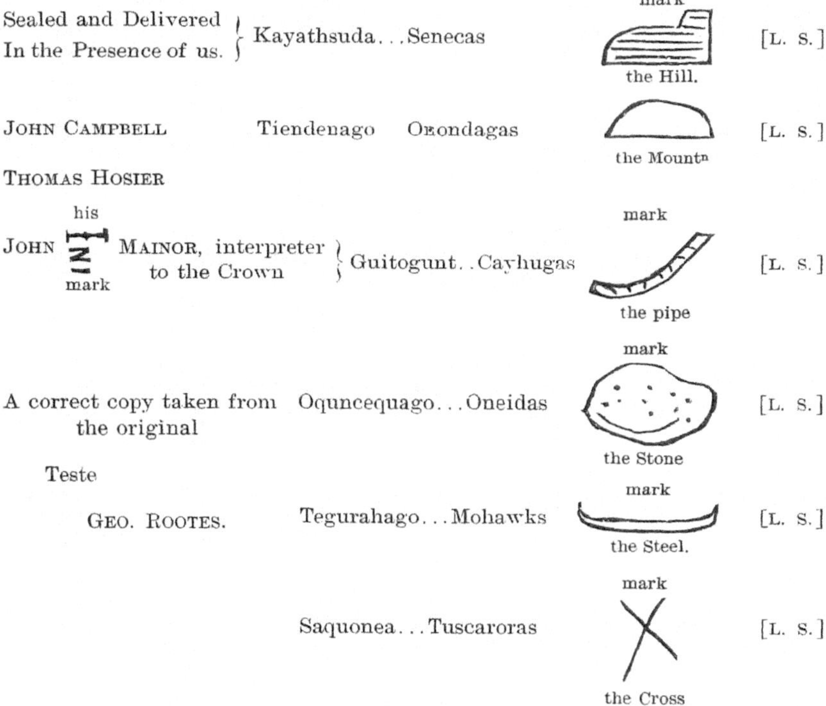

In one of the above-mentioned documents Fort Pitt is referred to as being in the State of Virginia. It appears that Virginia and Pennsylvania both claimed it, the former under a charter from James I. and the latter under a charter from Charles II. On Aug. 31, 1779, commissioners appointed by the two provinces met in Baltimore, and agreed upon the boundary, which was duly ratified by their respective legislatures. Since that time Pittsburg has remained in Pennsylvania.

The following are copied from parchments having reference to comparatively small tracts of land in the counties of Albemarle and Louisa:

George the Third by the Grace of God of Great Britain France and Ireland King Defender of the Faith &c. TO ALL TO WHOM these Presents shall come Greeting. KNOW YE that for divers good Causes and Considerations, but more Especially for and in Consideration of the Sum of *Twenty Five shillings* of good and Lawful Money, for our Use paid to our Receiver General of our Revenues in this our Colony and Dominion of Virginia, WE HAVE Given, Granted, and Confirmed, and by these Presents for us our Heirs and Successors, Do Give, Grant, and Confirm, unto Thomas Walker, one certain Tract or Parcel of Land Containing two hundred and twenty six acres, lying and being in the County of Albemarle, in the Coves and on the Ridges of one of the Ragged Mountains, and bounded as followeth to wit; Beginning at Pointers in Thomas Fitzpatrick's line running thence along the same North thirty two Degrees and a half East one hundred and twenty Poles to a Chestnut Oak, North eighty nine Degrees East one hundred and twenty four Poles to Pointers in Samuel Gay's Line, and with his Lines North twenty nine Degrees East one hundred and seventy eight Poles to Pointers, South eighty nine Degrees West one hundred and forty Poles to Pointers thence new lines, South fifty three Degrees West eighty nine Poles to Pointers, South thirty six Degrees West one hundred and eighty five Poles to Pointers in Jacob Moon's line, South thirty nine Degrees East eighty Poles to the Beginning. WITH ALL Woods, Under Woods, Swamps, Marshes, Low-grounds, Meadows, Feedings, and his due Share of all Veins, Mines and Quarries, as well discovered as not discovered, within the Bounds aforesaid and being Part of the said Quantity of Two hundred and twenty six Acres of Land, and the Rivers, Waters, and Water Courses therein contained, together with the Privileges of Hunting, Hawking, Fishing, Fowling, and all other Profits, Commodities, and Hereditaments whatsoever, to the same or any Part thereof belonging, or in any wise appertaining, TO HAVE, HOLD, Possess, and Enjoy, the said Tract or Parcel of Land, and all other the before granted Premises, and every Part thereof, with their and every of their Appurtenancas, unto the said Thomas Walker and to his Heirs and Assigns forever, To the only Use and Behoof of him, the said Thomas Walker, his Heirs, and Assigns forever, TO BE HELD of us our Heirs and Successors, as of our Manor of East Greenwich, in the County of Kent, in free and Common Soccage, and not in Capite or by Knights Service, YIELDING AND PAYING unto us, our Heirs, and Successors, for every fifty Acres of Land, and so proportionably for a lesser or greater Quantity than fifty Acres, the Fee Rent of one Shilling Yearly, to be paid upon the Feast of Saint Michael the Archangel, and also Cultivating and Improving three Acres part of every fifty of the Tract above mentioned within three Years after the Date of these Presents. PROVIDED always that if three Years of the said Fee Rent shall at any time be in Arrear and Unpaid, or if the said Thomas Walker his Heirs or Assigns do not within the Space of three Years, next coming after the Date of these Presents, Cultivate and Improve three Acres part of every fifty of the Tract above-mentioned, Then the Estate, hereby Granted shall Cease and be Utterly Determined, and thereafter it shall and may be Lawful to and for us our Heirs and Successors, to grant the same Lands and Premises with the Appurtenances unto such other Person or Persons as we our Heirs and Successors shall think fit. IN WITNESS whereof we have caused these our Letters Patent to be made. WITNESS our trusted and well beloved John Earl of Dunmore our Lieutenant and Governor General of our said Colony and Dominion at Williamsburg Under the Seal of our said Colony, the first Day of August, One thousand Seven hundred and Seventy two, In the twelfth Year of our Reign.

DUNMORE

There is a similar parchment dated 20th June, 1772, and signed by Dunmore. It is a grant from George III. to Thomas Walker of 350 acres of land

"Lying and being in the County of Louisa on the Branches of Great Creek and bounded as followeth to wit: Beginning at Robert Sharp's Corner several pines, running thence, on his lines, North Sixty nine Degrees West one hundred poles to a pine, thence North nine Degrees East one hundred and Sixty eight Poles to Sharps Corner pine in Biggar's line, thence on Biggar's line North twenty seven Degrees West twenty four Poles to Mathew Launders's Corner pine in Biggars Line, thence on Launders line South thirty nine Degrees East one hundred and eighty poles to William Hughson's Corner Pine on the Side of a hill in his line, thence on Hughson's line South forty Degrees East twenty two Poles to a pine, thence South twelve Degrees West two hundred and eighty poles to a Corner pine in Graves's line, thence on Graves's line North Seventy Degrees East one hundred and eighty seven poles to his Corner White Oak by the side of a Branch, thence South twenty poles to Fords Corner three pines in his line, thence on Fords line East forty poles to a pine in his line, thence North twelve Degrees East one hundred and Seventy four Poles to the Beginning."

The price of this last-mentioned tract of land was *thirty-five shillings*, which sum was paid by Dr. Walker to the Receiver General of the Revenues of the Colony, upon the same conditions with the preceding grant of 226 acres in Albemarle County.

The following parchment, found among Dr. Walker's papers, has reference to a grant from George II. to one James Flanegen, of a

"Certain Tract or parcel of Land containing two hundred and fifty acres lying and being in the County of Louisa and bounded as followeth to wit; Beginning at the said Flanegens Corner Pine in Silvanus Morris's line, thence on his line

South sixty two Degrees West one hundred and ninety six Poles crossing three small branches of Bunches Creek to his Corner two Spanish Oaks on the side of a Hill, thence new lines North sixty Degrees West one hundred and ninety six Poles to a Corner small Pine, thence North forty Degrees East one hundred and seventy two Poles to the beginning," etc.

The price of this piece of land was *twenty-five shillings* upon the same conditions as the two preceding. It ends as follows:

"WITNESS our Trusty and well beloved Sir William Gooch, Baronet, our Lieut. Governor and Commander in Chief of our said Colony and Dominion, at Williamsburg under the Seal of our said Colony, the twentieth day of August, One thousand seven hundred and forty seven, In the twenty first Year of our Reign.

WILLIAM GOOCH.

Dr. Walker probably received an academic education at the College of William and Mary, Virginia, but it is not known that he ever graduated in medicine. He probably served a certain length of time under some physician and was then licensed to practise by the County or other authorities, according to law. An original bill rendered by him for medical services in the case of Peter Jefferson, father of President Thomas Jefferson, U. S., was for many years to be seen at Castle Hill, Albemarle Co., Va.

Fredericksburg, situated on the Rappahannock River, Spottsylvania County, Va., was, at that time, like Yorktown, a point to which goods were directly imported from England. At Turkey Hill, Albemarle Co., Va., Thomas W. Page, Esqr., has in his possession an old-fashioned tall clock that has inscribed on its face "THOMAS WALKER, FREDERICKSBURGH, VA."

Dr. Walker is said to have been Commissary General of the Virginia troops under Washington in Braddock's army, and he was present at the defeat of the latter in 1755, near the present Pittsburg, Pa. When he returned to Castle Hill from this expedition, he brought with him a stallion that lived to be forty-eight years old.

William C. Rives, Esq., of Newport, R. I., has in his possession the fragment of a letter from Mr. Jackson, of Fredericksburg, Va., to Dr. Thomas Walker, written a short time after Braddock's defeat. In this letter Mr. Jackson inquires after Dr. Walker's health and also that of Col. (afterward General) George Washington. He concludes by saying that "if he had not known of Braddock's defeat and had read that the Royal forces had been so badly beaten by half naked savages, he would have disbelieved it and would have burned ye book."

Dr. Thomas Walker and Andrew Lewis were appointed Commissioners on the part of the government of Virginia to treat with the Six Nations of Indians at Fort Stanwix, New York, in 1768. There were also Commissioners from New York, and this treaty occurred during the administration of Governor Johnson of New York.

Dr. Thomas Walker and his son, John Walker, were Commissioners on the part of Virginia to treat with the Indians at Pittsburg, Penn., about 1777, the object being to conciliate them during the war of the Revolution. Commissioners were also appointed by the American Government. Dr. Thomas Walker was the president of the meeting.

Dr. Walker was a member of the Virginia House of Burgesses in 1775, for organizing a plan of defence, and was also placed on the second General Committee of Safety (see Journal of Convention, 16th Dec., 1775). He was also, in 1778, Commissioner with David Smith, on the part of Virginia, to complete the boundary line between Virginia and North Carolina, from Steep Rock Creek to the Tennessee line.

In 1728, Col. William Byrd, William Dandridge, and Richard Fitz Williams, with Thomas and Mayo, as surveyors, ran the boundary line between Virginia and North Carolina, from the sea-coast to Peter's Creek, now in Patrick County, Va., a distance of about 240 miles. In 1749, Col. Joshua Fry and Peter Jefferson (father of Thomas Jefferson who was President U. S.) were commissioned on the part of Virginia to continue the line from Peter's Creek to Steep Rock Creek—about 40 miles. Lastly, it was completed to the Tennessee line, in 1778, as above-mentioned. The total length is about 320 miles. The last portion of the line surveyed is still known as Walker's line.

Colonel Byrd's MS. of his part of the work is at Lower Brandon, on James River, Prince George County, Va. It is neatly bound in book form and a number of copies have been printed.

It may be stated here that Peter's Creek in Patrick County, Petersburg in Dinwiddie County, and Peter's Mountain in Albemarle County, Va., are said to have been named after Peter Jefferson, the father of President Thomas Jefferson, U. S.

Dr. Walker was intimately connected both by public and private relations with Gen. George Washington and Thomas Jefferson, to the latter of whom he was guardian. Dr. Walker was married twice, and both of his wives were second cousins (or first cousins once removed) of Gen. George Washington in the following way:

Col. John Washington and Laurence Washington, sons of Leonard Washington, of Wharton, County Lancaster, England, and Anne, his wife, emigrated to America together in 1659. They settled in Westmoreland County, Va., and became the progenitors of the Washington families in that State. Gen. George Washington was descended from Col. John Washington by his second wife,

Anne Pope, of Bridges Creek, Westmoreland Co., Va., as follows: Col. John Washington and Anne Pope, his second wife, had, among other children, Laurence Washington, who married, about 1680, Mildred Warner, of Gloucester County, Va., and had by her three children, viz.:

(1) John Washington, married, about 1712, Catherine Whiting, of Gloucester County, Va. Had a large family, of whom Catherine married Fielding Lewis.

(2) Augustine Washington, married, first, 20th April, 1715, Jane Butler, and secondly, 6th March, $173\frac{0}{1}$, Mary Ball, by whom he had, among others, Gen. George Washington, born 22d February, 1732, and Col. Samuel Washington.

(3) Mildred Washington, who married, first, about 1705, Roger Gregory, of King and Queen County, Va., "and had by him 3 daughters, Frances, Mildred, and Elizabeth, who married 3 brothers, Col. Francis Thornton, Col. John Thornton, and Reuben Thornton, all of Spottsylvania County, Va. She had for her second husband Col. Henry Willis, of Fredericksburgh, Va., and by him the present Col. Lewis Willis, of Fredericksburgh" (See Gen. Geo. Washington's letter, dated 2d May, 1792).

Francis Thornton, progenitor of the Thornton Family in Virginia, settled in Caroline County. He was the father of the abovenamed three brothers, viz.:

(1) Col. John Thornton, who married Frances Gregory, and had: (*a*) Mildred Thornton, who was the second of the five wives of Col. Samuel Washington, the brother of Gen. George Washington; (*b*) Elizabeth Thornton, who was the second wife of Dr. Thomas Walker.

(2) Col. Francis Thornton married Mildred Gregory, and had Mildred Thornton, who married Charles Washington, brother of Gen. George Washington.

(3) Reuben Thornton married Elizabeth Gregory. His daughter, Mildred, married, first, in 1738, Nicholas Meriwether, by whom she had one child, viz.: Mildred Meriwether, born 19th May, 1739; married Colonel Syme, of Hanover County, Va. Nicholas Meriwether died, and his widow, Mildred Thornton Meriwether, married, secondly, in 1741, Dr. Thomas Walker, of Castle Hill, Albemarle Co., Va., and was his first wife.

It will thus be seen that the mothers of Dr. Walker's two wives were sisters, who were first cousins of Gen. George Washington, and that Dr. Walker's two wives were themselves first cousins, who were second cousins (or first cousins once removed) of Gen. George Washington.

According to some statements, Col. Samuel Washington's second wife was Mildred, daughter of Col. Francis Thornton.

Dr. Thomas Walker, by marrying the widow Meriwether, became possessed of the Castle Hill estate, comprising about 11,000 acres of land in Albemarle County, Va., which originally was part of a grant of land from George II. to a certain (Nicholas?) Meriwether. Subsequently the estates of Turkey Hill, Peachylorum, Belvoir, Kinloch, etc., were cut off from the original Castle Hill estate for Dr. Walker's children and grandchildren.

The exact date of the founding of the Castle Hill House is not certainly known. The old part of the present house was not quite finished in 1764, when Hon. Francis Walker was born. Dr. Walker must, therefore, have lived in some other house previous to that time, which has been removed. He probably lived at Fredericksburg, Va., up to the time of his removal to Castle Hill. The house built by Dr. Walker, and which was nearly finished in 1764, fronted northwest, toward the mountain; but in 1824 an addition was built by Hon. William C. Rives, so that the house then fronted southeast. The two wings, or greenhouses, were added by Mr. Rives in 1840.

The following inscriptions were copied from tombstones in the Walker burying-ground at Castle Hill, by Dr. William C. Rives of New York, 16th May, 1889:

My Father
Col: Francis
WALKER
Born at Castle
Hill June 22, 1764
Died March 1806
[On foot-stone.]
F. W.

IHS
My Brother
Thomas Hugh
WALKER
Born May 1800
Died Sep: 1807
[On foot-stone.]
T. H. W.

My Mother
Mrs. Jane Byrd
WALKER
Born (Nelson)
May 1775
Died Jan. 1808
[On foot-stone.]
J. B. W.

According to Dr. Rives, the situation of the graves could only be conjectured by the position of the stones, some of which had fallen down. No other graves could be made out. They were inclosed by a brick wall, the entrance of which was probably formerly occupied by a gate, but which was perfectly open.

What is known as the Albemarle Pippin, probably the most deliciously flavored apple in the world, is nothing more than the Newtown Pippin of New York State, which is said to have been introduced into Albemarle County, Va., by Dr. Thomas Walker. The climate of Albemarle and nature of the soil are peculiarly adapted to the perfection of this justly celebrated fruit. These apples are so delicate that they decay very easily, and hence each apple should be culled separately and carefully packed in clean hay for preservation.

It was on the 4th of June, 1781, according to Lossing (see "Field Book of the Revolution"), when Tarleton, with his British troopers, on their way to Charlottesville, Va., appeared at Castle Hill and demanded breakfast. Among the rebels surprised there were William and Robert, brothers of Gov. Thomas Nelson, of Yorktown, Va., and Francis Kinloch. In their attempt to escape, the latter was pursued into the vineyard field by a British soldier, who shouted, "Stop, cousin Frank; you know I could always beat you running." Whereupon the cousin Frank surrendered to an old acquaintance and relative.

Living at Castle Hill at that time was a colored lad, about eleven years old, named THOMAS WILKES. Dr. Walker brought him to Castle Hill from King and Queen County, Va., and subsequently employed him as his body servant. He was also at one time fifer of the Eighty-eighth Virginia Regiment. He lived to an old age, and became known far and near as "Uncle Tom." He died about 1860, aged about 90 years.

According to Uncle Tom, Tarleton's men were mostly armed with halberds and spontoons. They are a sort of spear, and samples of these weapons are seen in the Tower of London, in the room called The Horse Armory. Tarleton was on his way to Charlottesville, Albemarle Co., Va., having received orders from Cornwallis to capture Gov. Thomas Jefferson (afterward President United States), and members of the Virginia Legislature, there assembled.

Tarleton was detained at Castle Hill about the breakfast, for more reasons than one. The cook stated that the soldiers forcibly carried off the food as fast as she could prepare it. This put Tarleton out of humor, and when he was told that some of his men were breaking open the stables and stealing the horses, he lost all patience and beame furious. The culprits were seized, and, according to Uncle Tom, punished in a terrible manner. Having been stripped to the waist, they were bound across tobacco hogsheads. In this position they were flogged with a perforated sole-leather paddle. The screams of the unfortunate creatures attested the severity of the punishment; but none except those who have heard Uncle Tom imitate their cries can fully appreciate it.

Meantime, a Mr. Jewitt, or Jouitte, of Louisa County, had ridden on ahead, and informed Governor Jefferson, who barely had time to escape into the woods. According to Lossing, *op. cit.*, Tarleton had pushed on to Castle Hill, "where he understood many influential Virginians were assembled. Several of these were captured, among whom were William and Robert, brothers of Gov. Thomas Nelson. . . . The delay for breakfast at Dr. Walker's was sufficient to allow most of the members of the Legislature at Charlottesville to escape. Mr. Jefferson had not been gone ten minutes when the British troopers rode up and found the Monticello mansion deserted."

According to Uncle Tom, Dr. Walker was accustomed to meet with Indian chiefs under an oxheart cherry tree that stood in the then rear of the house, but which subsequently died, and was removed about 1854. He said that he never heard the Indians talk much, as they eyed him very suspiciously. He, however, remembered to have heard one of the Sachems say with much excitement, "DOMI-NICKAH-HEE-HAY-SKEESH-SKEESH!"

Uncle Tom used to say that Dr. Walker had a remarkable dog named Bowser. The doctor went out once upon a time and remained absent among the Indians for the space of seven years. Upon his return to Castle Hill one evening, his dog, who had not seen him in all that time, recognized his voice, and broke through a shutter in getting out of a room to meet him. The identical shutter was at Castle Hill in 1852, and Uncle Tom always took great pride in showing it.

He also used to say that Dr. Walker was very careful with everything that might be of use. On a certain occasion he was going to split a nice piece of timber for kindling wood, but the doctor saw him and bade him put it into the barn. "If it is not wanted for some useful purpose in seven years," said he, "go there then and turn it over."

It may be said of Uncle Tom, that whenever he was much pleased with any one, he had a peculiar way of expressing his hope of seeing him again soon upon his taking leave, thus: "Good mornin', sir. I shall see you again, as the bull said to the haystack!"

For a history of Walker's Parish, in the County of Albemarle, see Bishop Meade, *op. cit.*, Vol. II., p. 41 *et seq.* "Thomas Jefferson (afterward President United States) and Nicholas Meriwether," says Bishop Meade, "laid off two acres for Walker's Church, by order of the Vestry of Fredericksville Parish. The land was given by Dr. Thomas Walker. An old mountain chapel stood here first, the age of which is not known," etc. The old mountain chapel was succeeded by Walker's Church, which, in 1855, was replaced by the beautiful Gothic edifice known as Grace Church. This building, an ornament of which any community may be proud, is made of freestone, quarried in the neighborhood, and the interior is finished off with carved oak and Virginia pine. The windows are of stained glass. The three marble tablets that stand in the rear of the chancel were the gift of the late Mrs. Henry Sigourney (Amélie Louise Rives), of Boston, Mass., who was lost on the ill-fated steamer *Ville du Havre*, 22d November, 1873. These tablets are framed in carved oak, and have inscribed upon them the Ten Commandments. Lewis Rogers, of New York, gave $3,000. The bell in the tower was presented by David Sears, Esq., of Boston, Mass. It weighs 1,575 pounds, and was cast by Mr. Hooper, of that city.

On the 1st January, 1845, according to the record on the Vestry-book of Walker's Parish, Albemarle Co., Va., Dr. Mann Page, of Turkey Hill, Francis K. Nelson, Esq., of Cloverfields, Hon. William C. Rives, of Castle Hill, and James Terrell, Esq., of Music Hall, residents of the said parish, were appointed a committee to take such necessary measures as they might deem expedient, for commencing and proceeding with the building of a new church. Owing to the estimated cost of the building, however, the corner-stone was not laid until about 1848. Soon after this occurred, Hon. William C. Rives was appointed American Minister to France, and was absent four years. Meantime, Dr. Mann Page and James Terrell, Esq., both died, so that for some time the work was postponed. Hon. William C. Rives returned to Castle Hill in the autumn of 1853, and it was chiefly due to the energy and devotion of Mrs. Rives that the building was completed early in 1855. It was named Grace Church, and was consecrated on the 9th May, 1855, by Bishop William Meade, of Virginia. Edward C. Mead, of Keswick, Thomas W. Page, of Turkey Hill, and Charlotte N. Meriwether, of Kinloch (afterward the second wife of Thomas J. Randolph, Jr.), all of Albemarle County, Va., were the first persons ever confirmed in the new building. They were confirmed by Bishop William Meade, of Virginia, who laid his hands first on Edward C. Mead. The first marriage occurred on March 15th, 1855, and was that of James Terrell Bacon, of Boston, Mass., to Miss Susan Stanford Lewis, of Albemarle. Their daughter Susie recently married Mr. Money, of Albemarle Co., Va.

In 1889 a tablet was placed in the church by the vestry, at the expense of Dr. R. C. M. Page, giving the date of its corner-stone laying and consecration. The following is an exact copy:

GRACE CHURCH
WALKER'S PARISH, ALBEMARLE COUNTY,
VIRGINIA.

THE CORNER-STONE WAS LAID
5th Oct. 1848,
BY THE REV. E. BOYDEN,
WHO WAS CALLED TO THIS PARISH IN 1839,
AND WAS ITS FAITHFUL RECTOR
DURING FORTY-ONE YEARS.
The Building,
FIRST OPENED FOR DIVINE SERVICE
22nd APRIL 1855,
WAS CONSECRATED
TO THE WORSHIP OF GOD
On the 9th of May of the Same Year
BY THE RT. REV. WILLLIAM MEADE, D.D.
Bishop of Virginia.

THE VESTRY HAVE CAUSED
THIS COMMEMORATIVE TABLET
To be Erected A.D. 1889.

The following clipping from the Charlottesville *Jeffersonian* regarding the Albemarle court-house will be of interest:

EDITORS JEFFERSONIAN: The question of a new Court-house being before the public, the following letter and account which my brother, Thos. W. Page, found among his great-grandfather's papers, may be of interest.

Yours truly,
FREDERICK W. PAGE.

Charlottesville, February 25, 1886.

(From an old photograph.)

GRACE CHURCH,

WALKER'S PARISH, ALBEMARLE CO., VA.

Consecrated 9th May, 1855.

W^{ms}BURG, March 6, 1762.

SIR: Colonel Richard Randolph has made application to me in Council in Relation to the Writ of adjournment for Albemarle Court-house. He alledges that the Spot of Ground on wch it is agreed the Court-house should be placed, was improperly call'd Hughes's Land; but that the property was in lien, he never having disposed of it to Hughes as was supposed. He further says that Mr. Hughes having some other Land not far off, advantage is proposed to be taken of the place having been call'd Hughes's Land, by setting the Court house on that Land belonging to Hughes. I should be very glad to know how this affair stands, for if the Spot proposed is acquiesced in, let the Land be whose it may, I need not give the Council any trouble about it by laying it before them; but if the point should be controverted, I must lay it before them for their Consideration and Determination thereon.

From my thorough knowledge of you, I rely on your setting this matter in its true Light to me, wch will oblige

Sir,

Your very humble

Servant,

FRAN.: FAUQUIER.

To Mr. Commissary Walker.

(Endorsed). "The Governor's Letter with ye copys of ye order of Court and Council for remov^{l} y^{e} Court House."

DR. THOS. WALKER.

DR.			CR.
1430 Acres Land @ £30 p. c.	£429	....Cash re'd of Stephen Hughes at twice	£183
2 years rent 6	12	....Bal. due	258
	441		441
Bal. per contra	258	....Oct. 30, cash of Col. Tucker	200
Int. from Jan'y 6, to Oct. 30	10 9. $7\frac{1}{2}$	....Bal. due	68 9. $7\frac{1}{2}$
	268. 9. $7\frac{1}{2}$		268. 9 $7\frac{1}{2}$
Bal. per contra	68. 9 $7\frac{1}{2}$		
$1\frac{1}{2}$ months' interest	8 6		
	£68. 18. $1\frac{1}{2}$	....Dec. 20, order on Alex. Mc-Cawl	£68 18 $1\frac{1}{2}$

1762, Dec 20th, E. E. RICHARD RANDOLPH.

(Endorsed). "Col. Richard Randolph's acct. for ye Court-house Land."

Dr. Thomas Walker married, first, in 1741, Mildred Thornton, widow of Nicholas Meriwether. She was born 19th March, 1721, and died 16th Nov., 1778, aged 57 years, and was buried at Castle Hill.

He married, secondly, about 1781, Elizabeth Thornton, first cousin of his first wife. There was no issue by this marriage. His second wife becoming a widow, married Alcock, a British officer, and removed from Castle Hill to Eldon, near Cobham, Albemarle Co., Va. In 1859 Eldon became the residence of Carter H. Page, Esq. Alcock had been a Revolutionary prisoner of war at Charlottesville, same county, Va.

While Dr. Walker was going to Fredericksburg, Va., to his second marriage, it is said that he was stopped by the British soldiers whom he met on the way, but when they ascertained the object of his journey, they let him through their lines. The children by his first marriage were as follows:

1. Mary Walker ("Capt. Moll, of local fame."—*Duke*), born at Castle Hill 24th July, 1742; married, about 1760, Nicholas Lewis, grandfather of the late Capt. Robert Lewis, of Castalia, Albemarle Co., Va., who married, about 1835, Sally Craven, of Pen Park, same county. Of their children, Thomas Lewis married, 1874, Jane Walker Page, of Millwood. (See Page Family, North End.)
2. Hon. John Walker, eldest son, born at Castle Hill, 13th February, 174$\frac{3}{4}$; removed to Belvoir, Albemarle Co., Va., and married, about 1764, Elizabeth Moore.
3. Susan Walker (called Suky), born at Castle Hill, 14th December, 1746; married, in June, 1764, Henry Fry, whose descendants now live in Albemarle County, Va.
4. Thomas Walker, Jr., second and only son to have male issue, was born at Castle Hill, Albemarle Co., Va., 17th March, 174$\frac{8}{9}$, and removed to Indian Fields, same county. He married, about 1773, Margaret Hoops, of Pennsylvania.
5. Lucy Walker, born at Castle Hill, 5th May, 1751; married, about 1771, Dr. George Gilmer, of Pen Park, Albemarle Co., Va. Children:
   (1) James Gilmer, born about 1772; died without issue.
   (2) Mildred Gilmer (called Milly), born about 1774; married, about 1794, Hon. William Wirt, Attorney-General, author of the "British Spy," etc.
   (3) George Gilmer, born about 1776; married, about 1801, Miss Hudson, and had (*a*) Thomas Walker Gilmer, Governor of Virginia, father of the late Rev. Thomas Walker Gilmer of the Presbyterian

Church who married Patty Minor of Albemarle Co., Va., and died, leaving one child, Thomas Walker Gilmer; Juliet Gilmer; James Gilmer, lawyer, removed to Texas; and Lizzie Gilmer, married St. George Tucker, and their daughter married a son of ex-President Tyler; (b) Christopher (called Kit); (c) John Harmer; (d) Anne, married Peter McGhee; (e) Mrs. Adams, who was the mother of Miss Mattie Adams; (f) Lucy married E. S. Pegram. Governor Gilmer was accidentally killed on board the *Princeton*, U. S. man-of-war, 28th February, 1844, by the bursting of a cannon. He was then Secretary U. S. Navy, his appointment having been made by President John Tyler, 14th February, 1844. Mr. Upshur, Secretary of State, was also killed at the same time. Mr. Gilmer was succeeded by John Y. Mason as Secretary U. S. Navy, and Mr. Upshur by John C. Calhoun, as Secretary of State. Hon. William Wilkins, of Pennsylvania, was at that time Secretary of War. President Tyler and Hon. and Mrs. William C. Rives were on board when the sad accident occurred.

(4) Peachy Gilmer, born about 1778, wife unknown. They had: (a) William Wirt Gilmer (called Billy Gilmer); died single. (b) Dr. Peachy Harmer Gilmer, married Isabella Walker; (c) George H. Gilmer, Judge of Pittsylvania County; (d) Francis W. Gilmer; (e) Mrs. Wilmer; (f) Mrs. Emina Gilmer Breckinridge, of Botetourt County, Va.

(5) Dr. John Gilmer, born about 1778; married, about 1805, Miss Minor, and had two daughters, one of whom died single; the other married Franklin Minor, whose descendants live in Albemarle County, Va.

(6) Lucy Gilmer, born about 1782; married, about 1802, Peter Minor, of Albemarle County, Va.

(7) Susan Gilmer, born about 1784.

(8) Harmer Gilmer, born about 1786.

(9) Francis Walker Gilmer, born about 1788; unmarried; Professor of Law at the University of Virginia, author and scholar. He was sent by Thomas Jefferson (ex-President United States) to England, for the purpose of procuring professors for the University of Virginia, near Charlottesville, Albemarle Co., Va.

6. Elizabeth Walker (called Betsey), born at Castle Hill, 1st August, 1753; married, about 1773, Rev. Matthew Maury, second rector of old Walker's (now Grace) Church, in Walker's Parish, Albemarle Co., Va., and had Reuben, Polly, Milly, Elizabeth, Kitty, John, Fontaine, Thomas, and Walker. Their descendants live in Albemarle County, Va.

7. Mildred Walker (called Milly), born at Castle Hill, 5th June, 1755; married, about 1775, Joseph Hornsby, of Williamsburg, James City Co., Va. No issue.

8. Sarah Walker, born at Castle Hill, 28th March, 1758; married, about

1778, Col. Reuben Lindsay, of Albemarle County, Va., and was his first wife. Children:

(1) Mildred Lindsay; probably died single.

(2) Sally Lindsay; married, about 1810, her first cousin, Capt. James Lindsay, of The Meadows, Louisa County, Va. He was the son of David Lindsay, who was the brother of Col. Reuben Lindsay. They had two children, one of whom died; the other, Mildred Lindsay, married, 1837, Alexander Taylor, and died leaving two children, viz.: Sally Lindsay Taylor, who married, 1858, Col. John M. Patton, and died 1872, aged 34, leaving children; and Fannie Taylor, who was smothered to death by wheat in Warwick & Barksdale's flouring mill, in Richmond, Va., 1850, aged 13 years.

9. Martha Walker, born at Castle Hill, 2d May, 1760; married, about 1780, George Divers, of Farmington, Albemarle Co., Va. No issue.

10. Reuben Walker, born 8th October, 1762, died 23d August, 1765, aged 3 years.

11. Hon. Francis Walker, born at Castle Hill, Albemarle Co., Va., 22d June, 1764; resided there. He married, 1798, Jane Byrd Nelson, of Yorktown, Va.

12. Peachy Walker, youngest, born at Castle Hill, 6th February, 1767; married, about 1787, Joshua Fry, of Kentucky, and had issue. Anne Fry, their daughter, married, about 1810, Mr. Bullit, of Kentucky, and had issue. Among the descendants of Joshua Fry and Peachy Walker, his wife, was James Speed, Attorney-General in Mr. Lincoln's cabinet.

V. HON. JOHN WALKER, of Belvoir, Albemarle Co., Va., eldest son and second child of Dr. Thomas Walker, of Castle Hill, same county, Va., and Mildred Thornton, the widow of Nicholas Meriwether, his first wife, was born at Castle Hill, 13th February, 1744, and died 2d December, 1809, aged 65 years. He was buried at Belvoir, although his death occurred in a house near Madison's Mill, Orange Co., Va., some distance from Orange Court House, while he was on his way to Philadelphia, Pa., to undergo a surgical operation. A ruptured artery was the immediate cause of his death. No operation had been performed. The hemorrhage occurred while Hon. Col. John Walker was in his carriage. He was speedily removed to the house aforesaid, but he expired a few moments afterward. His wife, Elizabeth Moore, daughter of Bernard Moore, of Chelsea, King William Co., Va., died about the same time—in December, 1809. She was ill at Belvoir when he left home for Philadelphia. Her sister, Anne Butler Moore, married, in 1770, Charles Carter, of Fredericksburg, Va., and was his second wife.

Their daughter, Anne Hill Carter, was born in 1773, and married General Lee (Light Horse Harry), of Revolutionary fame.

The following is a copy of the correspondence between Dr. Thomas Walker and Bernard Moore, in regard to the marriage of Hon. Col. John Walker to Elizabeth Moore:

May 27th, 1764.

Dear Sir: My son, Mr. John Walker, having informed me of his intention to pay his addresses to your daughter, Elizabeth, if he should be agreeable to yourself, lady and daughter, it may not be amiss to inform you what I feel myself able to afford for their support, in case of an union. My affairs are in an uncertain state; but I will promise one thousand pounds, to be paid in 1766, and the further sum of two thousand pounds I promised to give him; but the uncertainty of my present affairs prevents my fixing on a time of payment —the above sums are all to be in money or lands and other effects, at the option of my said son, John Walker.

I am, sir, your humble servant,

Thomas Walker.

Col. Bernard Moore, Esqr.,
in King William.

May 28th, 1764.

Dear Sir: Your son, Mr. John Walker, applied to me for leave to make his addresses to my daughter, Elizabeth. I gave him leave, and told him at the same time that my affairs were in such a state that it was not in my power to pay him all the money this year that I intended to give my daughter, provided he succeeded; but would give him five hundred pounds more as soon after as I could raise or get the money; which sums you may depend I will most punctually pay to him.

I am, sir, your obedient servant,

Bernard Moore.

To Thomas Walker,
Castle Hill, Albemarle County, Va.

Hon. John Walker was United States Senator from Virginia in 1790. He was also Confidential Aid to General George Washington during the Revolutionary War, and was also known as Colonel John Walker.

The following is a copy of a letter from General George Washington to Patrick Henry, in regard to the above-mentioned John Walker:

TO PATRICK HENRY, Governor of Virginia.

MORRISTOWN, 24th Feby, 1777.

DEAR SIR: Mr. Walker, I doubt not, informed you of the situation in which I have placed him, in order that he may obtain the best information, and, at the same time, have his real design hid from the world; thereby avoiding the evils which might otherwise result from such appointments, if adopted by other States. It will naturally occur to you, sir, that there are some secrets which cannot, or at least ought not, to be entrusted to paper, nay, which none but the Commander-in-Chief at the time should be acquainted with. If Mr. Walker's commission, therefore, from the Commonwealth of Virginia, should be known, it would, I am persuaded, be followed by others of the like nature from other States, which would be no better than so many marplots. To avoid the precedent, therefore, and from your character of Mr. Walker, and the high opinion I myself entertain of his abilities, honor and prudence, I have taken him into my family as an extra Aid-de-Camp, and shall be happy if, in this character, he can answer your expectations. I sincerely thank you, sir, for your kind congratulations on the latter success of the Continental arms (would God it may continue), and your polite mention of me. Let me earnestly entreat that the troops, raised in Virginia for this army, be forwarded on, by companies or otherwise, without delay, and as well equipped as possible for the field, or we shall be in no condition to open the campaign. With every sentiment of respect and sympathy,

I am, dear sir, &c., &c.,

GEORGE WASHINGTON.

(See "Writings of George Washington," by Jared Sparks, Vol. IV., p. 329. Boston: Russell, Odiorne & Metcalf; and Hilliard, Gray & Co., 1834.)

The location known as Belvoir is about three miles southwest from Castle Hill, Ablemarle Co., Va., and was first settled by LEWIS. The remains of the old Lewis family burying-ground were for a long time to be seen, but nearer to the mountain than the house built by Col. John Walker. The original Belvoir settlement was undoubtedly made by LEWIS, who married MERIWETHER. It was to the latter family that all the land in this part of the county was originally granted by George II. The Lewis house was somewhere near the old Lewis burial-ground, but has long since passed away.

Hon. Col. John Walker married Elizabeth Moore in 1764, and it was about that time that he built his first house. This house was taken down when the second house was to be built, and moved to Milton, on the Rivanna River, Albemarle Co., Va. It was afterward moved down to its present location, near Cobham, same county, and is the same that was occupied by Howell Lewis. The second house was built about 1790. This was destroyed by fire in the autumn of 1836. It was thought that the fire was occasioned by a defective flue (loose mortar in the chimney) in the garret, as it was first discovered at that point adjoining the southwest chimney. The following is the ground plan of this second Belvoir House, built by Hon. Col. John Walker in 1790:

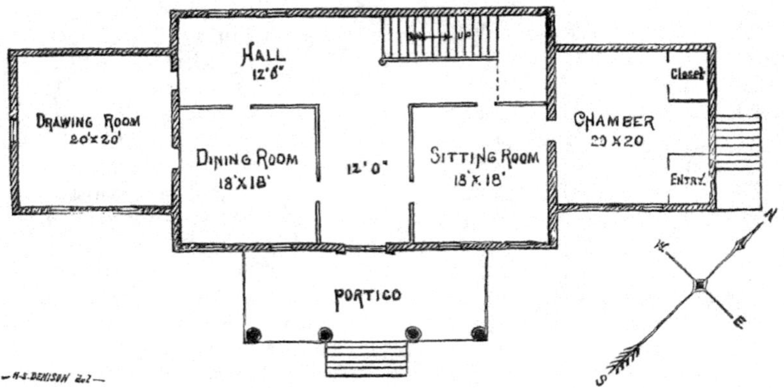

There were four rooms on the first floor and three rooms upstairs on the second floor. Above this was a very large garret. About fifty yards northeast from the house was the kitchen, and at the same distance southwest was an outhouse or office. Still further southwest were stables, near the mountain road.

Just in rear of the house was an ornamental garden, and behind this was the kitchen garden. At the north corner was a lot planted in fine trees and shrubs, and at the northern extremity of the latter was the cemetery. The road, with magnificent oaks and poplars on each side, wound gracefully along from the house to the public highway that runs between Gordonsville and Charlottesville, and entered it a little east of a point opposite old Walker's (now Grace) Church.

The Belvoir estate was inherited by Eliza Kinloch, only grandchild of Hon. Col. John Walker, and she married Hon. Hugh Nelson (see President Nelson). After the death of the latter, it was divided, and the home part fell to the youngest son, Dr. Robert W. Nelson, of Charlottesville, Albemarle Co., Va. He sold it in 1846 to D. C. Carver.

Hon. Col. John Walker married, in 1764, Elizabeth, daughter of Bernard Moore, of Chelsea, King William Co., Va. She was a granddaughter of Col. Sir Alexander Spottswood, Knight and Aid-de-Camp to the Duke of Marlborough at the battle of Blenheim. He was Governor of the Colony of Virginia, and founder of the so-called MOORE HOUSE, at Yorktown, York Co., Va.

(From a drawing by B. H. Toquet, New York, 1881.)

BELVOIR, ALBEMARLE COUNTY, VIRGINIA,
RESIDENCE OF UNITED STATES SENATOR JOHN WALKER, 1790.
Destroyed by fire, 1836.

They had only one child, viz.:

1. Mildred Walker, born at Chelsea, King William Co., Va., 1st August, 1765, and married, at Belvoir, 22d February, 1781, Francis Kinloch, of Charleston, S. C. They in turn had only one child:
   (1) Eliza Kinloch, born 31st December, 1781; married, 28th April, 1799, Hon. Hugh Nelson, fifth child and son of Gov. Thomas Nelson, of Yorktown, York Co., Va.

   Mildred Walker died 17th October, 1784, and Francis Kinloch married, secondly, Anne Middleton, of South Carolina. There is no surviving male issue of Francis Kinloch.

The following is copied from a letter in regard to the Kinloch family in South Carolina:

CHARLESTON, S. C., January 30th, 1883.

DR. R. CHANNING M. PAGE, New York City.

DEAR SIR: I am just in receipt of your favor of the 28th inst., and hasten to reply. Our name is usually pronounced KINLAW. The Francis Kinloch to whom you refer as having married, 22d February, 1781, Mildred Walker, of Belvoir, Albemarle Co., Va., has now no representative of the name. I know one of his granddaughters very well—Mrs. Singleton, of Columbia, S. C. This lady and her sons and one daughter are special friends of my own. The family of Kinloch, to which I belong, in this State, is large. We do not know of any positive relationship with the family of the above-named Francis Kinloch, but members of each family have talked it over, and we believe that such relationship does exist. My father came to this country from England when quite young; but originally his ancestors were from Scotland. It will afford me pleasure to meet you, should you come this way.

Very truly yours,

R. A. KINLOCH, M.D.

V. THOMAS WALKER, JR., OF INDIAN FIELDS, Albemarle Co., Va., fourth child and second son (being the eldest to have male issue) of Dr. Thomas Walker, of Castle Hill, Albemarle Co., Va., and Mildred Thornton, the widow of Nicholas Meriwether, his first wife, third child and second son of Thomas Walker, of King and Queen County, Va., and Susanna (Peachy), his wife, grandson (?) of Thomas Walker, of Gloucester County, Va., who was a member of the Virginia Assembly in 1662, progenitor of the Walker Family in Virginia, was born at Castle Hill, Albemarle Co., Va., 17th March, 1749. The mill on the public road near Indian Fields, now known as Cowherd's Mill, was built by Thomas Walker, and a stone in the front wall of the building has inscribed on it the initials "T. W.," also the date of its erection.

He married, about 1774, Margaret Hoops, of Carlisle, Pa., whose father is said to have educated Benjamin West, the artist. Some of their children are known to have died infants, and others are probably not recorded. He alone of the sons of Dr. Thomas Walker had male issue. Their children were as follows:

1. Jane Walker, born about 1775; married, about 1795, Mr. Rice, of Charlotte County, Va.
2. Elizabeth Walker, born about 1777; married, 1822, Mr. Michie, of Albemarle County, Va. No issue. She became blind, and was known as Cousin Betsey Michie; but retained her maiden name of Walker on the Maury monument at Grace Church. This monument was erected in memory of Rev. James Maury (father of Matthew), who was the first Rector of old Walker's Church. His wife was a Miss Walker—probably a cousin of Dr. Thomas Walker—and it was no doubt in this way that he became Rector of Walker's Church. The following is the inscription: "Sacred to the Memory of Rev. James Maury, first Pastor of Walker's Parish. Born April 8th, 1717. Died June 9th, 1769. This Monument was erected by Elizabeth Walker, as a tribute to his Piety, learning and worth." She was an authoress of considerable local fame; a novel of some length and merit by her was published in the *Southern Literary Messenger*. The monument marks the spot in old Walker's Church where the pulpit stood under which he was buried.
3. Maria Barclay Walker, born 1780; married, in 1805, Richard Duke, an architect, of Albemarle County, Va., by whom many of the ancient barns and machines in that county were constructed. He was the son of Clivears Duke, who was the son of Clevieures Duke, whose grandfather was Col. Henry Duke of Gov. Nicholson's Council, whose sister was Elizabeth Duke, wife of Nathaniel Bacon, the rebel. Children:
   (1) William Johnson Duke, eldest, born 1807; married, in 1844, Miss Anderson, of Kentucky, and died, leaving Richard, Florence, and Laura.
   (2) Lucy A. Duke; married, first, Wood, of Tennessee, and, secondly, Bills, of the same State.
   (3) Mary J. C. Duke; married Smith, deceased, of Texas.
   (4) Margaret Hoops Duke; died single.
   (5) Elizabeth Duke; married Rhodes, deceased.
   (6) Mildred Wirt Duke, married George Christopher Gilmer, called Kit, brother of Gov. Gilmer.
   (7) Hon. Richard Thomas Walker Duke, of Charlottesville, Albemarle Co., Va.; Member of Congress, Commonwealth's Attorney, etc.; married Miss Eskridge, and has two sons and one daughter.
   (8) Sallie F. Duke; married Deskins; she died, leaving one daughter.
   (9) Charles Carroll Duke, of Mississippi; married Hattie Walker, and has two daughters.

(10) Mattie L. Duke; single. Resided with Mrs. Smith, at Morea, University of Virginia.

4. Thomas Walker, Jr., born at Indian Fields about 1785; died infant.
5. Martha Walker, born about 1788; married, about 1808, Mr. Goolsby, of Kentucky.
6. John Walker, born about 1790; died infant.
7. Captain Meriwether Lewis Walker, born at Indian Fields, Albemarle Co., Va., about 1792; removed to Logan, same county, Va. He married, about 1817, Maria Lindsay, and had male issue.

(From a miniature painting.)

JANE BYRD NELSON,
WIFE OF HON. FRANCIS WALKER, OF CASTLE HILL.
Married 1798.

V. HON. FRANCIS WALKER, of Castle Hill, Albemarle Co., Va., eleventh child and fourth and youngest son of Dr. Thomas Walker, of same place, and Mildred Thornton, the widow of Nicholas Meriwether, his first wife, was born there 22d June, 1764, and died there in 1806, aged 42 years.

He was a Representative in the U. S. Congress from the counties of Orange and Albemarle, 1793–1795.

His watch that was worn by his sister-in-law, Maria Nelson, at the Virginia Richmond Theatre when it was destroyed by fire, 26th December, 1811, came into the possession of Dr. Robert W. Nelson, of Charlottesville, Albemarle Co., Va. A little diamond from this watch is now the property of Dr. R. C. M. Page, of New York City, who had it set in the back of his own watch, with the following inscription:

"This diamond belonged to Hon. Francis Walker's watch, by which was identified the body of his sister-in-law, Maria Nelson, who was burned in the Richmond Theatre, 26th Decr., 1811, æt. 17.

"LONDON, July 1st, 1889."

Hon. Francis Walker married, 1798, Jane Byrd, eldest child of Col. Hugh Nelson, of Yorktown, York Co., Va., and Judith Page, his wife. Their children were:

1. Jane Frances Walker, born in the Nelson House, Yorktown, York Co., Va., 17th February, 1799, and married, in Richmond, Va., 12th December, 1815, Dr. Mann Page, of Keswick (Turkey Hill), Albemarle Co., Va. She died at Turkey Hill, 7th February, 1873, aged 74 years. (See Page Family, North End.)
2. Thomas Hugh Walker, only son, born 1800; died infant, in 1805, aged 5 years.
3. Judith Page Walker, born at Castle Hill, Albemarle Co., Va., 24th March, 1802; married, 24th March, 1819, Hon. William C. Rives, U. S. Senator from Virginia. She died at Castle Hill, where she resided, 23d January, 1882, aged 80 years. Children:
   (1) Francis Robert Rives, eldest, of New York City, born at Castle Hill, 1822. He was Secretary of the U. S. Legation, in London, 1842–1845, when Hon. Edward Everett was Minister there, during President Tyler's administration. Married, 1848, Matilda Antonia, only child of George Barclay, of New York City. Both are dead. They had: (*a*) George Lockhart Rives; married, first, 1873, Caroline Kean, of Elizabeth City, N. J., who died, leaving issue; married, second, Mrs. Belmont, of New York, by whom he also has issue; (*b*) Ella Louisa Rives; married, 1875, David King, Jr., of Newport, R. I., and has children; (*c*) Francis R. Rives, Jr.; married, first, 1879, Georgia Fellows, of New York City, who died without issue; he married a second time and died without issue; (*d*) Constance Rives, married Borland and has issue; (*e*) Maud Rives, twin sister to Constance; married, May, 1882, Walker Breese Smith, of New York City, and has issue; (*f*) Reginald William Rives, married, and has issue.

(2) William Cabell Rives, of Newport, R. I., born at Castle Hill, in 1825; died, 1890. He married, 1849, Grace Winthrop Sears, of Boston, Mass. Children: (*a*) Dr. William C. Rives, married, 1876, Mary F. Rhinelander, of New York City; (*b*) Alice Rives, died single; (*c*) Arthur Landon Rives.

(3) Alfred Landon Rives, born in 1830. He graduated with distinction at the *école des ponts et chaussés*, Paris. He served with General Meigs in the construction of the new wing of the Capitol at Washington, D. C., in 1859–60. He married, 1859, Sadie, daughter of James B. McMurdo, of Richmond, Va. Children: (*a*) Amélie Louise Rives, the authoress, married Archie Chanler; (*b*) Gertrude Rives, and (*c*) Sadie Rives.

(4) Amélie Louise Rives, born in Paris, 8th July, 1832. She was named after the wife of Louis Philippe, who was a great friend of the family. She married, 1854, Henry Sigourney, of Boston, Mass. They, with three children and nurse, were lost on board the ill-fated steamship, *Ville du Havre*, 22d November, 1873, leaving one survivor, Henry Sigourney, Jr.

(5) Ella Rives, died single, 1891.

The following inscription is copied from the tablet in Grace Church, Albemarle Co., Va.:

In Memory
of
The Beloved Wife
of
WILLIAM CABELL RIVES,
Judith Page Walker,
Born 24th March 1802
Died 23d January 1882.
The Vestry of Grace Church
Have caused the following Inscription
to be placed on this tablet
In token of their estimation
of her life and character;
Through her Munificence
And untiring efforts,
This Beautiful House of Worship
was erected.
It stands a Monument
To her Piety, Zeal, and Self Consecration
to the
Master
Whom she loved and served.
Though dead, her works
do follow her.

There is one also to Mr. and Mrs. Henry Sigourney, who were drowned at sea.

Hon. William C. Rives was born in Nelson County, Va., 4th May, 1793, and died at Castle Hill, Albemarle Co., Va., 25th April, 1868, aged 75 years. He was educated at Hampden Sidney College, and also at William and Mary College. He removed his residence to Castle Hill in 1821.

1809–11, he studied law under Thomas Jefferson.

1814–15, Aide-de-camp to Gen. John H. Cocke, of Virginia.

1817–19, Member of the Virginia House of Delegates from Nelson County.

1821, Presidential elector.

1822–23, Member of the Virginia House of Delegates from Albemarle.

1823–29, Representative in the U. S. Congress.

1829–32, U. S. Minister to France, first time.

1832–34, 1836–39, 1841–45, U. S. Senator from Virginia.

1849–53, U. S. Minister to France, second time.

1853-68. Private life. Devoted his time to the internal improvements of Virginia, the Virginia Historical Society of which he was President, and his "History of the Life and Times of James Madison." In February, 1861, he was a delegate to the Peace Conference.

The following is an inscription on a tablet in Grace Church, Albemarle County, Va.:

In Memory
of
one of the Founders
of this Church.
WILLIAM CABELL RIVES, LL.D.
Statesman, Diplomatist, Historian.
Born 4th May, 1793,
Died 25th April, 1868.
Uniting a clear and capacious intellect,
A courageous and generous temper,
with sound learning
And commanding eloquence,
He won a distinguished place
among the foremost men
Whom Virginia has consecrated
To the service of the country;
While he added lustre to his talents,
By the purity and dignity
of his public career,
And adorned his private life
with all the virtues
which can grace the character
of Husband, Father, Friend and
CHRISTIAN.
"*Blessed are the dead which die in the* LORD."

VI. CAPTAIN MERIWETHER LEWIS WALKER, OF LOGAN (called after the Indian chief of that name), Albemarle Co., Va., sixth child and eldest surviving son of Thomas Walker, Jr., of Indian Fields, same county, Va., and Margaret Hoops, his wife, fourth child and second son (being the eldest to have male issue) of Dr. Thomas Walker, of Castle Hill, Albemarle Co., Va., and Mildred Thornton, the widow of Nicholas Meriwether, his first wife, third child and second son of Thomas Walker, of King and Queen County, Va., and Susanna (Peachy), his wife, grandson (?) of Thomas Walker, of Gloucester County, Va., member of the Virginia Assembly in 1662, and progenitor of the Walker Family in Virginia, was born at Indian Fields, about 1792, and died about 1861, aged about 69 years. He was generally known as Lewis Walker, or Captain Walker.

He married, about 1817, Maria, daughter of Col. Reuben Lindsay and Maria Tidwell, his second wife, and the sister of Elizabeth Lindsay, the wife of General William Fitzhugh Gordon, of Edgeworth, Albemarle Co., Va. Mrs. Maria L. Walker died about 1871, aged about 74 years, and her sister, Mrs. Gordon, who resided with her youngest son, Mason Gordon, at Charlottesville, Albemarle Co., Va., died August, 1886, aged 95.

The children of Captain M. Lewis Walker and Maria Lindsay, his wife, were:

1. Isabella Walker, called Belle, born about 1818; married, about 1836, Dr. Peachy Harmer Gilmer, and had:
   (1) Margaret W. Gilmer, burned to death in 1854, when the Indian Fields house was destroyed by fire.
   (2) Walker Gilmer.
2. DR. THOMAS L. WALKER, eldest son, born at Logan, Albemarle Co., Va., about 1820, removed to Lynchburg, Va. Being the eldest son of the eldest son, etc., he is the representative descendant of Dr. Thomas Walker, of Castle Hill, Albemarle Co., Va. He married, about 1855, Miss Dabney, and has issue.
3. Reuben Lindsay Walker, born at Logan, Albemarle Co., about 1828, removed to Richmond, Va. He married, first, about 1848, Miss Eskridge, of Staunton, Augusta Co., Va., by whom he had several children. Of these Francis Walker married, 1879, Miss Pryor, daughter of Judge Roger A. Pryor, of the Court of Common Pleas, New York City, but formerly of Virginia. R. Lindsay Walker married, secondly, about 1858, Sally Elam, and has issue.
4. Margaret Walker, born about 1832; married, about 1856, William H. Pryor.

PART IV.

PENDLETON FAMILY.

(From an etching by H. B. Hall, Morrisania, N. Y., 1872.)

JUDGE EDMUND PENDLETON,

EDMUNDSBURY, CAROLINE CO., VA.

Died 23d October, 1803, aged 82.

PENDLETON FAMILY.

The following is a brief account of the Pendleton family in Virginia:

Henry Pendleton, of Norwich, England, had two sons: (1) Nathaniel Pendleton, minister in the Established Church of England, who died without any known issue, and (2) Philip Pendleton.

I. PHILIP PENDLETON, OF NORWICH, ENGLAND, and New Kent County, Va., about the second son of Henry Pendleton, of the first-named place, was born there in 1650. He emigrated to the Colony of Virginia in 1674, and settling in that portion of New Kent County, Va., which now forms Caroline County, became the progenitor of the Pendleton Family in Virginia. He died in the last-named county in 1721, aged 71 years.

He went to England on a visit in 1680, and upon his returning to Virginia, he married, in 1682, Isabella Hert (pronounced Hart). They had three sons and four daughters, whose descendants are scattered in every direction.

II. HENRY PENDLETON, ELDEST SON AND CHILD of Philip Pendleton, of Norwich, England, and Caroline County, Va., progenitor of the Pendleton Family in Virginia, and Isabella Hert (pronounced Hart), his wife, was born in Caroline County, Va., in 1683, and died there in May, 1721, aged 38 years.

He married, in 1703, Mary, daughter of James Taylor. She was born in 1688, survived him, and married, secondly, Ed. Watkins. She died in 1770, aged 82. Henry Pendleton and Mary Taylor, his wife, had five sons and two daughters. The two daughters married Gaines, and one of them, Isabella, was the grandmother of General E. P. Gaines, of the United States army.

Of the five sons, we shall only notice JUDGE EDMUND PENDLETON and JOHN PENDLETON. The other three sons married Barbours, Turners, etc.

JUDGE EDMUND PENDLETON, of Edmundsbury, Caroline Co., Va., fifth child and son of Henry Pendleton, of the same county, and Mary Taylor, his wife, was born 9th September, 1721, and died at Richmond, Va., 23d October, 1803, aged 82 years. He married, first, in January, 1741, Elizabeth Roy, who died in November following, leaving one child, a son, who died infant.

He married, secondly, in June, 1743, Sarah Pollard, by whom he had no issue.

There are on record in the Virginia Land Registry Office, grants in his name numbering nearly 10,000 acres. The following autobiography is copied from the Richmond (Virginia) *Enquirer*, of the issue of April 11th, 1828:

"I was born September 9th, 1721; my father died some time before. In February, 1734-35, I was bound apprentice to Col. Benjamin Robinson, Clerk of Caroline Court. In 1737 I was made Clerk of the Vestry of St. Mary's Parish, in Caroline; with the profits I purchased a few books, and read them very diligently. In 1740 I was made Clerk of Caroline Court-Martial. In April, 1741, with my master's consent, I was licensed to practise law as an attorney, being strictly examined by Mr. Barradell. January 21st, 1741, I was married to Betty, daughter of Mr. John Roy, against my friends' consent, as also my master's, who, nevertheless, still continued his affection to me. My wife died November 17th, 1742. I was married a second time the 20th of January, 1745, to Sarah, the daughter of Mr. Joseph Pollard, who was born on the 4th day of May, 1725. I practised my profession with great approbation and success, more from my own good fortune and the kind direction of Providence than my own merit; and in October, 1745, my reputation at the County Courts prompted me to make an effort at the General Court, in which I continued until 1774, when the dispute with Great Britain commenced.

"In November, 1751, I was sworn Justice of the Peace for Caroline, and continued to November, 1777. In January, 1752, I was elected as a Burgess from Caroline. I was continued one of the representatives of that County without interruption until 1774, at which time I presided in Caroline Court and was County Lieutenant. In June of that year news arrived of the inimical designs of Parliament against the town of Boston, on which account the Assembly voted a fast, and were dissolved by the Government. A number of members stayed in Williamsburg, to keep the fast, when news arrived of the Boston Port Bill; when they collected, and recommended to the people to choose members for convention, to meet in August. I was chosen a member to that convention, which voted the utility of a General Congress of the States, to meet in Philadelphia the 1st of September. I was chosen, and attended that Congress, and a second in May, 1775. In August, 1775, I was appointed President of the Committee of Safety, and in December following, President of the Convention, on the death of Mr. Randolph, and re-chosen President of the new one in May, 1776. In October, 1776, I was elected to the chair of the House of

Delegates, which sat under the new Constitution. In March, 1777, by a fall from a horse, I had my hip dislocated, and have been unable to walk ever since, except on crutches; however, the good people of Caroline the next month chose me as delegate, in hope of my recovery, but I could not attend the May session, and another Speaker was appointed, in which, however, I was highly honored by all the candidates having promised to resign the Chair when I should come. I attended on crutches in the October session, but meant then to take leave of all public business, and retire; but the General Court and Court of Chancery being established, I was prevailed on by some worthy members to consent to be nominated as a Chancery Judge, in which I was elected to the Presidency of the whole three by a unanimous vote.

"In 1779, when the Court of Appeals was organized, and made to consist of the Judges of the General Court, Chancery and Admiralty, the Chancellors were to have the first rank, and of course I presided in that Court. In 1788, when a new arrangement was made of the Superior Courts, and that of Appeals, to consist of separate Judges, I maintained my rank in that Court, and so may be considered as having been now fifteen years at the head of the Judiciary Department.

"In 1788, when a State Convention was to meet to consider of a new proposed plan of Federal government, and all the officers of the State made eligible, my good old friends in Caroline again called me to their representation in convention, and that respectable body to preside over them, indulging me in sitting in all my official duties, usually performed standing. Thus, without any classical education, without patrimony, without what is called the influence of what is called family connection, and without solicitation, I have attained the highest offices of my country.

"I have often contemplated it as a rare and extraordinary instance, and pathetically exclaimed: 'Not unto me, O Lord, but unto Thy Name be the praise.' In His providence, He was pleased to bestow on me a docile and unassuming mind, a retentive memory, a fondness for reading, a clear head and upright heart, with a calm temper, benevolent to all, though particular in friendship with but few; and if I had uncommon merit in public business, it was that of superior diligence and attention.

"Under the Regal Government I was a Whig in principle, considering it as designed for the good of society, and not for the aggrandizement of its officers, and influenced in my legislative and judicial character by that principle, when the dispute with Britain began, a redress of grievances, and not a revolution of government was my wish; in this I was firm but temperate, and whilst I was endeavoring to raise the timid to a general united opposition by stating to the uninformed the real merits of the dispute, I opposed and endeavored to moderate the violent and fiery, who were plunging us into rash measures, and had the happiness to find a majority of all the public bodies confirming my sentiments, which, I believe, was the corner-stone of our success. Although I so long, and to so high a degree, experienced the favor of my country, I had always some enemies; few indeed, and I had the consolation to believe that their enmity was unprovoked, as I was ever unable to guess the cause, unless it was my refusing to go lengths with them as their partisan.

"July 20th, 1793. EDMUND PENDLETON."

"R. D. W.," in the Richmond (Virginia) *Daily State*, 26th May, 1881, says: "Judge Edmund Pendleton was the first President of the Supreme Court of Appeals of Virginia, and his autobiography will, I think, commend itself to you as worthy of publication, and as presenting the record of a life which affords an example that ought to be cherished. Our young men would do well to read his life and be strengthened to follow on in his slow, steady, useful and brilliant career. Judge Pendleton died at the age of eighty-two years, in the full enjoyment of his mental faculties, and almost literally in the discharge of his official duties."

III. JOHN PENDLETON, OF CAROLINE COUNTY, Va., elder brother of Judge Edmund Pendleton, was about the fourth child and son of Henry Pendleton, of same county, and Mary Taylor, his wife, and was born in said county, about 1723, and died in April, 1799, aged about 76 years. He married twice, it is said, but the names of his wives are unknown. By one of these marriages, probably the first, he had:

1. Edmund Pendleton, eldest, born in Caroline County, Va., about 1748, removed to White Plains, same county, and married, about 1773, Mildred Pollard.
2. Son Pendleton, married and had two daughters but no male issue.

There were several other sons, all of whom went West except Henry Pendleton, who settled in Louisa County, Va., and raised a large family.

IV. EDMUND PENDLETON, OF WHITE PLAINS, Caroline Co., Va., eldest son of John Pendleton, of same county, was born there about 1748. He married, about 1773, Mildred Pollard, called Milly, youngest sister of Sarah Pollard, who was the second wife of Judge Edmund Pendleton. They had the following children:

1. Edmund Pendleton, Jr., eldest, born at White Plains, Caroline Co., Va., 18th April, 1774, removed to Edmundton, same county. He married, first, 23d August, 1794, Jane B. Page. He married, secondly, 16th May, 1798, Lucy Nelson.
2. Mildred Pendleton, born about 1776 at White Plains, Caroline Co., Va., married, about 1798, Thomas Page, about the seventh surviving son of Hon. John Page, of North End, Gloucester (now Matthews) Co., Va., and Jane Byrd, his wife. (See Page Family, North End.)

There were probably other children of Edmund Pendleton and Mildred Pollard, his wife, but they are not known.

V. Edmund Pendleton, Jr., of Edmundton, Caroline Co., Va., eldest son and child of Edmund Pendleton, of White Plains, same county, and Mildred (called Milly) Pollard, his wife, eldest son and child of John Pendleton, of same county (the names of his two wives being unknown), about the fourth child and son of Henry Pendleton, of same county, and Mary Taylor, his wife, eldest son and child of Philip Pendleton, of Norwich, England, and Caroline County (formed out of New Kent County), Va., progenitor of the Pendleton Family in Virginia, and Isabella Hert (pronounced Hart), his wife, was born at the second above-named place, 18th April, 1774. The date of his death is unknown.

The estate, called Edmundton, was given to him by his great-uncle, Judge Edmund Pendleton. He married, first, 23d August, 1794, Jane Burwell, eldest daughter and about the second child of John Page, of Caroline County, Va., and Elizabeth (called Betty) Burwell, his wife. The latter was the mother of Capt. Hugh N. Page, U. S. Navy, and others, and was burned to death in the Richmond (Virginia) Theatre, 26th December, 1811. (See Page Family, North End.) Edmund Pendleton had one child by the first marriage, viz.:

1. Elizabeth Page Pendleton, born at Edmundton, Caroline Co., Va., about 1795; married, 18th April, 1817, John C. Sutton, of Norfolk City, Va. She died, leaving eleven children.

Edmund Pendleton, Jr. (his first wife dying), married, secondly, 16th May, 1798, Lucy, second child and daughter of Col. Hugh Nelson, of Yorktown, York Co., Va., and Judith Page, his wife. (See President Nelson.) The children by the second marriage were as follows:

1. Hugh Nelson Pendleton, eldest, born at Edmundton, Caroline Co., Va., 13th April, 1800, removed first to Clarke and then to Wythe County, Va. He married, first, 20th February, 1829, Lucy Nelson, and, secondly, about 1840, Elizabeth Digges.
2. Mildred Pendleton, born at the same place, 21st March, 1802, married, 17th November, 1825, Edmund A. Pendleton, of Augusta, Ga. Children:
   (1) Edmund Lewis Pendleton, born 28th January, 1827, married, October, 1850, Catista E. Norton, of Vermont, and had one daughter, Edmonia Pendleton, married F. S. Mosher, of Augusta, Ga.

(2) William Pendleton, born 21st June, 1828, married, 24th September, 1862, Zemula C. Walker, of Augusta, Ga. Has four sons.

(3) John Pendleton, born 15th March, 1834; single.

(4) Hugh Pendleton, twin brother of John, born 15th March, 1834, married, December, 1867, Rebecca Jones, of Nottoway County, Va. Has two sons and two daughters.

(5) Judith Page Pendleton, born about 1836, married, in 1858, Richard B. Williams, of Richmond, Va. She died April, 1863, without issue.

(6) Armistead Franklin Pendleton, born 25th September, 1838; married in March, 1868, Isabella Garvin, of Augusta, Ga., and has two daughters and one son.

(7) Anne Elizabeth Pendleton, born 9th October, 1844; single.

3. Judith Page Pendleton, born at Edmundton, Caroline Co., Va., 8th December, 1803, married, June, 1826, Robert H. Harrison, of the same county, and died leaving two children, viz.:

(1) William L. Harrison, married, about 1832, Lama A. Lumpkin, of Dover, King William Co., Va., and had Robert, Rosa, Annie, Mary, and Lama.

(2) Mary F. Harrison, married Dr. James E. Williams, of Richmond, Va. No issue.

4. Dr. Francis Walker Pendleton, born at Edmundton, Caroline Co., Va., 7th December, 1808, removed to Warsaw, Richmond Co., Va. He married, January, 1834, Sarah F., daughter of Daniel Turner, of Caroline County, Va., and had:

(1) Robert Carter Pendleton, died a youth.

(2) Nannie F. Pendleton, born 1840.

(3) Mildred E. Pendleton, born 1841, married, about 1861, Tasker Crabbe, of Richmond County, Va. She died, leaving one child, Fannie Crabbe.

5. Rev. William Nelson Pendleton, born in Richmond, Va., 26th December, 1809; removed to Lexington, Rockbridge Có., Va., where he died, 15th January, 1883, aged 74 years.

He married, in 1831, Anzolette Page, of Rugswamp, Hanover Co., Va., who died 15th January, 1884, just exactly one year after the death of her husband. (See Page Family, Rosewell.) Their children were:

(1) Susan Pendleton, married, about 1852, Ed. Lee, who died without issue.

(2) Mary Pendleton.

(3) Rose Pendleton.

(4) Alexander S. Pendleton, only son, called Sandy, born about 1839; died September, 1864. He married, 1863, Kate Corbin, of Moss Neck, Caroline Co., Va. (See Secretary Nelson.) They had one child that died infant. Mrs. Kate Corbin Pendleton married, secondly, Brooke, of Lexington, Rockbridge Co., Va., and has issue.

(5) Nancy Pendleton.
(6) Lella Pendleton; married, and has issue.

6. Robert Carter Pendleton, born at Edmundton, Caroline Co., Va., 14th September, 1812; died single, at Uniontown, Pa., in 1836, aged 24 years.
7. James L. Pendleton, born at Edmundton, Caroline Co., Va., about 1815; removed to Richmond, Va. He married, in 1840, Annalethia, daughter of Samuel S. Carter, of Richmond, Va. She died there in 1881. He died many years before. Their children were:
   (1) Samuel H. Pendleton, born about 1841, removed to New York City; married, 1864, Sallie A., daughter of Philip H. Pendleton, of Port Royal, Caroline Co., Va. They had one child, Arthur Pendleton. They now reside at Elizabeth, N. J.
   (2) Hugh Thomas Pendleton, died single, 3d July, 1863.
   (3) Emma Walker Pendleton, married, 1882, Robert C. Little, of Columbus, Ga.
   (4) Martha Carter Pendleton, married, 1871, Joseph M. Furqurean, of Richmond, Va., and has several children.
   (5) William J. Pendleton, married, about 1875, Mary J., daughter of John M. Royall, of Richmond, Va.
8. Guerdon H. Pendleton, born at Edmundton, Caroline Co., Va., 4th April, 1817; removed to Clarke County, Va. He died about 1877, aged about 60 years. He married, 11th May, 1854, Jane Byrd, daughter of Mann Randolph Page. (See Page Family, North End.)

VI. Hugh Nelson Pendleton, of Clarke County, Va., eldest son and child of Edmund Pendleton, Jr., of Edmundton, Caroline Co., Va., and Lucy Nelson, his second wife (there was no male issue by the first wife), eldest son and child of Edmund Pendleton, of White Plains, same county, and Mildred (called Milly) Pollard, his wife, eldest son and child of John Pendleton, of same county (names of his two wives unknown); about the fourth child and son of Henry Pendleton, of the same county, and Mary Taylor, his wife, eldest son and child of Philip Pendleton, of Norwich, England, and Caroline County (formed out of New Kent County), Va., progenitor of the Pendleton Family in Virginia, and Isabella Hert (pronounced Hart), his wife, was born at the second above-named place, 13th April, 1800. He died recently, exact age unknown.

He married, first, 20th February, 1829, Lucy, only child of Chancellor Robert Nelson (ninth child and youngest son of Gov. Thomas Nelson, Yorktown, York Co., Va.) and Judith Carter

Page, his wife, who was the ninth surviving child and youngest daughter of Gov. John Page, of Rosewell, Gloucester Co., Va., and Frances (called Fannie) Burwell, his first wife.

Hugh Nelson Pendleton and Lucy Nelson, his first wife, had only one child, viz.:

1. Julia Pendleton, born about 1830; died in 1865, aged about 35. She married, about 1853, James Allen, of Bedford County, Va., who died in August, 1862. They left one child, viz., Hugh Allen, who is the sole surviving descendant of Chancellor Robert Nelson.

Hugh Nelson Pendleton married, secondly, about 1840, Eliza beth, daughter of Dudley Digges, of Louisa County, Va., and Alice Page, widow of Dr. John A. Smith, of Yorktown, York Co., Va., his wife. Alice Page, the widow Smith, was the second surviving daughter and about the sixth child of Gov. John Page and Frances (called Fannie) Burwell, his first wife.

Hugh Nelson Pendleton and Elizabeth Digges, his wife, had the following children:

1. Dudley Digges Pendleton, eldest, born about 1841; removed to Shepherdstown, Jefferson Co., W. Va. Being the eldest son of the eldest son, etc., he was the Representative Descendant of the Pendleton Family in Virginia, from John Pendleton, who belonged to the third generation of that family in Virginia. Dudley D. Pendleton married, about 1868, Helen Boteler, of Shepherdstown. He was accidentally caught in machinery while threshing wheat, 25th August, 1886, and so crushed that he died a few hours afterward, leaving his widow and several children.
2. Robert Nelson Pendleton, born about 1843; married, about 1868, Fannie Gibson, and removed to Wythe County, Va.
3. Kenneth Pendleton, born about 1845; died young.

For further information about the Pendletons, the reader is referred to the "History of St. Mark's Parish," Culpepper County, Va., by Rev. Philip Slaughter, D.D. Published by Innes & Co., Baltimore, Md., 1877.

PART V.

RANDOLPH FAMILY.

(From an old print.)

JOHN RANDOLPH,

Roanoke, Charlotte Co., Va.

Died 24th May, 1833, aged 60.

RANDOLPH FAMILY.

The following is a somewhat incomplete account of the Randolph Family in Virginia.

I. Col. William Randolph, of Turkey Island, on James River, Henrico Co., Va., the first of his family in Virginia, was born in Yorkshire, England, about 1651. He removed to Warwickshire, England, and emigrated from that place to Virginia about 1674. He died 15th April, 1711, aged about 60 years. The following inscription was copied from his tombstone at Turkey Island, and sent to the author in May, 1884, by Dr. Robert C. Randolph, of Newmarket, Clarke Co., Va.

> Col. Wm Randolph of Warwickshire, but late of
> Virginia, Gent. died April 11th 1711.
> Mrs. Mary Randolph his only wife, she was the daughter
> of Mr. Henry Isham by Catherine his wife. He was of
> Northamptonshire, but late of Virginia, Gent.

Col. William Randolph was a member of the House of Burgesses and of the Royal Council in Virginia. He married, about 1680, Mary, daughter of Henry Isham, of Bermuda Hundred on James River, and Catherine, his wife, whose maiden name is unknown. Their children, according to the order arranged by John Randolph of Roanoke, were as follows:

1. William Randolph, Jr., known as Councillor Randolph, eldest, born at Turkey Island, Henrico Co., Va., November, 1681; resided there. He married, about 1705, Elizabeth Beverly.
2. Thomas Randolph, born at Turkey Island, Henrico Co., Va., about June, 1683; removed to Tuckahoe on James River, Goochland Co., Va. He married, about 1710, Judith Churchill.
3. Isham Randolph, born at Turkey Island, Henrico Co., Va., December, 1684; removed to Dungeness, Goochland Co., Va. He married, in 1717, Jane Rogers, of London, England.

4. Richard Randolph, born at Turkey Island, Henrico Co., Va., about May, 1686; removed to Curls Neck on James River, same county, and married, about 1714, Jane Bolling.
5. Henry Randolph, born about October, 1687, died, unmarried, in England. He left his part of the Curls estate to his brother Richard.
6. Sir John Randolph, Knight, born at Turkey Island, Henrico Co., Va., about April, 1689; removed to Williamsburg, James City Co., Va. He married, about 1718, Susanna Beverly, sister of his brother William's wife.
7. Edward Randolph, born about October, 1690, removed to Bristol, England. He married, about 1715, Miss Grosvenor, of that place, and had issue. Of these, Edward married Lucy Harrison, and Elizabeth and Mary married Yates, of Gloucester County, Va. Mary's husband was the Rev. Robert Yates. Their daughter, Catherine, married Dr. Robert Wellford, a surgeon in the English army, who settled in Fredericksburg, Va. His son, William Wellford, married Susan R. Nelson. (See SECRETARY NELSON.)
8. Mary Randolph, born at Turkey Island, Henrico Co., Va., about 1692; married, about 1712, Capt. John Stith. Their only son was Rev. William Stith, President of William and Mary College, and Historian of Virginia. According to Bishop Meade, Rev. William Stith "wrote his history in 1740, and died, in 1752, at William and Mary College." He married, in February, 1744, Judith Randolph, of Tuckahoe.
9. Elizabeth Randolph, youngest, was born about 1695. She married, about 1711, Richard Bland, of Jordan's Point, on James River, Va., and was his second wife. She died 22d January, 1720. Among their children were:
   (1) Mary Bland, born about 1712, married, about 1728, Henry Lee, of Lee Hall. Their third son, and fourth child, Henry Lee, was born about 1733, and married, about 1755, Lucy Grymes, Washington's Lowland Beauty, by whom he had General Lee (Light Horse Harry), born 29th January, 1756, who was the father of Gen. Robert E. Lee.
   (2) Richard Bland, of Jordan's Point, on James River, Va., was their eldest son. He was a member of the Virginia House of Burgesses; of the Virginia Convention of 1775, and of the First American Congress at Philadelphia. He married Anne Poythress.
   (3) Theodoric Bland, the last and 5th surviving child. Born, 1720, soon before his mother died.

II. WILLIAM RANDOLPH, known as COUNCILLOR RANDOLPH, of Turkey Island, Henrico Co., Va., eldest son and child of William Randolph of Yorkshire and Warwickshire, England, and Turkey Island, Henrico Co., Va., progenitor of the Randolph Family in Virginia, and Mary Isham, his wife, was born at the first-named place in November, 1681, and resided there. He died 19th October, 1741, aged 61.

The following is the inscription copied from his original tombstone at Turkey Island:

> Here lies the HONOURABLE WILLIAM RANDOLPH ESQR.
> oldest son of COLONEL WILLIAM RANDOLPH of this
> place, and of Mary his wife, who was of the
> ancient and estimable family of Ishams of
> Northamptonshire; having been easily introduced
> into business, and passed through many inferior
> offices of Government, with great reputation and
> eminent capacity. He was at last, by his Majesty's
> happy choice and the universal approbation of his
> Country, advanced to the Council. His experience
> in men and business, the native gravity of his
> person and behaviour, his attachment to the interests
> of his Country, knowledge of the laws in general,
> and of the laws and constitution of his Colony in
> particular, his integrity above all calumny or
> suspicion, the acuteness of his parts and the
> extensiveness of his genius together with the solidity
> of sense and judgment in all he said or did,
> rendered him not only equal but an ornament
> to the high office he bore, and have made him
> universally lamented as a most able and impartial
> Judge and as an upright and useful magistrate in
> all other respects. Neither was he less conspicuous
> for a certain majestic plainness of sense and
> honour which carried him through all parts of
> private life with an equal dignity of reputation;
> and deservedly obtained him the character of
> the just good man in all the several duties
> and relations of life—Natus November 1681
> Mortuus Oct. 19th 1741
> Anno Ætatis 61.

The foregoing inscription was copied September 5th, 1874, for Dr. Robert C. Randolph, of Newmarket, Clarke Co., Va., by Mrs. Charles Nelson Carter, of Shirley, on James River. The stone is a slab near that of the father, Col. William Randolph, the first of the Randolph Family in Virginia. The brick house, which for a long time was the only part of the original Turkey Island mansion left, does not now exist.

Councillor William Randolph married, about 1705, Elizabeth, daughter of Peter Beverly, of Gloucester County, Va., and Eliza Peyton his wife, who was a daughter of Robert Peyton, descended from a family of that name in Norfolk, England. Councillor William Randolph and Elizabeth Beverly, his wife, had the following children:

1. Beverly Randolph, eldest, born at Turkey Island, Henrico Co., Va., about 1706, resided there. He married, about 1731, Miss Lightfoot, and died without issue.
2. Peter Randolph, born at Turkey Island, Henrico Co., Va., about 1708; removed to Chatsworth, same county. He married, about 1733, Lucy, daughter of Robert Bolling, and had William, Beverly, Robert, and Anne. Beverly was born at Chatsworth, in 1754, and married Martha Cooke, by whom he had issue. He died at his residence, Green Creek, in February, 1797. He succeeded Edmond Randolph as Governor of Virginia, 1st December, 1788, and served until 1st December, 1791, when he was succeeded in that office by Gen. Henry Lee (Light Horse Harry), the father of Gen. Robert E. Lee.
3. William Randolph, born about 1710; removed to Wilton, Henrico (?) Co., Va. He married, about 1735, Anne, daughter of Benjamin Harrison, of Berkeley (Harrison's Landing), on James River, Va., and Anne Carter, his wife. Their children were: (1) William Randolph, born about 1736. He was probably the father of Elizabeth Randolph, who married William Berkeley. (2) Peyton Randolph, born about 1738; married, about 1763, Lucy Harrison, his cousin, and had Betty, Kidder, and Peyton. The latter married Anne, daughter of James Innes, Attorney-General of Virginia. His only son, James Innes Randolph, married Susan, daughter of Capt. Addison Armistead, U. S. army. Of the sons of that marriage is Innes Randolph, Esq., of Baltimore, Md. (3) Anne Randolph, born about 1740; married, about 1760, Benjamin Harrison, of Brandon, on James River, Prince George Co., Va., and died without issue. (4) Elizabeth Randolph, born about 1742; married, about 1762, Philip Grymes, of Middlesex County, Va.; probably the brother of Lucy Grymes, who married Governor Thomas Nelson, of Yorktown, Va. (5) Lucy Randolph, born about 1744; married, about 1764, Lewis Burwell, of Kings Mill (Kingsmel), York Co. (?), Va. He was probably the brother of Elizabeth (called Betty) Burwell, wife of John Page, of Caroline County, Va. (See Page Family, North End.)
4. Daughter Randolph, born about 1718; married Price.
5. Elizabeth Randolph, born about 1725; married, about 1745, Col. John Chiswell, and had four surviving children: (1) Lucy Chiswell, married, 24th November, 1770, Col. William Nelson, of The Dorrill, Han-

over Co., Va. (See Secretary Nelson.) (2) Susan R. Chiswell, married Speaker John Robinson of the Virginia House of Burgesses, and had issue. Mrs. Susan N. Wellford, who married Philip Burwell, of Chappel Hill, Clarke Co., Va., was named after her. (3) Daughter Chiswell, married Warner Lewis. (4) Elizabeth Chiswell, married Charles Carter of Ludloe, whose mother was Mary Walke, the wife of Charles Carter of Clere.

Col. John Chiswell and Elizabeth Randolph, his wife, had no surviving sons, so that the surname of Chiswell in Virginia has become extinct. It was pronounced "Chizzle" in those days, and is believed to have been originally written De Choiseul.

II. THOMAS RANDOLPH, of Tuckahoe, on James River, Goochland Co., Va., second son and child of William Randolph, of Yorkshire, England, and Turkey Island, Henrico Co., Va., progenitor of the Randolph Family in Virginia, and Mary Isham, his wife, was born at Turkey Island, Henrico Co., Va., about 1683. He married, about 1710, Judith Churchill, of Middlesex County, Va. There appears to be some uncertainty as to who was the wife of Thomas Randolph, of Tuckahoe. According to Rev. P. Slaughter, in his "History of Bristol Parish," p. 214, she was a Miss Fleming. This corresponds with the statement made in Browning's "Americans of Royal Descent," p. 298. On the other hand, Mrs. Ellen Wayles Randolph Harrison, of Edge Hill, Albemarle Co., Va., states that her name was Judith Churchill, and that no marriage between Randolph and Fleming took place until a later period. Mrs. Harrison suggested, however, that application for correct information on this point should be made to Wilson M. Cary, of Baltimore, Md. In reply to a letter from the author on the subject Mr. Cary wrote under date of 8th March, 1883, as follows:

"In the conflict of authorities as to the wife of Thomas Randolph, of Tuckahoe, I have always accepted Richard Randolph's account rather than that of John Randolph, of Roanoke, because the former was a professed antiquary and more likely to be correct than the eccentric and erratic statesman who probably took no pains to verify his opinion by general research. There being no extracts from parish records, there is nothing left but to choose between their statements, aided by such corroborating testimony as one can obtain at this late day."

In view of this statement, we shall assume that the wife of Thomas Randolph, of Tuckahoe, was named Judith Churchill.

Their children were as follows:

1. William Randolph, born at Tuckahoe, Goochland Co., Va., in 1712, married, about 1735, Maria Judith, second child and only daughter of Hon. Mann Page, of Rosewell, Gloucester Co., Va., and Judith Wormeley, his first wife.
2. Judith Randolph, born about 1724; married, February, 1744, Rev. William Stith, President of William and Mary College, also Historian of Virginia.
3. Mary Randolph, born about 1726; married, about 1746, William Keith. Chief Justice John Marshall, of the United States, was descended from them.

III. WILLIAM RANDOLPH, of Tuckahoe, on James River, Goochland Co., Va., eldest son and child of Thomas Randolph, of the same place, and Judith Churchill, his wife, was born there in 1712, and died 1745.

He married, about 1735, Maria Judith, second child and only daughter of Hon. Mann Page, of Rosewell, Gloucester Co., Va., and Judith Wormeley, his first wife. Their children were as follows:

1. Mary Judith Randolph, born about 1736; married, about 1756, Edmund Berkeley, Jr., of Barnelms, Middlesex Co., Va., and was his first wife. He was the eldest son of Col. Edmund Berkeley, of the same place, and Mary Nelson, his wife, who was the only daughter and about the second child of Thomas Nelson, known as Scotch Tom, of Yorktown, Va., and Margaret Reid, his first wife. They had only one child, who married Joseph Clayton. Edmund Berkeley, Jr., married, secondly, Mary Burwell, sister of Colonel Burwell, of Carter Hall, Clarke Co., Va., and had Norborne, Carter, William, Elizabeth (called Betsey) who married Churchill and was the grandmother of J. Churchill Cooke and others, Lucy who married Hepanon, Alice who married Fontaine, Sally, and Lewis.
2. Mary Randolph, born about 1738; married, about 1758, Tarlton Fleming, of Rock Castle, Goochland Co., Va. This was the first connection between the Randolphs and Flemings.
3. Thomas Mann Randolph, born at Tuckahoe, Goochland Co., Va., in 1741. He was the only son, and married, 18th November, 1761, Anne Cary.
4. Priscilla Randolph, probably unmarried.

IV. THOMAS MANN RANDOLPH, of Tuckahoe, on James River, Goochland Co., Va., only son of William Randolph, of the same place, and Maria Judith Page, his wife, was born there in 1741.

He married, first, 18th November, 1761, Anne, eldest daughter and child of Col. Archibald Cary, of Ampthill, Chesterfield Co., Va., and Mary Randolph, of Curls Neck, on James River, Henrico Co., Va., his wife. Their children were as follows:

1. Mary Randolph, born 9th August, 1762; married, about 1782, David Meade Randolph, of Presqu' Isle, on James River, Va. She was known as "The Queen." Of their children, Beverly was a clerk in the United States Treasury Department, at Washington, D. C., and three of his sons, James, Maury, and Richard, were in the employment of the Baltimore and Ohio Railroad Company.
2. Henry Cary Randolph, born about 1763; died infant.
3. Elizabeth Randolph, born about 1765; married, about 1785, Robert Pleasants, of Filmer.
4. Thomas Mann Randolph, Jr., eldest surviving son, and Governor of Virginia, was born at Tuckahoe, Goochland Co., Va., about 1767, and removed to Edge Hill, Albemarle Co., Va. He married, in 1790, Martha, daughter of Thomas Jefferson, President U. S.
5. William Randolph, born at Tuckahoe, about 1769; married, about 1794, Lucy Bolling, daughter of Beverly Randolph, of Cumberland Co., Va., and died, leaving two sons, viz.:
   (1) William Fitzhugh Randolph, married Jane Cary, daughter of Randolph Harrison, of Clifton, Cumberland Co., Va. She became entirely blind. Her two sons, Beverly and William Eston, resided near her at Millwood, Clarke Co., Va. Of these, William married Susan, daughter of Dr. Robert C. Randolph, of Newmarket, Clarke Co., Va. Her only daughter married George Tabb, of Gloucester County, Va.
   (2) Beverly Randolph, married Miss Mayor, of Pennsylvania, and died, leaving one son, William Mayor Randolph, who removed to St. Louis, Mo.
6. Archibald Cary Randolph, born about 1771; died infant.
7. Judith Randolph, born about 1773; married, about 1793, her cousin, Richard Randolph, of Bizarre, who was the brother of John Randolph, of Roanoke. They had one son, who died a deaf-mute, and left quite a large property to be divided among his heirs according to law. Of these, Col. Thomas Jefferson Randolph, of Edge Hill, Albemarle Co., Va., received about *forty dollars!*
8. Anne Cary Randolph, born at Tuckahoe about 1775; married, about 1795, Gouverneur Morris, of Morrisania, N. Y., U. S. Minister to France.
9. Jane Cary Randolph, born about 1777, married, about 1797, Thomas Eston Randolph, of Bristol, England, and had:
   (1) Mann Randolph, Captain U. S. Navy.
   (2) Dr. James Randolph, of Tallahassee, Fla., married Miss Heywood.

(3) Lucy Randolph, married Parkhill, of Jacksonville, Fla.
(4) Harriet Randolph, married Dr. Willis; no issue.
(5) Elizabeth Randolph, married Francis Wayles Eppes.
(6) Dr. Arthur Randolph, of Tallahassee, Fla., married Miss Duval, and has issue.

10. Dr. John Randolph, born at Tuckahoe, Goochland Co., Va., about 1779; removed to Middle Quarter, same county. He married, about 1804, Judith Lewis, of Amelia County, Va. They had several children, the eldest of whom, William Lewis Randolph, married Margaret, daughter of Col. Thomas Jefferson Randolph, of Edge Hill, Albemarle Co., Va., and had: (*a*) William L. Randolph, Jr., married, 1866, Agnes Dillon, of Savannah, Ga. They reside near Charlottesville, Albemarle Co., Va., and have five children; (*b*) Margaret Randolph, married Ed. C. Anderson, and had four children.
11. George Washington Randolph, born about 1781; died infant.
12. Harriet Randolph, born about 1783; married, about 1803, Richard S. Hackley, of New York, Consul to Cadiz. He died, leaving two daughters, one of whom married Captain Talcott, and had several sons and daughters. One of the sons, Randolph Talcott, removed to Richmond, Va.
13. Virginia Randolph, born at Tuckahoe, Goochland Co., Va., 31st January, 1786. She married, at Monticello, Albemarle Co., Va., 28th August, 1805, WILSON JEFFERSON CARY, of Carysbrooke, Fluvanna Co., Va. He was the great-nephew of United States President Thomas Jefferson. Their children were:
(1) COL. WILSON MILES CARY, born at Carysbrook, Fluvanna Co., Va., 1806; removed to Baltimore County, Md., and represented that county for six years in the Maryland State Senate. He married, in 1832, Jane Margaret, daughter of Peter Carr and Hetty Smith, his wife. The latter was niece of Gen. Samuel Smith, of Baltimore, Md. Their children were as follows: (*a*) Sarah Nicholas, married J. Howard McHenry, of Baltimore; (*b*) Virginia, died infant; (*c*) Hetty, married, first, Maj.-Gen. John Pegram, and, secondly, Prof. Newell Martin, of Johns Hopkins University, Baltimore; (*d*) Virginia Randolph, died young; (*e*) WILSON MILES, attorney, of Baltimore, Md., representative of the Cary Family of Virginia, born 1838; (*f*) John Brune, married Fannie E., daughter of William S. Daniel, of Jefferson County, W. Va.; (*g*) Jenny; (*h*) Sidney Carr, of the firm of Cary & Co., merchants, Baltimore, Md.
(2) Archibald Cary, born at Carysbrook Fluvanna Co., Va.; removed to Cumberland County, Md. He married Monimia, daughter of Thomas, ninth Lord Fairfax, and died, leaving three children: (*a*) Falkland, a brilliant youth, died young; (*b*) Constance, married Burton N. Harrison, of Mississippi, removed to New York

City; (*c*) Clarence, married, 1878, Elizabeth, daughter of Howard Potter, of the banking firm of Brown Bros., New York City.
(3) Jane Blair Cary, married Rev. E. D. Smith, of New York City.
(4) Mary Randolph Cary, married Dr. Orlando Fairfax.
(5) Martha Jefferson Cary, married her first cousin, Gouverneur Morris, of Morrisania, N. Y.

Thomas Mann Randolph, of Tuckahoe, married, secondly, about 1790, Gabriella Harvey, by whom he had another Thomas Mann Randolph, who was, consequently, the half-brother of Gov. Thomas Mann Randolph, of Edge Hill.

The said Thomas Mann Randolph, son of Gabriella Harvey, married, first, Harriet Wilson, and had:

(1) John Randolph, married Margaret Timberlake, of Washington, D. C.
(2) Mary Randolph, married John, son of Professor Chapman, M.D., of Philadelphia, Pa.
(3) Margaret Randolph, married F. A. Donkins.
(4) Harriet, married Albert S. White.

Thomas Mann Randolph, son of Gabriella Harvey, married, secondly, Miss Patterson, and had:

(1) Henry Randolph, of Washington, D. C., clerk in one of the departments there.
(2) Daughter Randolph, married Mr. Howard, of Baltimore, Md.

V. Thomas Mann Randolph, Jr., of Edge Hill, Albemarle Co., Va., Governor of Virginia, was the fourth child and eldest surviving son of Thomas Mann Randolph, of Tuckahoe, Goochland Co., Va., and Anne Cary, his wife, and was born at Tuckahoe about 1767.

He was Governor of Virginia 1819–1821, and was a Presidential Elector in 1825.

He married, in 1790, Martha, daughter of U. S. President Thomas Jefferson, and Martha Wayles, his wife. Their children were:

1. Anne Cary Randolph, born 1791; married, about 1810, Charles Bankhead, and had:
   (1) Daughter; married John Carter.
   (2) Thomas M. R. Bankhead; died in Arkansas, without issue.
   (3) John Bankhead; lives in Missouri, and has a family.
   (4) William Bankhead; removed to Alabama.
2. Thomas Jefferson Randolph, eldest son, born at Edge Hill, Albemarle Co., Va., 1792; he resided there, and married, 1815, Jane Nicholas.

3. Ellen Randolph, born about 1794; died infant.
4. Ellen Wayles Randolph, born about 1796; married, about 1824, Joseph Coolidge, of Boston, Mass., and had:
   (1) Joseph R. Coolidge; married Julia Gardiner.
   (2) Bessie; died infant.
   (3) Ellen R. Coolidge; married Edmund Dwight.
   (4) Sidney Coolidge; killed in the United States army, at Chattanooga, 1864.
   (5) Algernon Coolidge, twin brother of Sidney; married Mary Lowell.
   (6) Thomas Jefferson Coolidge, minister to France, succeeding Whitelaw Reid, during the administration of President Benjamin Harrison; married Mehitabel (Hettie) Appleton.
5. James Madison Randolph, born about 1798; died single.
6. Cornelia Jefferson Randolph; died single.
7. Mary Jefferson Randolph; died single.
8. Virginia Randolph, born about 1801; married, about 1821, N. P. Trist, who made the Treaty of Hidalgo Guadaloupe, after the Mexican war (1848), and had:
   (1) Thomas Jefferson Trist, deaf-mute; married Ellen Lyman, also a deaf-mute, of Boston, Mass. No issue.
   (2) Martha Jefferson Trist; married John Burke, of Alexandria, Va., and had seven children.
   (3) Dr. H. B. Trist; married Anna Warring, of Savannah, Ga., and has seven children also.
9. Benjamin Franklin Randolph, born about 1805; married, about 1828, Sarah Carter, and had:
   (1) Meriwether Lewis Randolph; married Louisa Hubard, and has five children.
   (2) Septimia Anne Randolph, married Dr. David Meikleham, and had William Morland Meikleham, who married in New York and lives in Fordham, with three children—Alice Scott, Randolph, and Ellen Wayles.
10. Meriwether Lewis Randolph, born about 1808; married, about 1830, Eliza Wharton. No issue.
11. George Wythe Randolph, born about 1815; married, about 1852, Mary E. Adams (the widow Pope). No issue.

VI. Col. Thomas Jefferson Randolph, of Edge Hill, Albemarle Co., Va., eldest son and second child of Governor Thomas Mann Randolph, Jr., of the same place, and Martha Jefferson (daughter of U. S. President Thomas Jefferson), his wife, third child and eldest son of Thomas Mann Randolph, Sr., of Tuckahoe, Goochland Co., Va., and Anne Cary, his wife, eldest son and child of William Randolph, of the last-named place, and Maria Judith Page, his wife (who was the daughter of the first Mann Page and Judith Wormeley, his first wife), eldest son and child of Thomas Randolph, of the same place, and Judith Churchill, his wife, second son and child of William Randolph, of Yorkshire, England, and Turkey Island, Henrico Co., Va., progenitor of the Randolph Family in Virginia, and Mary Isham, his wife, was born at the first above-named place in 1792, and died there in 1875, aged 83 years. He was buried at Monticello, in the Jefferson graveyard.

He was a Presidential Elector in 1845, and was President of the National Democratic Convention, which met in Baltimore, Md., in 1873. He was also chosen President of the Philadelphia Centennial Exhibition of 1876; but, as already stated, died a short time before its opening. He married, in 1815, Jane, daughter of Gov. Wilson Cary Nicholas, of Warren, Albemarle Co., Va. Their children were:

1. Margaret Smith Randolph, born about 1816; married, about 1836, William Lewis Randolph.
2. Patsey Jefferson Randolph, born about 1817; married, about 1838, J. C. Randolph Taylor, of Albemarle County, Va., and had:
   (1) Bennet Taylor; married, about 1865, Lucy Colston, and had six children.
   (2) Jane Randolph Taylor.
   (3) Susan Beverly Taylor; married John Blackburn.
   (4) Jefferson Randolph Taylor, lawyer. Resides at Charlottesville, Albemarle Co., Va.
   (5) Margaret Randolph Taylor.
   (6) Charlotte Taylor; died infant.
   (7) Cornelia Jefferson Taylor.
   (8) Stevens Mason Taylor.
   (9) Edmund Randolph Taylor.
   (10) Sidney W. Taylor; died infant.
   (11) I. C. Randolph Taylor; died infant.
   (12) Moncure Robinson Taylor.
3. Cary Anne Nicholas Randolph, born about 1820; married, about 1840, Frank G. Ruffin, of Albemarle County, Va., and had:
   (1) Jefferson Randolph Ruffin.
   (2) William Roane Ruffin; married, about 1868, Miss McIlvaine, of Petersburg, Dinwiddie Co., Va., and has several children.
   (3) Wilson Cary Nicholas Ruffin; married, about 1870, Mary Harvey.
   (4) George Randolph Ruffin; removed to Texas.
   (5) Frank Gildart Ruffin, Jr.
   (6) Eliza McDonald Ruffin.

(7) Cary Randolph Ruffin.

4. Mary Buchanan Randolph, born about 1821; died infant.

5. Mary Buchanan Randolph (No. 2), born about 1823; resides, unmarried, at Edge Hill, and is principal of the school there. She very much resembles the portrait of Thomas Jefferson (President U. S.).

6. Ellen Wayles Randolph, born about 1825; married, about 1860, William B. Harrison, of Upper Brandon, on James River, Charles City Co., Va., and was his second wife. She resided at Edge Hill after the death of her husband. Two children, viz.:
   (1) Jane Nicholas Harrison.
   (2) Jefferson Randolph Harrison.

7. Maria Jefferson Carr Randolph, born about 1827; married, about 1848, Charles Mason, and had:
   (1) Jefferson Randolph Mason; removed to San Antonio, Tex.
   (2) Lucy Roy Mason.
   (3) John Enoch Mason, Commonwealth's Attorney, King George County, Va.

8. Caroline Ramsay Randolph, born about 1828; resided, unmarried, at Edge Hill, Albemarle Co., Va.

9. Thomas Jefferson Randolph, Jr., eldest son, born at Edge Hill, Albemarle Co., Va., about 1830; removed to Shadwell, same county; he married, first, about 1854, Mary Walker Meriwether, who died July, 1863, leaving:
   (1) Frank Meriwether Randolph; married Charlotte Macon.
   (2) Thomas Jefferson Randolph, Jr.
   (3) Margaret Douglas Randolph; died young.
   (4) Francis Nelson Randolph; died young.
   (5) George Geiger Randolph.

He married, secondly, in 1865, Charlotte N. Meriwether, and had one child, viz., Mary Walker Randolph. He was accidentally killed by a blast on the Chesapeake and Ohio Railroad, about 1870, aged about 40 years. His second wife died about 1876.

10. Dr. Wilson Cary Nicholas Randolph, born at Edge Hill, Albemarle Co., Va., about 1832; removed to Charlottesville, same county. He married, about 1855, Mary Holliday, of that place, and had:
   (1) Virginia Rawlings Randolph.
   (2) Wilson C. N. Randolph, Jr.
   (3) Mary Walker Randolph.
   (4) Julia Minor Randolph.

11. Jane Nicholas Randolph, born about 1834; married, about 1856, R. Garlick H. Kean, and had:
   (1) Launcelot Kean.
   (2) Patsey Cary Kean.
   (3) Jefferson Randolph Kean.
   (4) Robert Garlick Hill Kean, Jr.

12. Meriwether Lewis Randolph, born at Edge Hill, Albemarle Co., Va.,

about 1836; died there in 1870, aged about 34 years. He married, 1869, Anna Daniel, and left one child that died infant.

13. Sarah Nicholas Randolph, authoress, born at Edge Hill, Albemarle Co., Va., about 1838. She removed to Maryland, and became the principal of the Patapsco Institute there. Died, unmarried, in Baltimore, Md., 25th April, 1892.

II. ISHAM RANDOLPH, of Dungeness, on James River, Goochland Co., Va., third son of William Randolph, of Yorkshire, England, and Turkey Island, Henrico Co., Va., progenitor of the Randolph Family in Virginia, and Mary Isham, his wife, was born at Turkey Island about 1690.

He married, in 1717, Jane Rogers (or Rodgers) of Shadwell Street, London, England, and their children were:

1. Jane Randolph, born in London, England, 1720; married, 1738, Peter Jefferson, of Shadwell near the Rivanna River, Albemarle Co., Va. This place was evidently named Shadwell after Shadwell Street, London, England, and not because shad-fish formerly came up the Rivanna River to that point. Of their children, were:
   (1) THOMAS JEFFERSON, President of the United States of America, eldest, born 1743; died 4th July, 1826, aged 83 years. He married, 1772, Martha, daughter of John Wayles, of The Forest, Charles City Co., Va., and had two surviving children, viz.: (*a*) Martha Jefferson; married, 1790, Governor Thomas Mann Randolph, of Edge Hill, Albemarle Co., Va., father of Col. Thomas Jefferson Randolph, of the same place. (*b*) Maria Jefferson; married, 1796, John Wayles Eppes, of Bermuda Hundred, Chesterfield Co., Va., and had one child, viz., Francis Eppes, of Poplar Forest, Bedford Co., Va., who married, first, 1822, Elizabeth, daughter of Thomas Eston Randolph, of Ashton, Albemarle Co., Va., and had Jane, John, Jefferson, Rev. William, and Elizabeth. He married, secondly, Mrs. Crouch, by whom he had four or five children.
   (2) Randolph Jefferson.
   (3) Martha Jefferson; married John Bolling.
   (4) Daughter Jefferson; married Dabney Carr.
   (5) Daughter Jefferson; married Lewis.
   (6) Daughter Jefferson; married Marks.
2. Susanna Randolph, born about 1743; married, about 1764, Carter Henry Harrison, of Clifton, grandson of Robert (King) Carter, and had:
   (1) Robert Harrison, removed to Kentucky, and married Anne Cabell. He was the grandfather of Carter H. Harrison, who was Mayor of Chicago.
   (2) Anne Harrison, married Thomas Drew.
   (3) Peyton Harrison, married Elizabeth Barclay.

(4) Elizabeth Harrison, married Bradley.
(5) Randolph Harrison, of Clifton, Cumberland Co., Va., married, 20th March, 1790, at Dungeness, his first cousin, Mary Randolph. He was born at Clifton, 11th February, 1769.
(6) Carter Henry Harrison, Jr., graduated at William and Mary College. He died in 1800 when just beginning to practise law.

3. Thomas Isham Randolph, eldest son; born at Dungeness, Goochland Co., Va., about 1745; resided there. He married, about 1768, Jane, third child and daughter of Col. Archibald Cary.
4. William Randolph, born about 1747; removed to Bristol. He married Miss Little.
5. Mary Randolph; married, about 1770, Charles Lewis.
6. Elizabeth Randolph; married, about 1771, John Railey.
7. Dorothy Randolph; married, about 1773, John Woodson, of Goochland County, Va.
8. Anne Randolph, born about 1755; married, first, about 1775, Daniel Scott, by whom she had no issue. She married, secondly, Jonathan Pleasants, and had Samuel and Jane. She married, thirdly, James Pleasants, of Goochland County, Va., and had:
   (1) James Pleasants, Governor of Virginia.
   (2) Susan Pleasants; married Webster.

III. Thomas Isham Randolph, of Dungeness, on James River, Goochland Co., Va., eldest son of Isham Randolph, of the same place, and Jane Rogers, his wife, was born there about 1745.

He married, about 1768, Jane, third child and daughter of Col. Archibald Cary, of Ampthill, Chesterfield Co., Va., and Mary Randolph, of Curls, his wife. Their children were as follows:

1. Archibald (called Archie) Cary Randolph, eldest, born about 1769, at Dungeness, Goochland Co., Va. He married, about 1794, Lucy, daughter of Col. Nathaniel Burwell, of Carter Hall, Clarke Co., Va., and had:
   (1) Isham Randolph, eldest, killed by lightning at Benlomond, near Dungeness, Goochland Co., Va.; unmarried.
   (2) Dr. Philip Grymes Randolph, U. S. army, born about 1769; married, about 1784, Mary O'Neal, of Washington, D. C., and died leaving two daughters: (*a*) Mary Conway Randolph, married Beverly Randolph of the U. S. Navy, and (*b*) Henrietta Randolph, married Pendleton. Beverly Randolph and Mary, his wife, had Beverly, died young, 2d March, 1865; Nathaniel, also died young, 3d January, 1874; Mary Harrison, married, 26th June, 1877, Perry W. Charington, of England; Grymes, married Ruth, daughter of Benjamin O'Fallon, of St. Louis, Mo., and Miss Carter, his wife, who was descended from Councillor William Randolph and Robert

(King) Carter, William Fitzhugh, Eston, and Julian. One of the brothers married Rebecca Rosalie O'Fallon, sister of Ruth.

Dr. Philip Grymes Randolph was at one time chief clerk in the U. S. War Department and bearer of dispatches to Spain under General Jackson's administration.

(3) Susan Grymes Randolph; married, about 1839, Dr. Robert Powell Page, of The Briars, Clarke Co., Va., and was his second wife. (See Page Family, Broadneck.)

(4) Mary (called Polly) Cary Randolph, married Dr. Matthew Page. (See Page Family, Rosewell.)

(5) Dr. Robert C. Randolph, of Newmarket, Clarke Co., Va.; died in 1886. He married, about 1830, Lucy Nelson, only child of William Wellford and Susan R. Nelson, his wife. She was the great-great-granddaughter of Councillor William Randolph, and great-granddaughter of Secretary Thomas Nelson. (See Secretary Nelson.) They had: (*a*) Bettie Burwell Randolph, married Warren C. Smith, of Clarke Co., Va., and has two sons and three daughters; (*b*) Dr. Archie Cary Randolph, eldest son, married 29th September, 1881, Mrs. Susan Henry, *née* Burwell; no surviving issue; (*c*) Col. William Wellford Randolph, married, 1863, Ada Stewart, of King George County, Va. He was killed at the battle of the Wilderness, May 6th, 1864, leaving one son, William Wellford, Jr.; (*d*) Philip Burwell Randolph, died at the University of Virginia, 1857, while a student; (*e*) Thomas Hugh Burwell Randolph, married Eliza Page Burwell, daughter of George H. Burwell, of Carter Hall, Clarke Co., Va., and had one son, Robert Carter; (*f*) Robert Carter Randolph, Jr., died single in 1864; (*g*) Susie Wellford Randolph, married William Eston Randolph, of Halifax County, Va., and has two daughters and one son, Henry Isham. These three children trace their lineage back to six of the seven sons of William Randolph I., of Turkey Island; (*h*) Isham Randolph, of Chicago, chief engineer of the Chicago and Western Indiana Railroad, married Mary, daughter of George Taylor, formerly of Richmond, Va., and has one son, Robert Isham; (*i*) Polly Cary Randolph, youngest. Three others died infant. All of the children of Dr. Robert C. Randolph and Lucy Nelson Wellford, his wife, are descended from five of the seven sons of William Randolph I., and their daughter Susan's children from six. The seventh son of William Randolph I., Edward, removed to Bristol, England, and so became separated.

(6) Lucy Burwell Randolph; married Rev. Eleazar Hutchinson, and had several children: (*a*) Robert Randolph Hutchinson, of St. Louis, Mo., (*b*) Lewis Burwell Hutchinson, of Mississippi, and (*c*) Mary Talcott Hutchinson, who married Robert Anderson, of Scotland. There were others who died young.

2. Isham Randolph, born at Dungeness, Goochland Co., Va., about 1770;

removed to Richmond, Va. He married, about 1795, Nancy Coupland, of the same place, and had:

(1) Julia Randolph, born about 1805; married, 1st February, 1827, Thomas Nelson Page, of Shelly, Gloucester Co., Va. (See Page Family, Rosewell.)

(2) Jane Randolph.

(3) Fannie P. Randolph, born about 1808; married, 1827, William N. Page, of Ça Ira, Cumberland Co., Va. (See Page Family, North End.)

(4) D. Coupland Randolph, born about 1810; married, 1857, Harriet R. Page, of Union Hill, Cumberland Co., Va. (See Page Family, North End.)

3. Thomas Randolph, twin brother of Isham. He married, first, Miss Skipwith, and had one child, a daughter, who married Walkins, but without issue. He married, secondly, Miss Lawrence, granddaughter of Governor Findley, of Kentucky (?), and had Mary, who married William Sheets. They had several children. Mrs. Sheets removed to Indianapolis, Ind. He was killed at the battle of Tippecanoe, Indiana, November 5th, 1811. In this battle Gen. William Henry Harrison, grandfather of President Benjamin Harrison, gained a complete victory over the Indians led by the famous chief Tecumseh, and the latter was killed. This victory gave General Harrison the soubriquet of Tippecanoe, and hence the origin of the political campaign phrase when he was elected President of the United States with John Tyler, of Virginia, as Vice-President, of "Tippecanoe and Tyler too." Thomas Randolph and Joe Devies, two friends and gallant spirits, were both killed in this battle and buried together under an oak-tree on which their initials were cut. Some beautiful lines were subsequently published by Mrs. Mary Sheets, called "The Lost Initials."

4. Mary Randolph, born at Ampthill, Chesterfield Co., Va., 1st February, 1773; married, 20th March, 1790, her first cousin, Randolph Harrison, of Clifton, Cumberland Co., Va., and had fourteen children as follows:

(1) Thomas Randolph Harrison, born at Clifton, 27th February, 1791, died at Dover, Goochland Co., Va., 3d November, 1833, aged 42. He married at Cartersville, Cumberland Co., Va., 2d December, 1812, Eliza Cunningham, and had: (*a*) John, born 20th September, 1813; (*b*) Mary Burleigh, born August 1st, 1815; (*c*) William Mortimer, born August 4th, 1817, and married Caroline Lambert. Their daughter Mary married Major Drewry, of Westover, Charles City Co., Va. Major Drewry formerly resided at Drewry's Bluff on James River, but subsequently removed to Westover, the old Byrd estate. Elizabeth (called Lizzie), the second daughter of William Mortimer Harrison and Caroline Lambert, his wife, married Robert Carter Wellford, of Sabine Hall, Richmond Co., Va.; (*d*) Eliza Cunningham, born October 19th, 1819; (*e*) Jane Cary, born August 14th, 1821; (*f*) Edward C., born March 10th, 1823; (*g*) Thomas Randolph, born September 30th, 1825; (*h*) Burleigh

Cunningham, born August 30th, 1827; (*i*) Archibald Tayloe, born October 28th, 1829; (*k*) Randolph, born August 28th, 1831, removed to California.

(2) Carter Henry Harrison, born at Clifton, Cumberland Co., Va., 28th August, 1792, removed to Glentivar, same county. He married, 16th January, 1819, at Richmond, Va., Janetta Fisher, and had many children. He died at Bremo, Hanover Co., Va., in October, 1843, aged 51 years.

(3) Archibald (called Archie) Morgan Harrison, born September 6th, 1794; married, first, at Blackheath, 27th February, 1817, Kitty Heth; and, secondly, at Glenavon, Fluvanna Co., Va., 22d November, 1837, Fanny Taylor, who, becoming a widow, married Ellis, of Richmond, Va. Archie Harrison died at Carysbrook, Fluvanna Co., Va., 17th March, 1842, leaving three children, but it is not known by which of his two wives: (*a*) Mrs. Kidder Taylor; (*b*) Mrs. Robert Morrison; (*c*) Henry Harrison.

(4) Jane Cary Harrison, born at Glentivar, Cumberland Co., Va., 9th February, 1797; married there, in September, 1817, William Fitzhugh Randolph, of Fauquier County, Va. She died November 28th, 1883, at The Moorings, Clarke Co., Va.

(5) Randolph Harrison, of Elk Hill, Goochland Co., Va., born 17th February, 1799; married, at Wilton, Logan Co., Ky., 6th September, 1821, Miss Heningham Carrington Wills. He died at Norfolk, Va., 18th May, 1844. Their children were: (*a*) Elizabeth, born 1st March, 1823, married at Elk Hill, 28th December, 1848, Alexander B. Gordon, of Baltimore, Md., and had two sons, Randolph Harrison and Heningham, and three daughters, Margaret, Emily, and Mary Nicholas; (*b*) William Morton, died infant; (*c*) Mary Randolph, born 26th November, 1825, died infant 26th May, 1832; (*d*) Julian, born 6th February, 1826, resided at Millview, a part of the Elk Hill estate. He was killed by the accidental discharge of a pistol, 17th July, 1877. He married, first, 7th June, 1849, Lavinia Beverly Heath, by whom he had Heath, Julian, Walter, Belle, Fannie, and Virginia, and Lulie who died; and, secondly, he married, 12th June, 1866, at Narragansett Pier, R. I., Miss Lilly Johnston, by whom he had Hebe, Lizzie, Peyton Randolph, Bernard, and Alexander; the latter died infant. Hebe Johnston, sister of Lilly Johnston, married Joseph H. Craig, of Lexington, Ky., and had Richard and Joseph. Young Joseph J. Craig and his cousin, Peyton R. Harrison, at present reside in New York; (*e*) Heningham, died infant, September, 1829; (*f*) Louisa, born 2d October, 1829, married at Elk Hill, 26th May, 1853, Alexander B. Hagner, of Annapolis, Md., no issue; (*g*) Randolph, born 12th February, 1830, resided at Elk Hill; married, November, 1853, Elizabeth Williamson, of Norfolk Va., and had issue. He afterward removed to Williamsburg, James City Co., Va.

(6) Rev. Peyton Harrison, of Baltimore, Md., born at Clifton, 19th November, 1800. He married, first, at Richmond, Va., in 1825, Jane, daughter of Judge Dabney Carr, who was a nephew of President Thomas Jefferson. They had five sons, only one of whom, Harry Tucker, survives. He lives near Baltimore. There were also five daughters, of whom two survive: Virginia, married Hoge, and Willie Irving, married Turnbull. The children that died were Mrs. Betty Atkinson, Randolph, Dabney Carr, Peyton, William Wirt, Mrs. Hunter, and Nannie. Rev. Peyton Harrison married, secondly, at Philadelphia, in 1863, Ellen Smith, by whom he had one son, Sam Graeme, who resides in Baltimore.

(7) William Mortimer Harrison, born at Clifton, 23d September, 1802; was drowned 19th May, 1811, in the Rivanna River, Albemarle Co., Va., while a schoolboy at Edge Hill, and was buried at Monticello. His father, who was at Clifton, dreamed three times during the night that he had seen his son William struggling in the water. Before daylight a messenger arrived with the fatal news. When Mr. Harrison heard the knock on the door he remarked to his wife that he feared his dream had come true.

(8) Mary Randolph Harrison, born at Clifton, September 10th, 1804; married, 8th February, 1827, at the same place, William Byrd Harrison, of Upper Brandon, on James River, Prince George Co., Va., and was his first wife. She died at Upper Brandon, 3d September, 1851. Children: (*a*) Randolph Harrison, of Ampthill, Cumberland Co., Va., married Harriet Hielman; (*b*) Col. Benjamin Harrison, of The Rowe, Charles City Co., Va.; married, 11th November, 1854, Polly R. Page. Col. Harrison was killed at the battle of Malvern Hill, in the summer of 1862, as before stated. (See Page Family, North End.) There were several children; (*c*) Shirley Harrison; (*d*) Dr. George Harrison, of Washington, D.C.; married, 1876, Jennie, daughter of Dr. Robert Stone, of that city, and Margaret Ritchie, his wife. Dr. Stone was the first to see President Lincoln after the assassination. Dr. George Harrison and Jennie Stone, his wife, have several children.

(9) Susanna Isham Harrison, born at Clifton, September 13th, 1806; married there, December 15th, 1837, Rev. Samuel Blain. They removed to Louisville, Ky. Children: (*a*) Daniel, minister in the Presbyterian church; (*b*) Mary Randolph; (*c*) Randolph Harrison; (*d*) Charlotte, married Charles Richardson, and died leaving several children; (*e*) Lucia Cary. They all live in Louisville, Ky., except Daniel.

(10) Lucia Cary Harrison, born at Clifton, 19th May, 1809; married, 19th March, 1829, at the same place, Nelson Page, of The Fork, Cumberland Co., Va., and was his first wife. She died at that place, August 8th, 1842. Their children were: (*a*) Mary Randolph, called Polly, who married Col. Benjamin Harrison and had issue

as before stated; and (*b*) Lucius Cary, died young. (See Page Family, North End.)

(11) Catherine Lilbourne Harrison, born at Clifton, 3d July, 1811; married there, 2d October, 1831, John S. McKim, of Baltimore, Md., and had: (*a*) Emily; (*b*) Mary Randolph; (*c*) Margie Telfair; (*d*) Telfair; (*e*) Carter Henry, and (*f*) Rev. Randolph Harrison McKim, of Washington, D. C. The latter married, in 1862, Miss Philips, of Staunton, Augusta Co., Va., and had several children. Of these Dr. McKim, formerly of the Chambers Street Hospital, New York, and late of Washington, D. C., died a few years ago unmarried.

(12) Williana Mortimer Harrison (called Willie), born at Clifton, 17th May, 1813; married, 5th October, 1836, Henry Page Irving, who removed to California. She died at Richmond, Va., 7th February, 1847. They had two sons: (*a*) Joseph Kincaid, who went to school at Hanover Academy, 1855–56. He died, of wounds received in battle, at Staunton, Augusta Co., Va., in 1864; (*b*) Henry, died infant, a few days before his mother in 1847, aged 2 years.

(13) Virginia Randolph Harrison, born 24th May, 1815; died at Richmond, Va., 10th December, 1830, aged 15.

(14) Nannie Hartwell Harrison, born at Clifton, 18th February, 1819; married, 18th June, 1847, at Upper Brandon, Dr. John Bolling Garrett, of Cloverplains, Albemarle Co., Va., and had three charming daughters.

II. Sir John Randolph, of Williamsburg, James City Co., Va., fourth son and child of William Randolph, of Yorkshire, England, and Turkey Island, Henrico Co., Va., progenitor of the Randolph Family in Virginia, and Mary Isham, his wife, was born at the last-named place in 1693, and died 15th March, 1737, aged 44 years. Upon a mural tablet that was placed to his memory in William and Mary College, destroyed by fire in 1859 (the college has been partially burned a number of times—usually from careless management), he was called "Johannes Randolph, Eques." It is proper, therefore, in speaking of him to say Sir John Randolph, as he was Eques or Knight, and not Armiger or Esquire, nor Generosus, which signifies Gentleman or Gent.

He married, about 1718, Susanna, daughter of Peter Beverly, of Gloucester County, Va., and sister of Elizabeth, the wife of William Randolph, the eldest son, who was known as Councillor Randolph. According to the above-mentioned mural tablet, Sir John Randolph and Susanna Beverly, his wife, had the following children:

1. John Randolph, born at Williamsburg, James City Co., Va., about 1727; married, about 1752, Miss Ariana, daughter of Edmund Jennings.
2. Peyton Randolph, born at Williamsburg, James City Co., Va.; died in Philadelphia, Pa., 22d October, 1775, aged 53 years. He was Attorney-General for Virginia, Speaker of the Virginia House of Burgesses, and President of the First American Congress. Married Elizabeth Harrison. No issue.
3. Beverly Randolph, married Miss Wormeley.
4. Mary Randolph, born at Williamsburg, James City Co., Va.; married, about 1743, Philip Grymes, of Brandon, Middlesex Co., Va. Children:
   (1) Philip Grymes, Jr., married, about 1762, Elizabeth, daughter of William Randolph, of Wilton, and Anne Harrison, his wife.
   (2) Lucy Grymes, married, about 1761, Gov. Thomas Nelson, of Yorktown, York Co., Va.
   (3) Susan Grymes, married Nathaniel Burwell, of The Grove, York Co., Va., and afterward of Carter Hall, Clarke Co., Va.
   (4) Mary Grymes, married, about 1777, Robert Nelson, of Malvern Hill, Charles City Co., Va., younger brother of Gov. Thomas Nelson, and was his first wife. There were perhaps others.

III. John Randolph, of Williamsburg, James City Co., Va., eldest son and child of Sir John Randolph, of the same place, and Susanna Beverly, his wife, fourth son and child of William Randolph, of Yorkshire, England, and Turkey Island, Henrico Co., Va., progenitor of the Randolph Family in Virginia, and Mary Isham, his wife, was born at the first-named place about 1727. He was Attorney-General for the colony of Virginia.

He married, about 1752, Ariana, daughter of Edmund Jennings, of Annapolis, Md., who was Attorney-General for Maryland and Virginia, and their children were as follows:

1. Edmund Randolph, born at Williamsburg, James City Co., Va., 10th August, 1753; died in Frederick County, Va., 12th September, 1813, aged 60. He did not follow his father to England when the war of the American Revolution broke out, but remained, and was adopted by his uncle, Peyton Randolph, who was President of the First American Congress.

   Edmund Randolph was the First Attorney-General of the United States of America, 1790, having been Governor of the State of Virginia, 1786–88. He married, 29th August, 1776, Elizabeth, daughter of Robert Carter Nicholas, Speaker of the House of Burgesses and Treasurer of Virginia, and had:
   (1) Peyton Randolph, married Maria Ward, who had been engaged to John Randolph, of Roanoke.

(2) Lucy Randolph, married Judge Peter Vivian Daniel, and had issue.
(3) Daughter Randolph, married Preston.
(4) Daughter Randolph, married Bennet Taylor, of Albemarle County, Va.

Edmund Randolph succeeded Patrick Henry as Governor of Virginia, 1st December, 1786, and was followed in that office by his kinsman, Beverly Randolph, 1st December, 1788. On the 2d August, 1794, he succeeded Thomas Jefferson as Secretary of State, which office he held until 19th August, 1795, when he retired to private life.

2. Ariana Randolph, born at Williamsburg, James City Co., Va., about 1750; went with her father to England when the war broke out. She married Ralph Wormeley. Their son was an admiral in the British navy. He had three daughters, viz.: (*a*) Mrs. Latimer, of Baltimore, Md.; (*b*) Catherine Preble Wormeley, resides at Newport, R. I.; (*c*) Ariana, married Daniel S. Curtis, of Boston, Mass.

II. Richard Randolph, of Curls Neck, on James River, Henrico Co., Va., fifth son and child of William Randolph, of Yorkshire, England, and Turkey Island, Henrico Co., Va., progenitor of the Randolph Family in Virginia, and Mary Isham, his wife, was born at Turkey Island, Va., about 1695.

He married, about 1714, Jane, daughter of John Bolling, of Cobbs, Chesterfield Co., Va., and Mary Kennon, his wife. Jane Bolling was of the fourth generation in descent from Pocahontas. Richard Randolph and Jane Bolling, his wife, had:

1. Richard Randolph, Jr., born at Curls Neck, in 1715; married, about 1750, Anne, daughter of David Meade, of Nansemond County, Va., and had issue. The following epitaph was copied in 1874, by Mrs. Charles Carter, *née* Nelson, daughter-in-law of Mr. Hill Carter, of Shirley-on-James River, Va., from the original tombstone at Curls Neck: "This Monument is erected by Ryland Randolph in memory of his Parents, Richard and Ann Randolph, of Curles. The former died 6th June, 1786, aged 71 years, and the latter December, 1814, aged 83 years."

The above-mentioned Mrs. Charles Carter was a direct descendant from Councillor William Randolph through Secretary Nelson, of Yorktown, Va. When she made the above copy, in 1874, it was the only tombstone at Curles (or Curls) that bore a legible inscription.

2. Mary Randolph, born at Curls Neck, about 1727; married, 31st May, 1744, Col. Archibald Cary, of Ampthill, Chesterfield Co., Va. Of their children, Mary Cary (called Polly) married Major Carter Page, of The Fork, Cumberland Co., Va., and was his first wife.
3. Jane Randolph, born about 1729; married, about 1750, Anthony Walke, of Princess Anne County, Va. Their son was Rev. Anthony Walke.

6. John Randolph (two others died young), born at Curls Neck, Henrico Co., Va., about 1737; removed to Roanoke, Charlotte Co., Va. He married, about 1769, Frances, daughter of Theodrick Bland, and had:
   (1) Richard Randolph, of Bizarre, born about 1770; married, 1790, his cousin Judith, daughter of Thomas Mann Randolph, of Tuckahoe.
   (2) Theodrick Bland Randolph, born 1771; died 1792, single.
   (3) JOHN RANDOLPH, OF ROANOKE, Charlotte Co., Va., born 3d June, 1773. Died unmarried, in Philadelphia, 24th May, 1833. He was buried at Roanoke, his residence, in Charlotte County, Va., but his remains have since been removed to Holywood Cemetery, Richmond, Va.
   (4) Jane Randolph.

Judge Roger A. Pryor, of New York City, has in his possession a little book that formerly belonged to John Randolph, of Roanoke, entitled: "Petite Dictionnaire de la Langue Française." In it is a book-plate on which is engraved the Randolph coat-of-arms with the two mottoes: "Nil Admirari" at the top, and "Fari qui sentiat" at the bottom. The coat-of-arms may be described as follows:

ARMS: Gules (red), with a cross bearing three stars (the tincture of the latter not indicated).

CREST: Antelope's head couped, holding a bone in his mouth. No tinctures indicated

This description and the motto, "Nil admirari," correspond with those sent to the author 2d June, 1884, by Isham Randolph, engineer, of Chicago, a son of the late Dr. Robert C. Randolph, of Clarke County, Va.

For further information in regard to the Randolphs, the reader is referred to the "History of Bristol Parish," Dinwiddie County, Va., by Rev. Philip Slaughter, D.D. Published by Randolph & English, Richmond, Va., 1879.

FINIS.

INDEX.

18

www.ingramcontent.com/pod-product-compliance
Lightning Source LLC
LaVergne TN
LVHW020540100826
845148LV00010B/1546
* 9 7 8 0 7 8 8 4 3 0 6 2 6 *